HISTORY COMICS

THE NATIONAL PARKS
PRESERVING AMERICA'S WILD PLACES

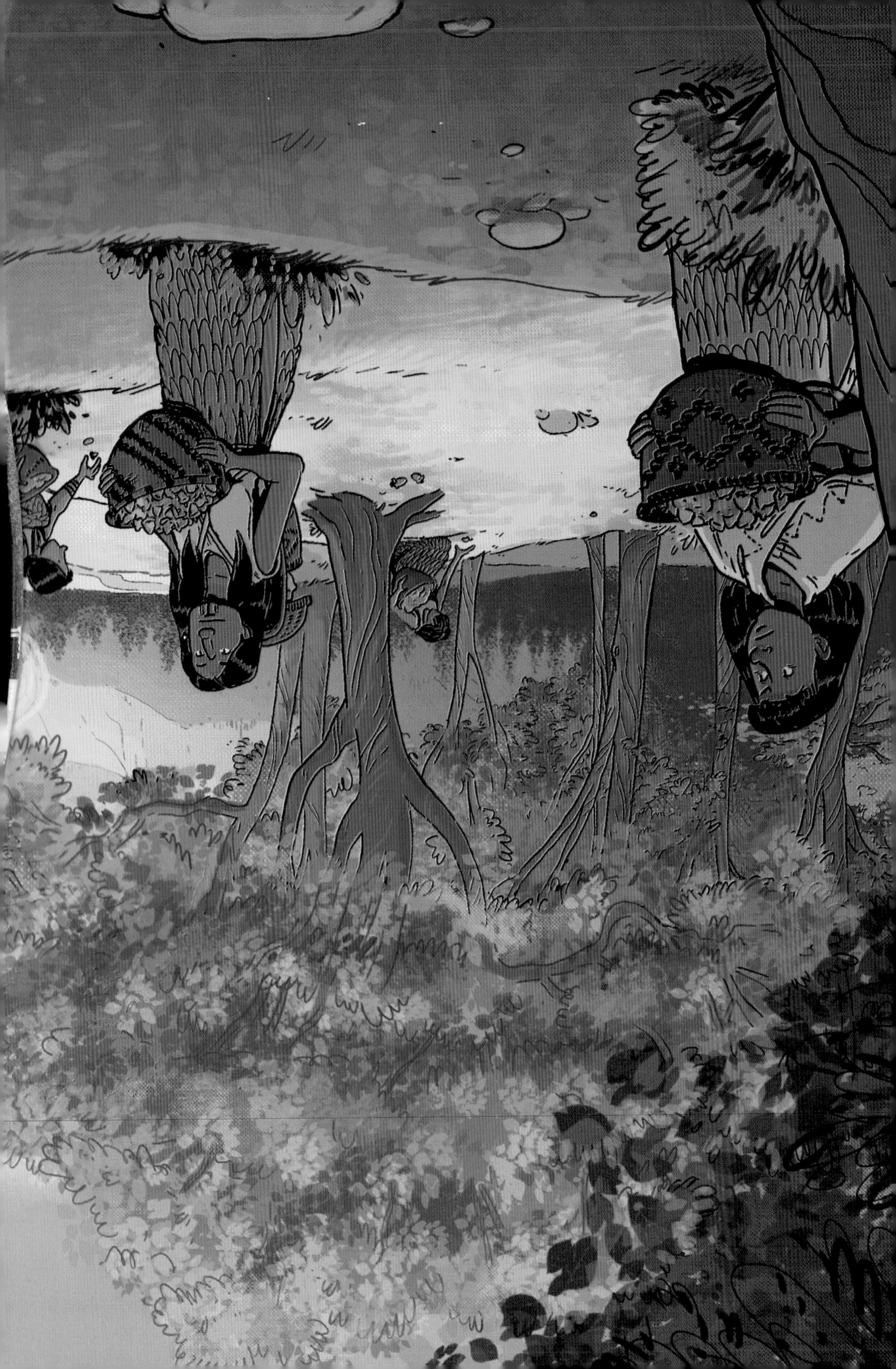

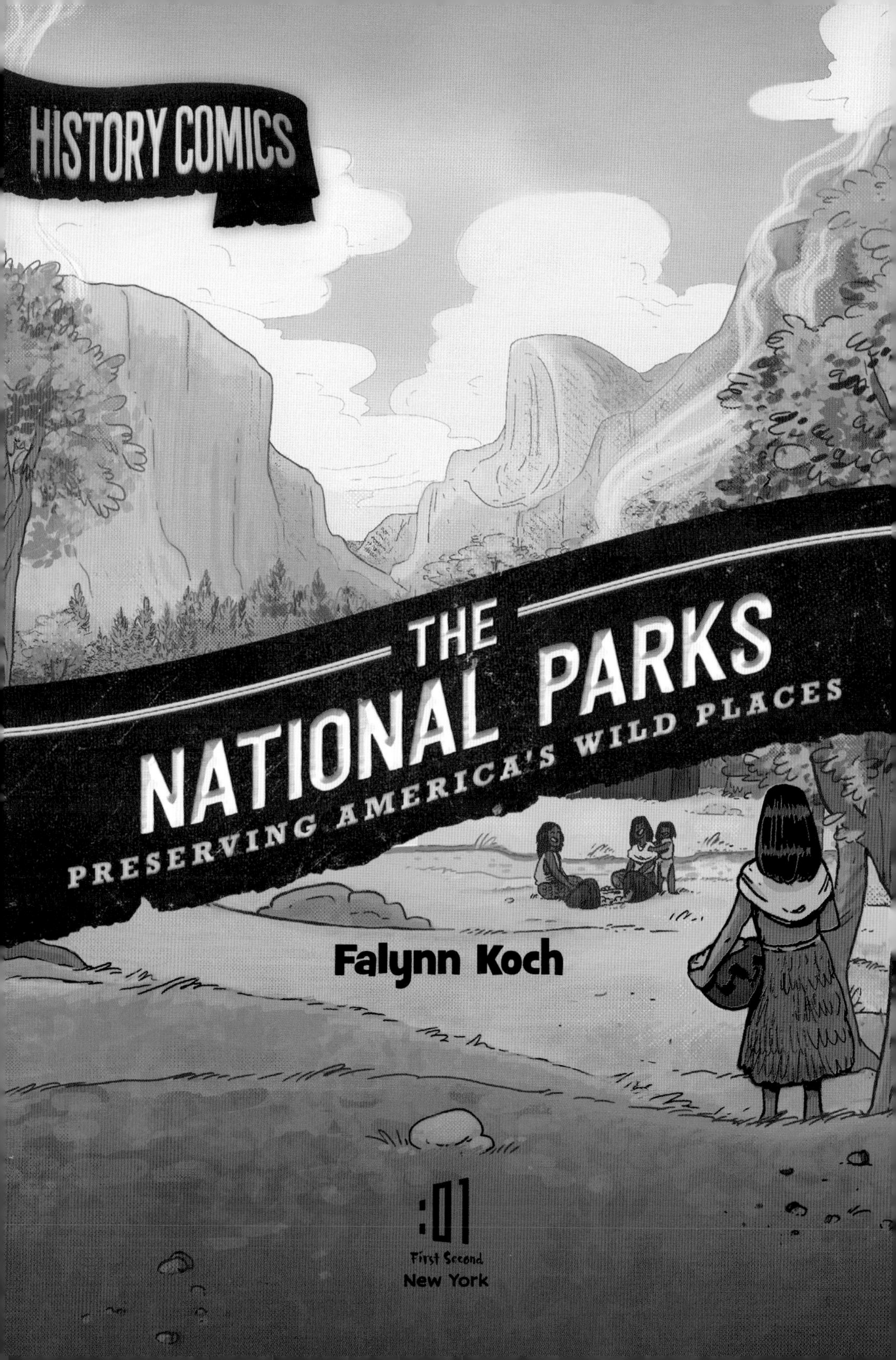

HISTORY COMICS

THE NATIONAL PARKS

PRESERVING AMERICA'S WILD PLACES

Falynn Koch

:01
First Second
New York

First Second

Published by First Second
First Second is an imprint of Roaring Brook Press, a division of Holtzbrinck Publishing
Holdings Limited Partnership
120 Broadway, New York, NY 10271
firstsecondbooks.com
mackids.com

Library of Congress Control Number: 2021916380

Our books may be purchased in bulk for promotional, educational, or business use. Please
contact your local bookseller or the Macmillan Corporate and Premium Sales Department
at (800) 221-7945 ext. 5442 or by email at MacmillanSpecialMarkets@macmillan.com.

First edition, 2022
Edited by Dave Roman
Cover design by Sunny Lee
Series design by Andrew Arnold
Interior book design by Falynn Koch and Sunny Lee
With special thanks to Elise McMullen-Ciotti

Drawn and colored in Photoshop with the use of Kyle Webster brushes.
Lettered with the Soliloquous font from Comicraft.

Printed in China by Toppan Leefung Printing Ltd., Dongguan City, Guangdong Province

ISBN 978-1-250-26588-3 (paperback)
10 9 8 7 6 5 4 3

ISBN 978-1-250-26587-6 (hardcover)
10 9 8 7 6 5 4 3

Don't miss your next favorite book from First Second! For the latest updates go to
firstsecondnewsletter.com and sign up for our enewsletter.

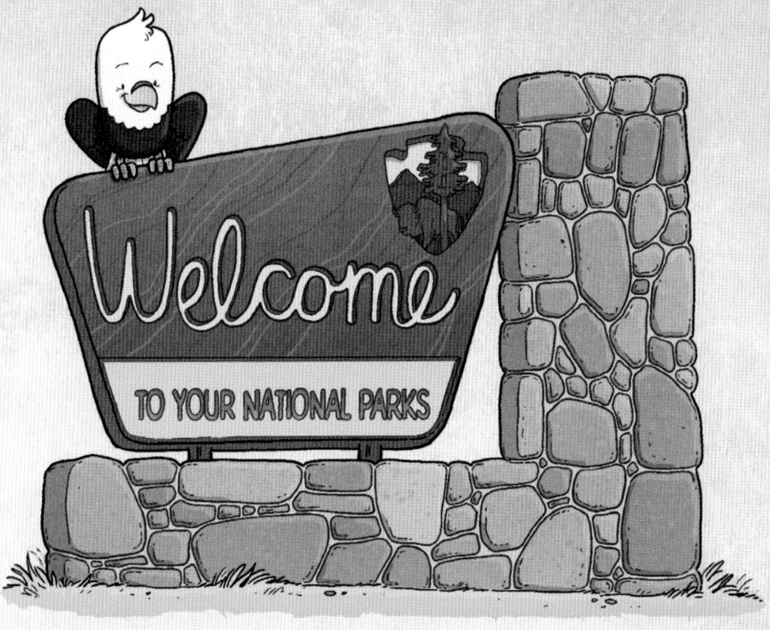
Welcome
TO YOUR NATIONAL PARKS

The national parks have been called "America's Best Idea." This notion has been echoed by many over the years, but it leaves much to consider. First, we should appreciate the fact that there are a number of "Americas." Not only does America include Canada, but it also includes Mexico and the countries of Central America and South America, which means that there are versions of America that do not look the same to everyone. Whether the setting is urban, suburban, rural, or remote, the experiences of each American may look very different when compared to one another.

Something that we can all agree on, I hope, is the fact that our national parks are truly special places (set aside by law) for the benefit of all present and future generations. Our national park model is so popular that it's been adopted and adapted in more than a hundred countries around the world.

In the United States, these diverse places are part of a nationwide system of recreational areas, historic sites, monuments, landscapes, seashores, ecosystems, and other designations that represent our nation's best way to engage with history and connect with the beauty and serenity of nature.

The iconic logo of the National Park Service features an arrowhead as its frame and background. This image serves to humbly remind us that all of these places are on land that was home to the many Native American nations: revered grounds, mountain ranges, valleys, and streams, which are integral to the enduring cultures of the Indigenous people who lost so much during the evolution of our country.

In many ways, the designation of national parks fulfills parts of the founders' original vision for the United States. Contributing to "a more perfect Union," these cherished places give every visitor a chance to reflect on all that has taken place before us and the kind of future we can make together.

Because they are open to all, national parks contribute to a sense of justice and equality, and since they are places where people make memories, they add to our ideal of national tranquility.

In the wake of brutal wars, national parks have been used as places for wounded and tired soldiers to refresh and renew, adding to the "common defense" mentioned in the Preamble to the Constitution; most certainly, the satisfaction, learning, and relaxation these parks offer are among the blessings of liberty.

Yet, national parks are still only what we make them. Nature is strong and powerful, but also requires protection. Americans learn over and over again that they must take care of these places by not littering or intruding on the experiences of others.

Growing up, I dreamed of many things, but one of my fondest ambitions was to become a National Park Ranger. I was a child of the 1960s, living in Washington, D.C., during a very tumultuous time for the city. But there were a number of great things about growing up in the nation's capital, which is filled with monuments and memorials that are all part of the National Park System.

The house where I grew up was just blocks from a number of places that had been Civil War fortifications, built to protect Washington, which for years had already been part of the National Park System. My parents and grandparents were involved with voter registration drives and Civil Rights campaigns. They took my brother and me down to the National Mall to witness parts of the March on Washington and the Poor People's Campaign. What I did not know at the time is that even the National Mall and the Lincoln Memorial were part of our system of national parks. They did for me what national parks do best—they encouraged me to reflect on the past and dream about the future. And with a focused education and a willingness to travel to new places, my dream of becoming a National Park Ranger eventually came true!

For over thirty years, I was able to live and work in breathtaking locations, and immerse myself in some of the most interesting aspects of our nation's history. It was a great honor to be called upon to work in parks set aside for their natural beauty, monumental importance, and connection to American history, as well as for the stories of notable people who help us gain a fuller understanding of the nation we live in.

Over the span of my career, I was a National Park Ranger in places as varied as:

- Prince William Forest Park (Virginia)
- The Lincoln Memorial, Thomas Jefferson Memorial, and Washington Monument on the National Mall (Washington, D.C.)
- Bent's Old Fort National Historic Site (southeastern Colorado on the Santa Fe Trail)
- The Frederick Douglass National Historic Site (southeastern Washington, D.C.)
- The Booker T. Washington National Monument (western Virginia)
- Fort Davis National Historic Site (West Texas)
- Fort Laramie National Historic Site (Wyoming on the Oregon Trail)
- Rocky Mountain National Park (Colorado)

My training and experience with the National Park Service led to my serving as a staff member by a Presidential Commission, becoming an Assistant Regional Director for the Intermountain Region of the National Park Service and then continuing my federal service working as a Guest Curator for Military History for the Smithsonian Institution's National Museum of African American History and Culture.

Altogether, it has been a profound experience for me and my family. My children literally grew up in national parks! I personally found it endlessly fulfilling to work with and make friends with Americans from all backgrounds and walks of life. My job allowed me to connect with a wide array of communities, from American Indians living on reservations to Hispanic/Latinx and African American families in a wide variety of small towns and big cities across the American landscape.

I no longer pin on a badge or put on the flat-brimmed Ranger hat to go to work, but my dreams for a better United States very much include a system of national parks as well as a National Park Service that exists to manage and protect them.

Old habits are hard to break and I still serve the national parks as a longtime participant in Volunteers-In-Parks (VIP), an opportunity that is open to you as well in almost every national park regardless of where you live. In addition, if you are a young person, you can learn more about national parks as you earn Junior Ranger badges both in person and online at national park sites across the country.

Perhaps the best idea that we ever had as a nation is *you*, a citizen who cares about both the past and the future. A citizen who contributes to a larger good and, on some level, uses, protects, and promotes wonderful places that can do so much good for people, whether they are U.S. citizens or from elsewhere.

After reading this book, your job is to get out and enjoy the national parks. They were set aside as special places for everyone!

There will never be an end to the good that national parks are and the good that they do.

—**William Gwaltney,** Retired Assistant Regional Director, National Park Service

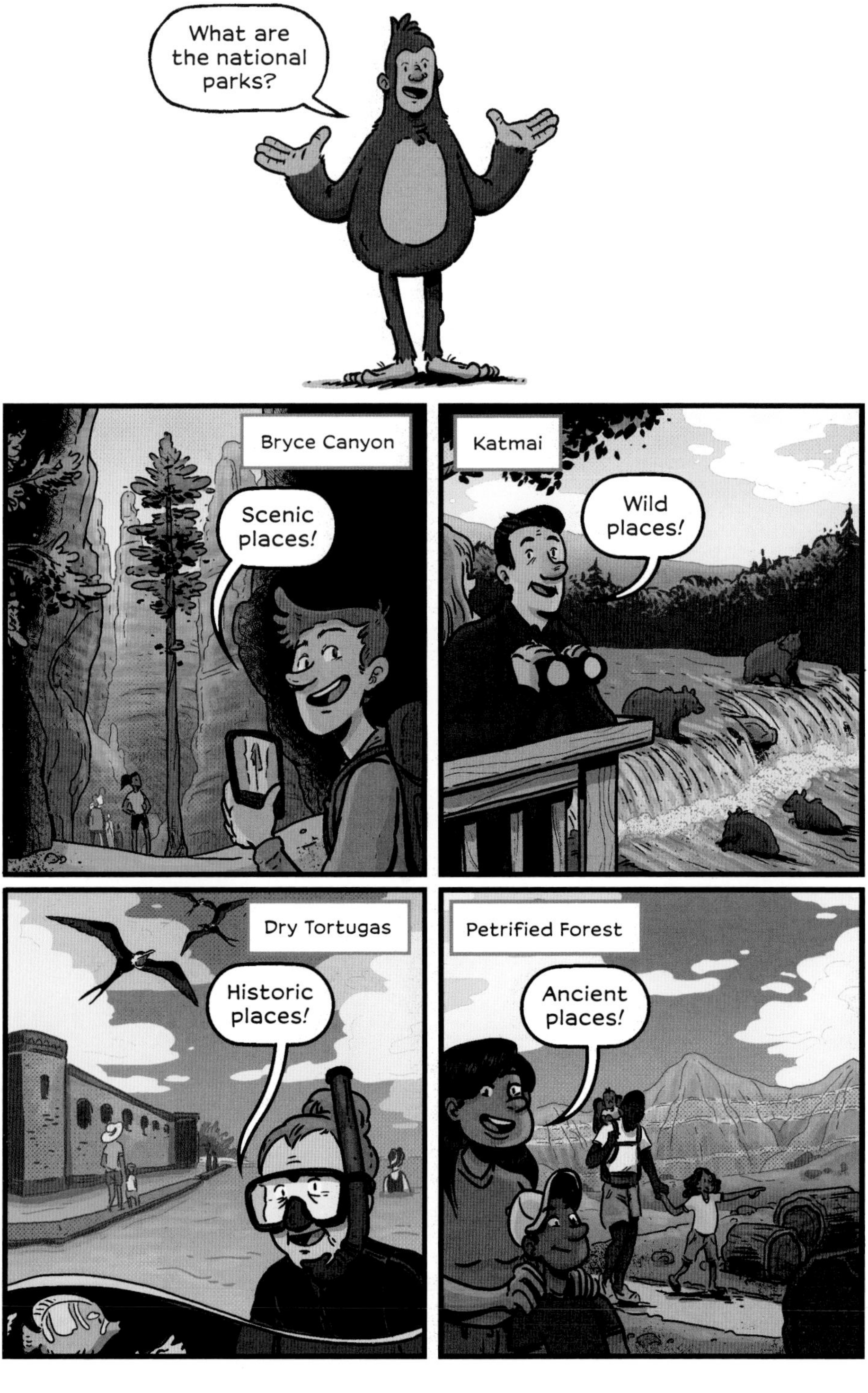
What are the national parks?
Bryce Canyon
Scenic places!
Katmai
Wild places!
Dry Tortugas
Historic places!
Petrified Forest
Ancient places!

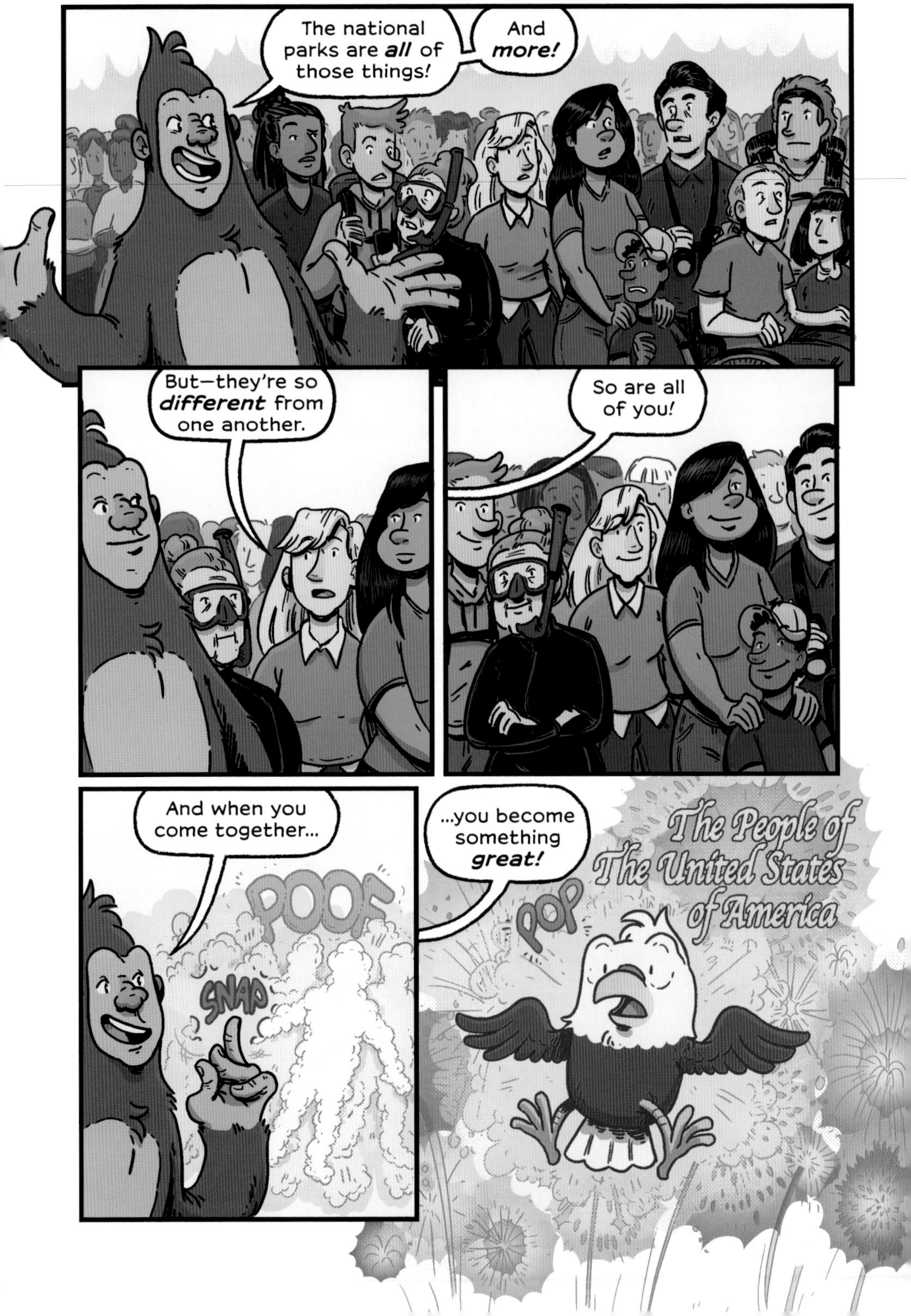

The national parks are *all* of those things!
And *more!*
But—they're so *different* from one another.
So are all of you!
And when you come together...
POOF
SNAP
...you become something *great!*
POP
The People of The United States of America

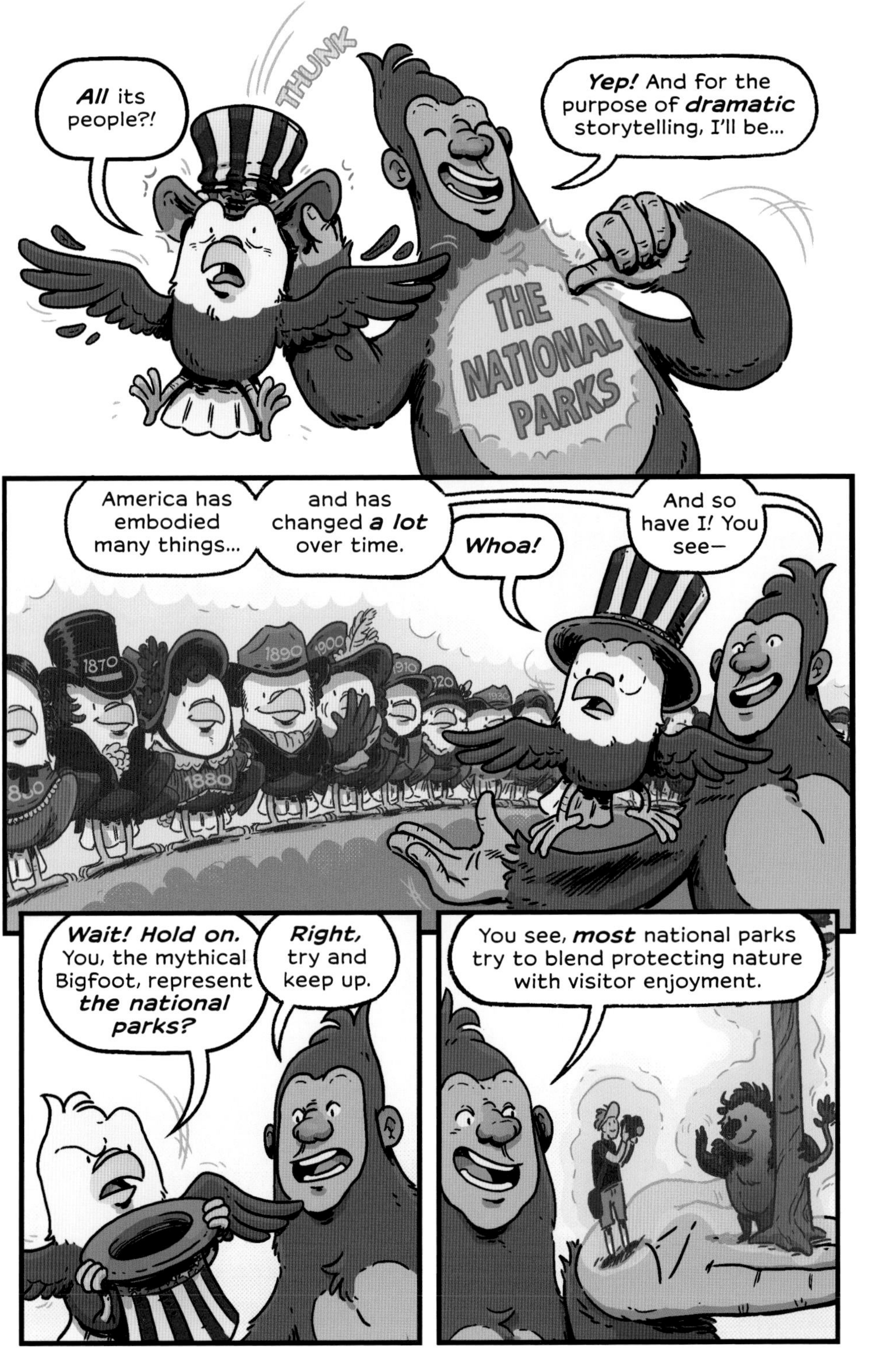
All its people?!
THUNK
Yep! And for the purpose of ***dramatic*** storytelling, I'll be...
THE NATIONAL PARKS
America has embodied many things...
and has changed ***a lot*** over time.
Whoa!
And so have I! You see—
1870
1890
1900
1910
1920
1880
Wait! Hold on. You, the mythical Bigfoot, represent ***the national parks?***
Right, try and keep up.
You see, ***most*** national parks try to blend protecting nature with visitor enjoyment.

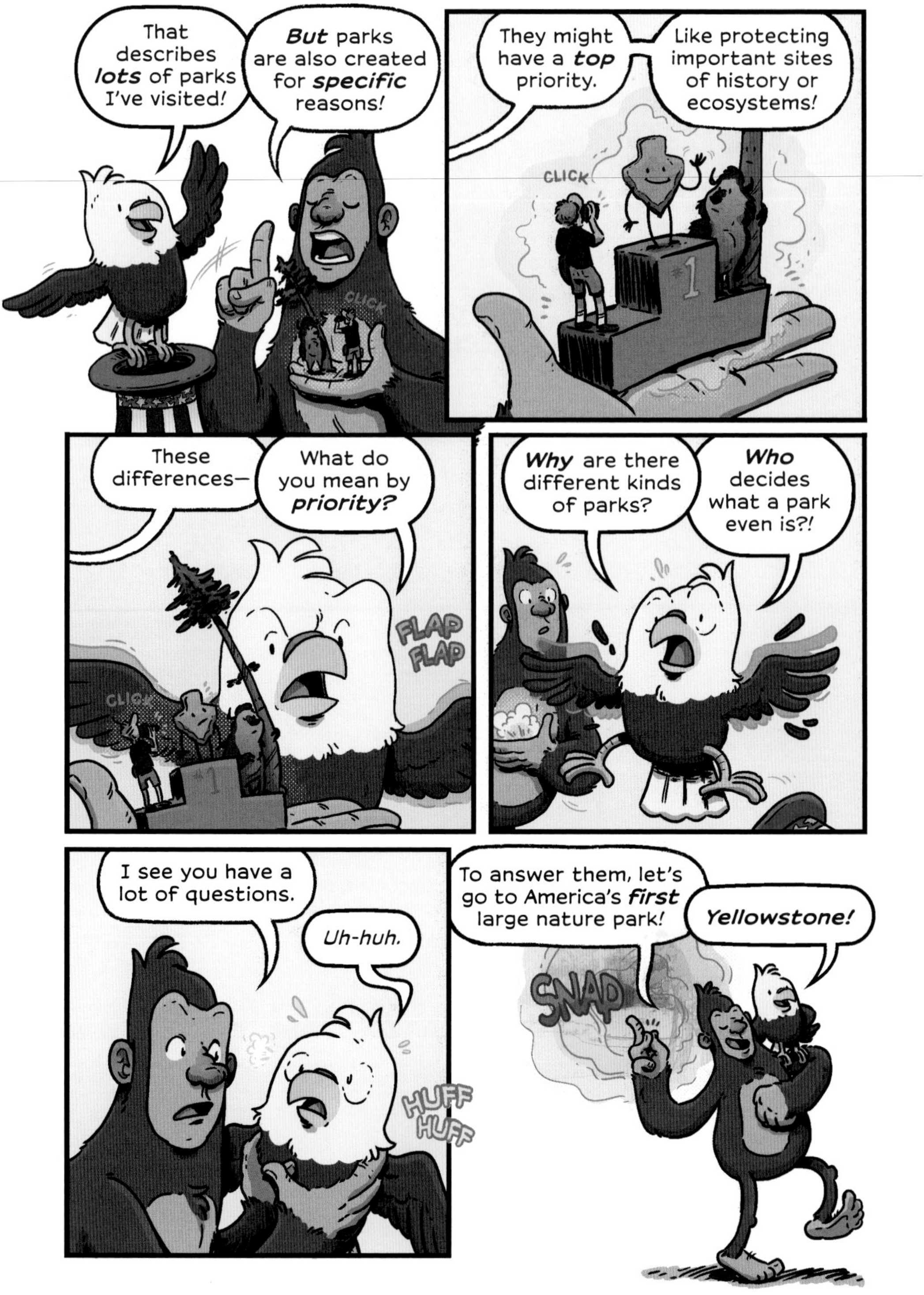
That describes *lots* of parks I've visited!
But parks are also created for ***specific*** reasons!
CLICK
They might have a ***top*** priority.
Like protecting important sites of history or ecosystems!
CLICK
These differences—
What do you mean by ***priority?***
FLAP FLAP
CLICK
Why are there different kinds of parks?
Who decides what a park even is?!
I see you have a lot of questions.
Uh-huh.
HUFF HUFF
To answer them, let's go to America's ***first*** large nature park!
SNAP
Yellowstone!

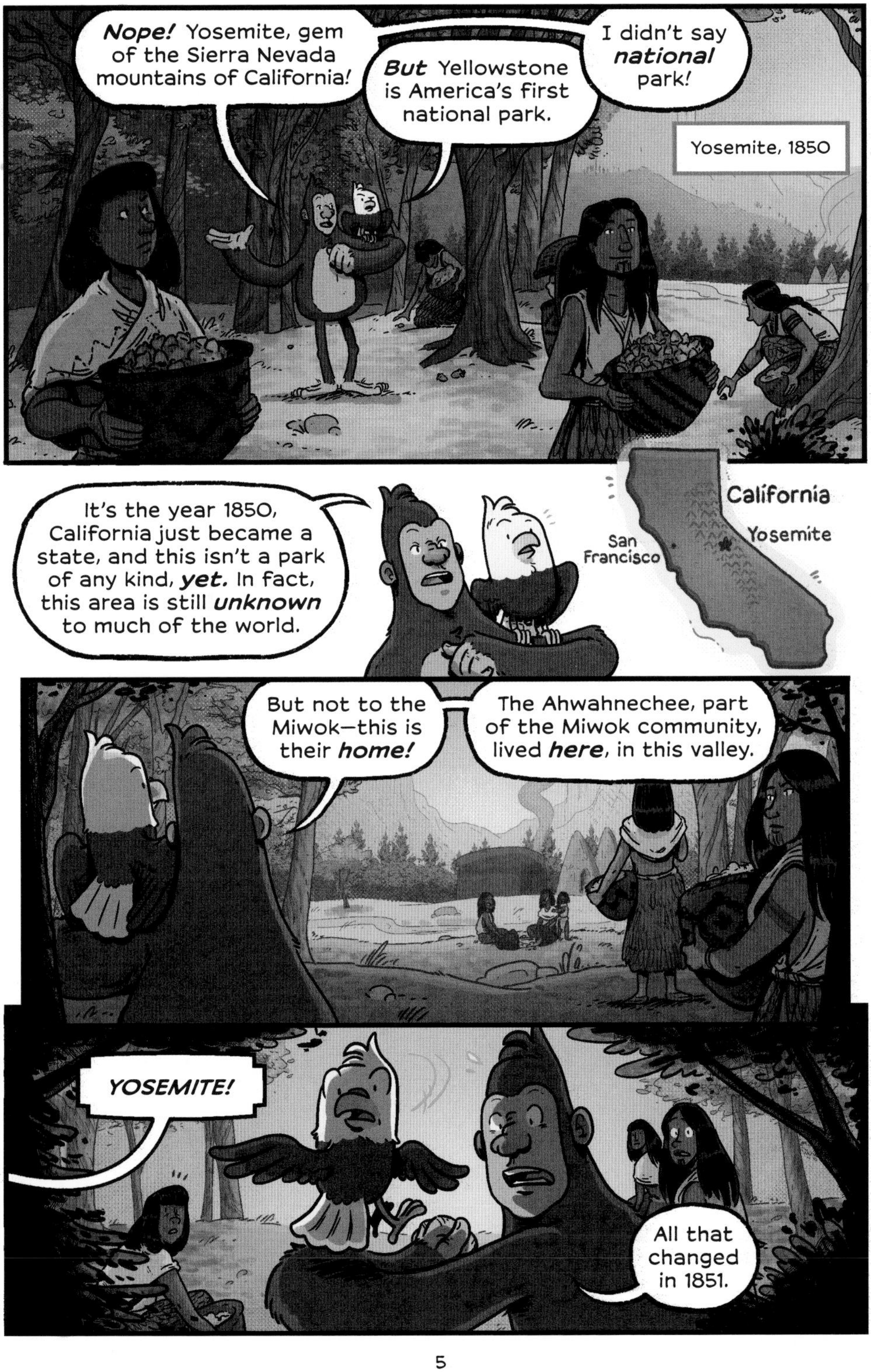
Nope! Yosemite, gem of the Sierra Nevada mountains of California!
But Yellowstone is America's first national park.
I didn't say **national** park!
Yosemite, 1850
It's the year 1850, California just became a state, and this isn't a park of any kind, **yet.** In fact, this area is still **unknown** to much of the world.
California
San Francisco
Yosemite
But not to the Miwok—this is their **home!**
The Ahwahnechee, part of the Miwok community, lived **here**, in this valley.
YOSEMITE!
All that changed in 1851.

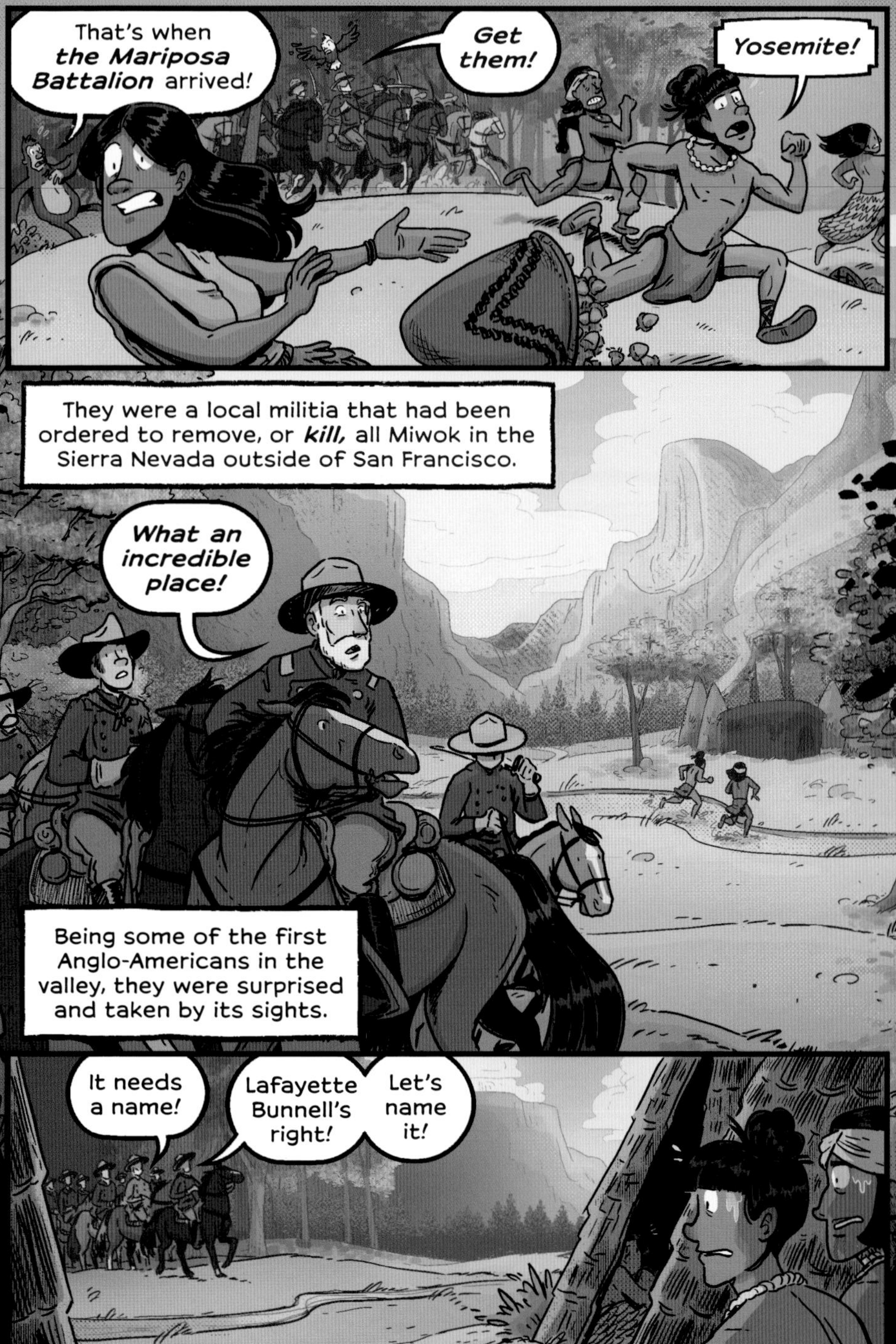
That's when *the Mariposa Battalion* arrived!
Get them!
Yosemite!
They were a local militia that had been ordered to remove, or ***kill,*** all Miwok in the Sierra Nevada outside of San Francisco.
What an incredible place!
Being some of the first Anglo-Americans in the valley, they were surprised and taken by its sights.
It needs a name!
Lafayette Bunnell's right!
Let's name it!

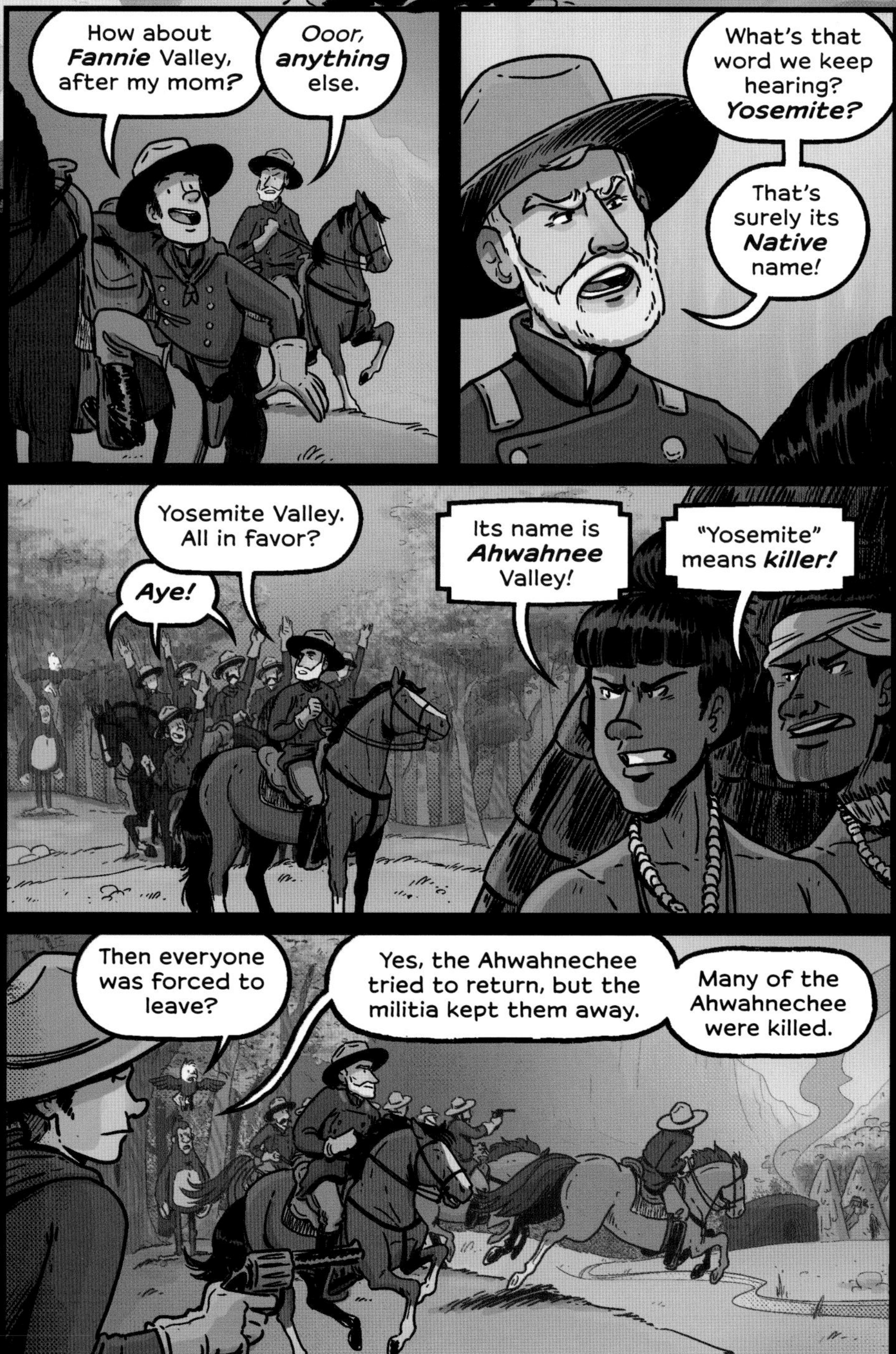
How about *Fannie* Valley, after my mom?
Ooor, *anything* else.
What's that word we keep hearing? *Yosemite?*
That's surely its *Native* name!
Yosemite Valley. All in favor?
Aye!
Its name is *Ahwahnee* Valley!
"Yosemite" means *killer!*
Then everyone was forced to leave?
Yes, the Ahwahnechee tried to return, but the militia kept them away.
Many of the Ahwahnechee were killed.

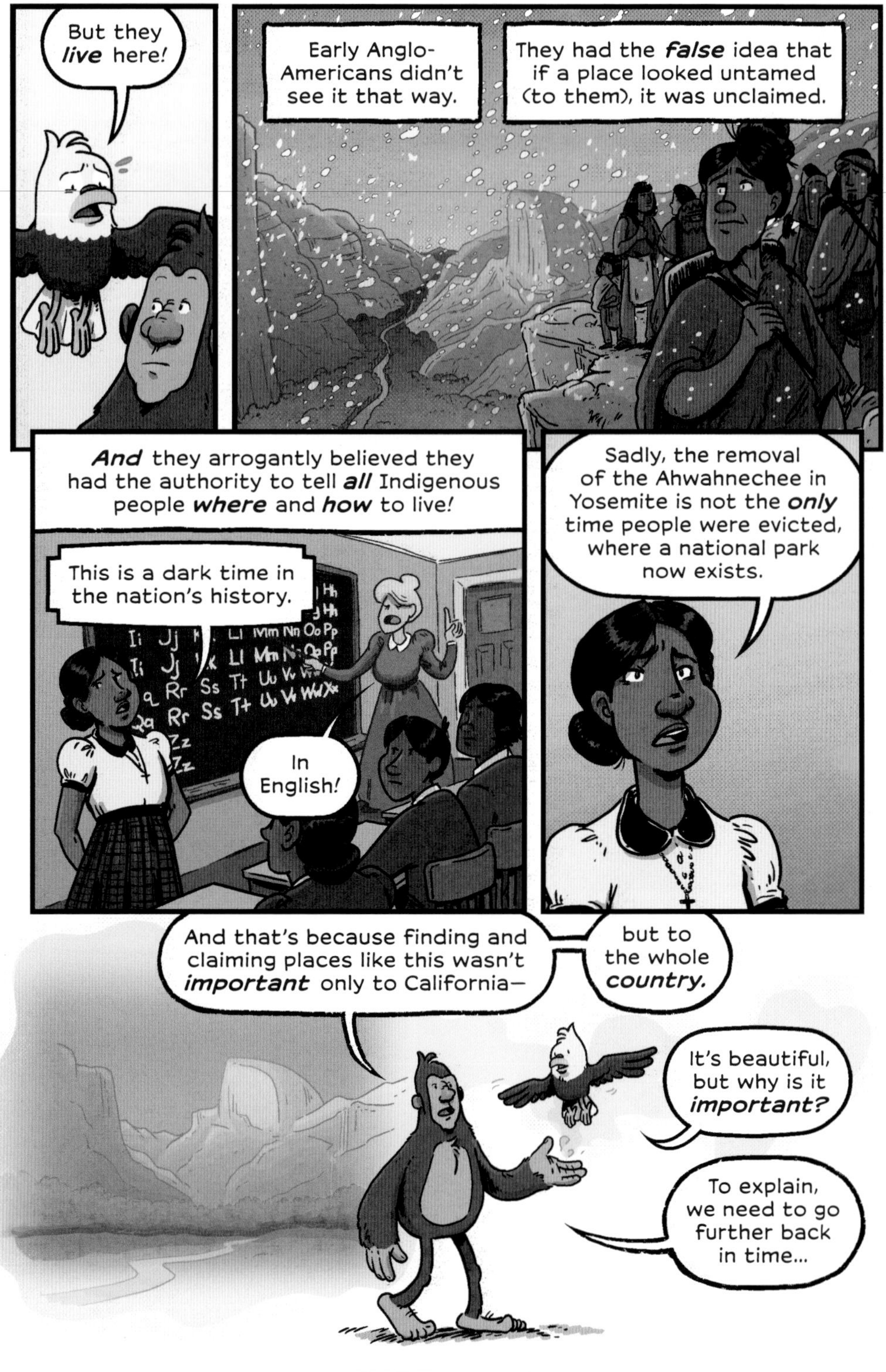
But they *live* here!
Early Anglo-Americans didn't see it that way.
They had the *false* idea that if a place looked untamed (to them), it was unclaimed.
And they arrogantly believed they had the authority to tell *all* Indigenous people *where* and *how* to live!
This is a dark time in the nation's history.
In English!
Sadly, the removal of the Ahwahnechee in Yosemite is not the *only* time people were evicted, where a national park now exists.
And that's because finding and claiming places like this wasn't *important* only to California—
but to the whole *country.*
It's beautiful, but why is it *important?*
To explain, we need to go further back in time...

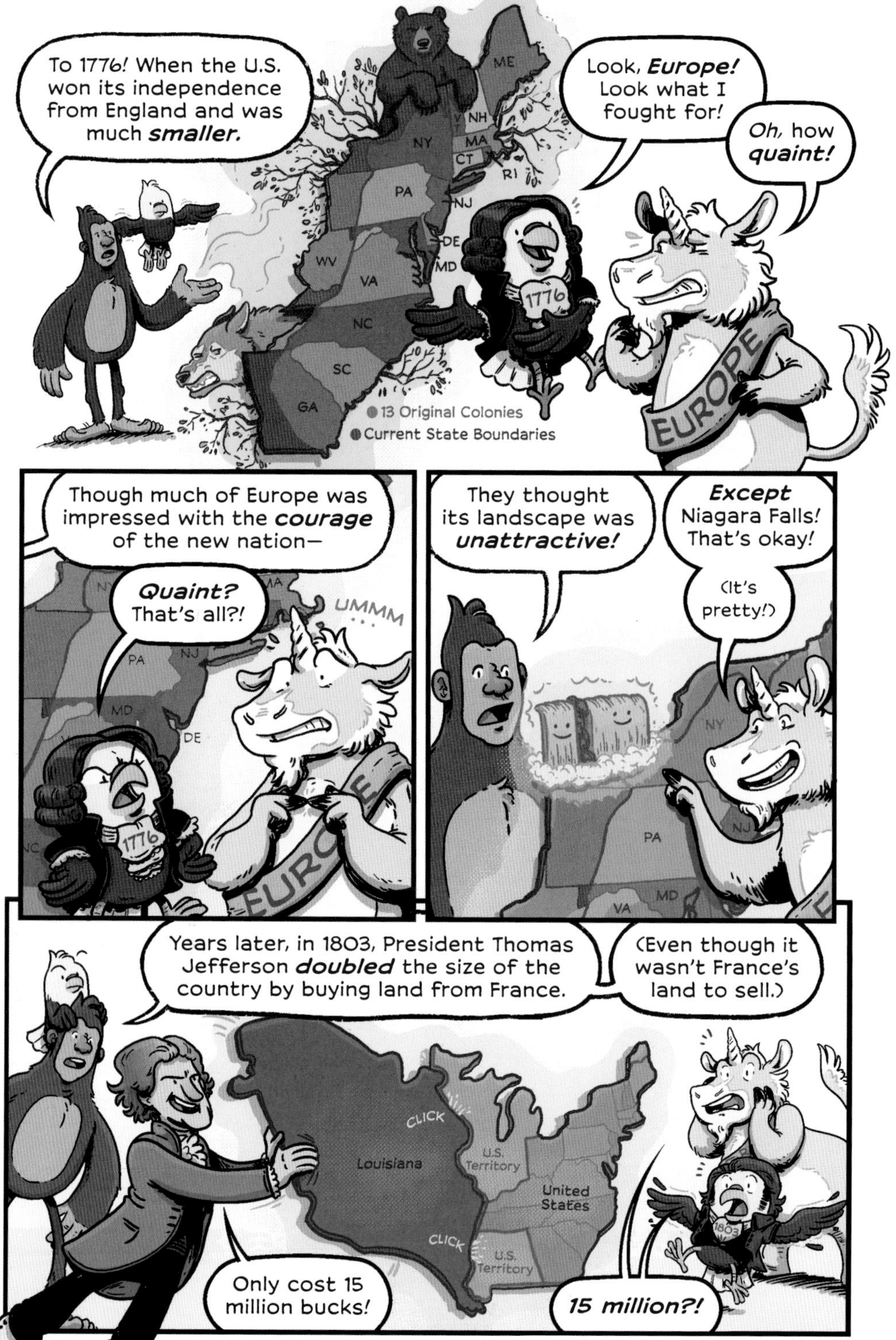
To 1776! When the U.S. won its independence from England and was much ***smaller.***
ME
NH
VT
MA
NY
CT
RI
PA
NJ
DE
MD
WV
VA
NC
SC
GA
13 Original Colonies
Current State Boundaries
Look, ***Europe!*** Look what I fought for!
Oh, how ***quaint!***
1776
EUROPE
Though much of Europe was impressed with the ***courage*** of the new nation—
Quaint? That's all?!
UMMM . . .
They thought its landscape was ***unattractive!***
Except Niagara Falls! That's okay!
(It's pretty!)
Years later, in 1803, President Thomas Jefferson ***doubled*** the size of the country by buying land from France.
(Even though it wasn't France's land to sell.)
CLICK
Louisiana
U.S. Territory
United States
CLICK
U.S. Territory
Only cost 15 million bucks!
15 million?!
1803

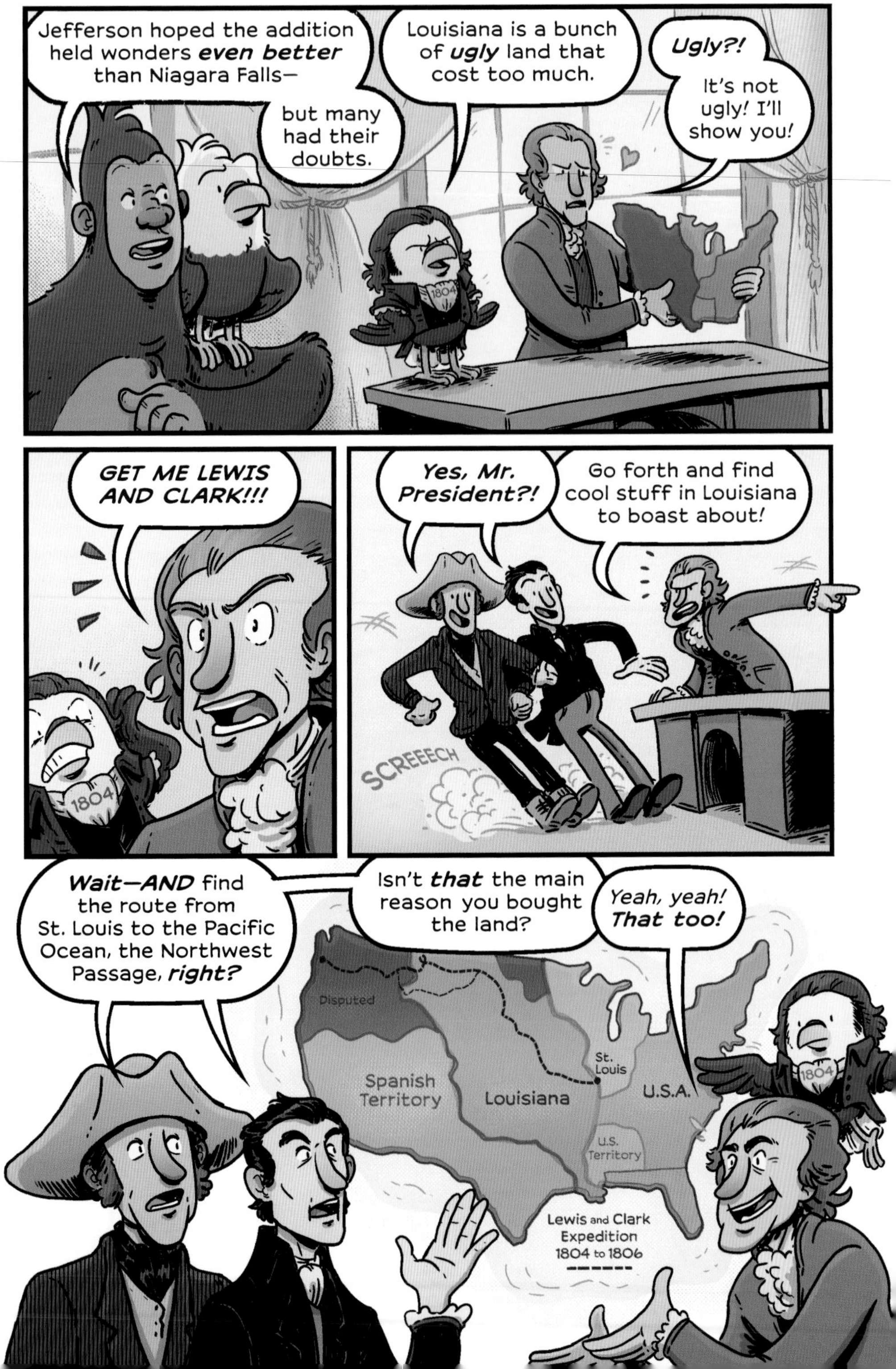
Jefferson hoped the addition held wonders *even better* than Niagara Falls—
but many had their doubts.
Louisiana is a bunch of *ugly* land that cost too much.
Ugly?!
It's not ugly! I'll show you!
1804
GET ME LEWIS AND CLARK!!!
1804
Yes, Mr. President?!
Go forth and find cool stuff in Louisiana to boast about!
SCREEECH
Wait—AND find the route from St. Louis to the Pacific Ocean, the Northwest Passage, *right?*
Isn't *that* the main reason you bought the land?
Yeah, yeah! That too!
Disputed
Spanish Territory
Louisiana
St. Louis
U.S.A.
U.S. Territory
Lewis and Clark Expedition 1804 to 1806
1804

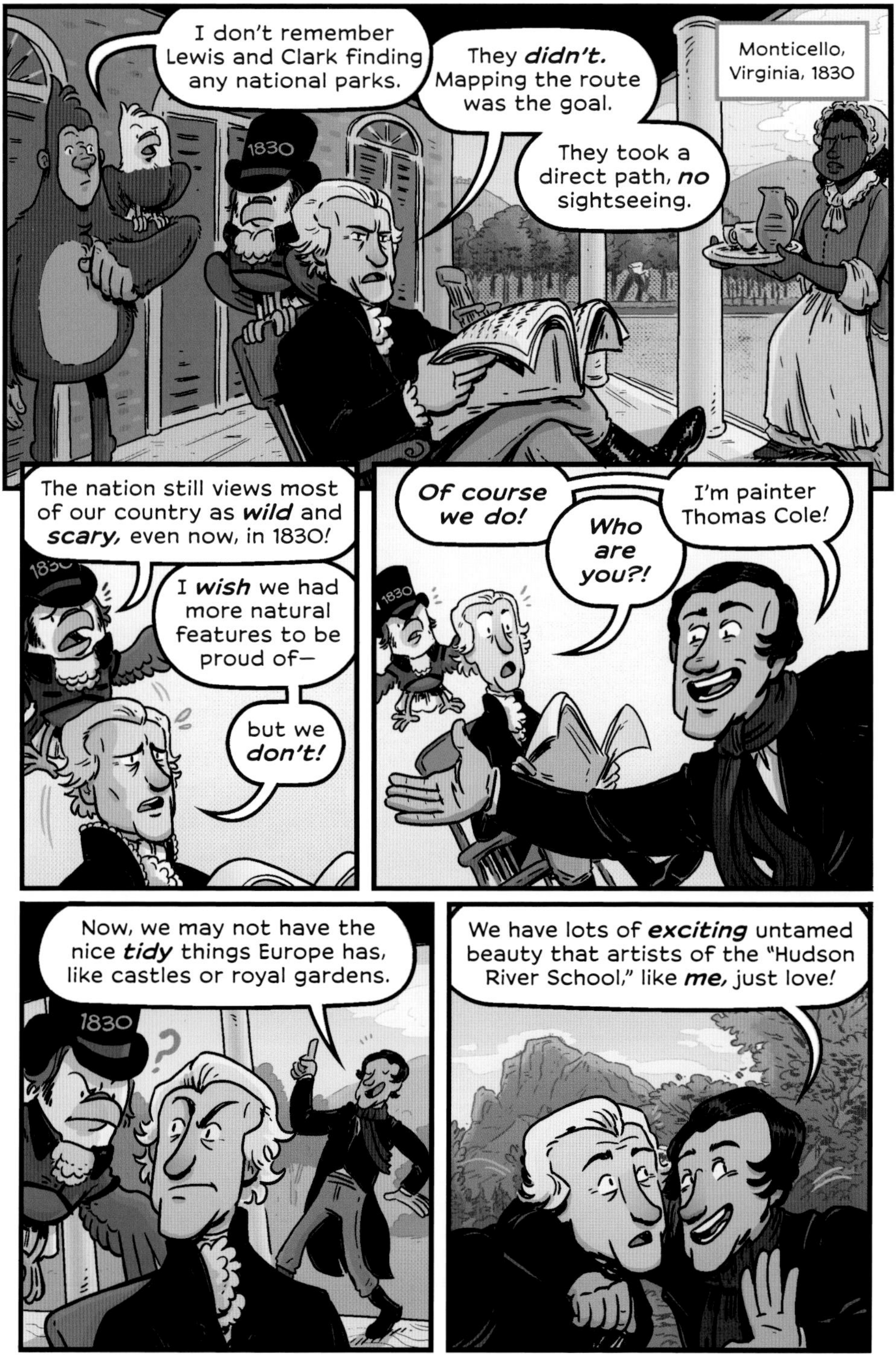
Monticello, Virginia, 1830
I don't remember Lewis and Clark finding any national parks.
They ***didn't.*** Mapping the route was the goal.
They took a direct path, ***no*** sightseeing.
1830
The nation still views most of our country as ***wild*** and ***scary,*** even now, in 1830!
I ***wish*** we had more natural features to be proud of—
but we ***don't!***
Of course we do!
Who are you?!
I'm painter Thomas Cole!
Now, we may not have the nice ***tidy*** things Europe has, like castles or royal gardens.
?
We have lots of ***exciting*** untamed beauty that artists of the "Hudson River School," like ***me,*** just love!

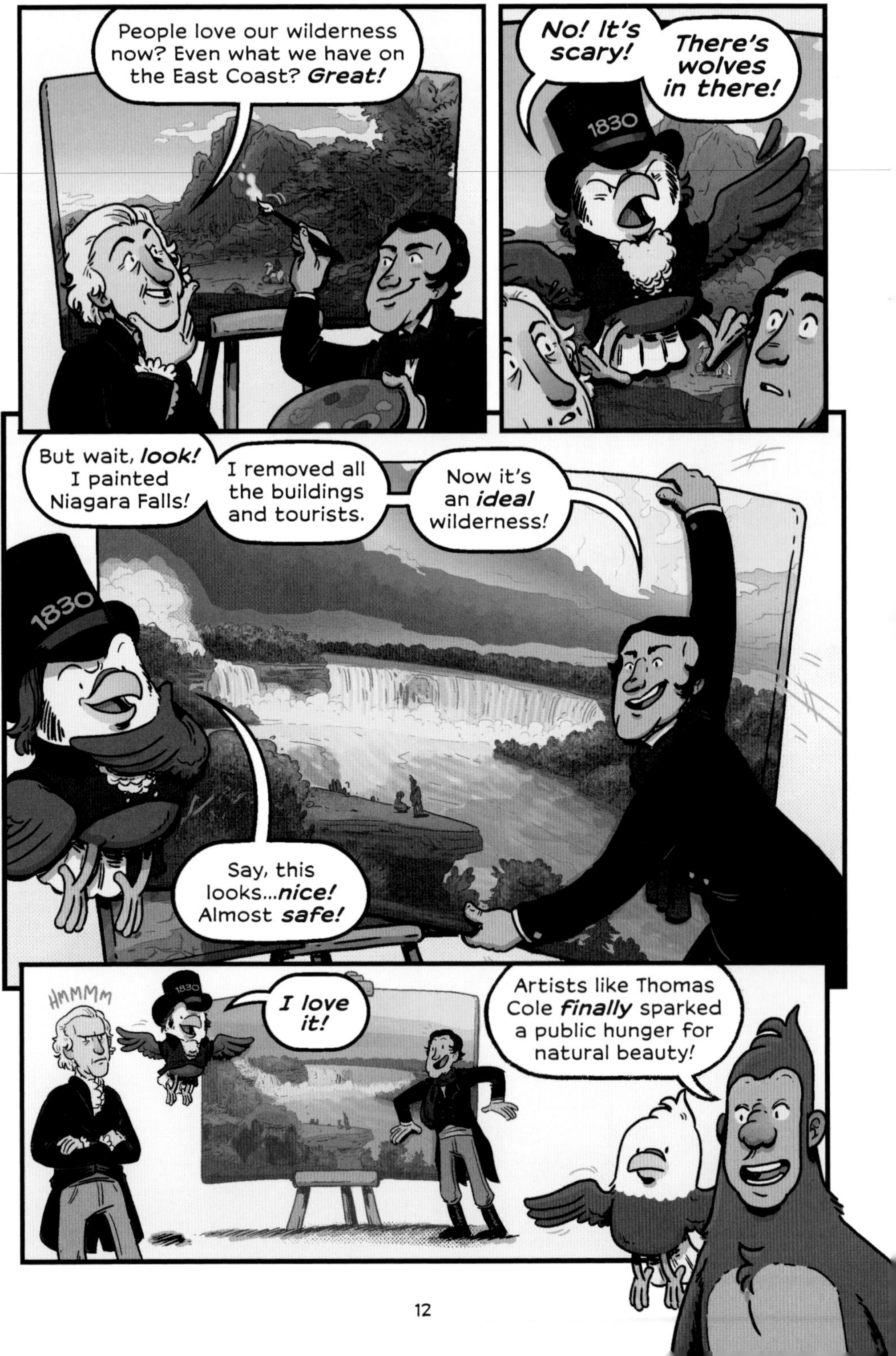
People love our wilderness now? Even what we have on the East Coast? ***Great!***
No! It's scary!
There's wolves in there!
But wait, ***look!*** I painted Niagara Falls!
I removed all the buildings and tourists.
Now it's an ***ideal*** wilderness!
1830
Say, this looks...***nice!*** Almost ***safe!***
HMMMM
I love it!
Artists like Thomas Cole ***finally*** sparked a public hunger for natural beauty!

Years later, that hunger *grew* when news of waterfalls in California—

a *thousand* times taller than Niagara Falls—

spread across the country—and the world!

Um, it's only *14* times taller.

Yosemite Valley was the marvel the nation had been waiting for. And by 1855, people who knew very little about the area were eager to *capitalize* on it.

Here we are, *Yosemite Falls!*

Aah, this is nature we can *really* brag about!

Take that, *Europe!*

Get sketching, Thomas Ayres! The world needs to see this place!

Yes, Mr. Hutchings!

Another painter?

Just take a photo!

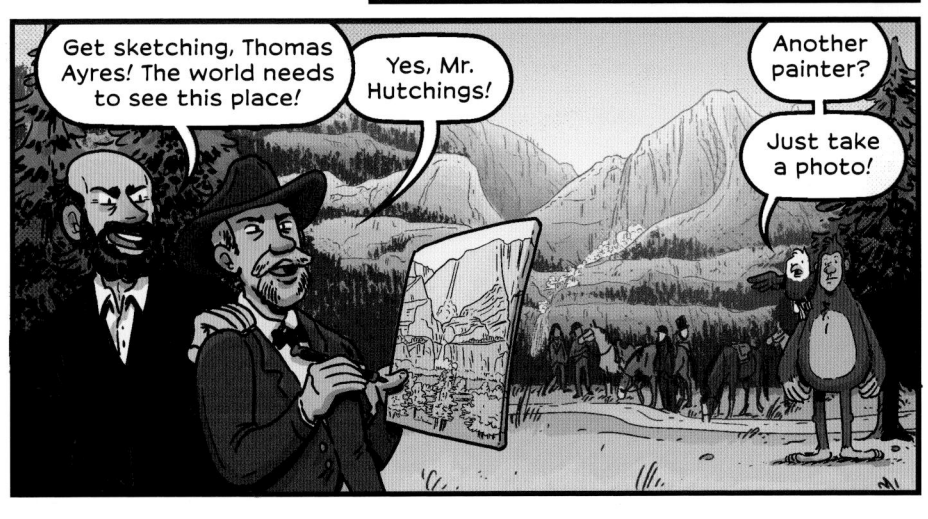

13

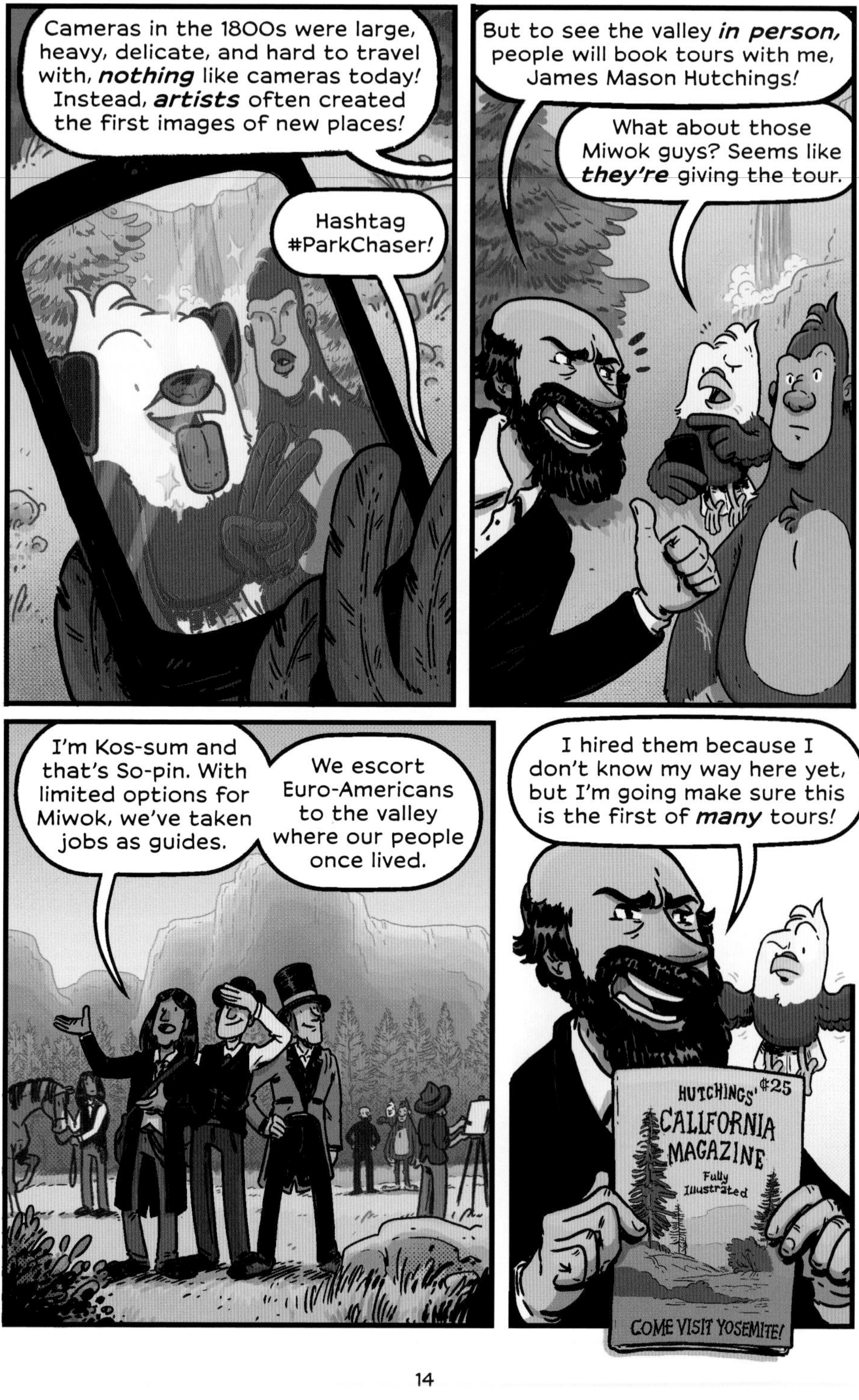
Cameras in the 1800s were large, heavy, delicate, and hard to travel with, *nothing* like cameras today! Instead, *artists* often created the first images of new places!
Hashtag #ParkChaser!
But to see the valley *in person,* people will book tours with me, James Mason Hutchings!
What about those Miwok guys? Seems like *they're* giving the tour.
I'm Kos-sum and that's So-pin. With limited options for Miwok, we've taken jobs as guides.
We escort Euro-Americans to the valley where our people once lived.
I hired them because I don't know my way here yet, but I'm going make sure this is the first of *many* tours!
HUTCHINGS' ¢25
CALIFORNIA MAGAZINE
Fully Illustrated
COME VISIT YOSEMITE!

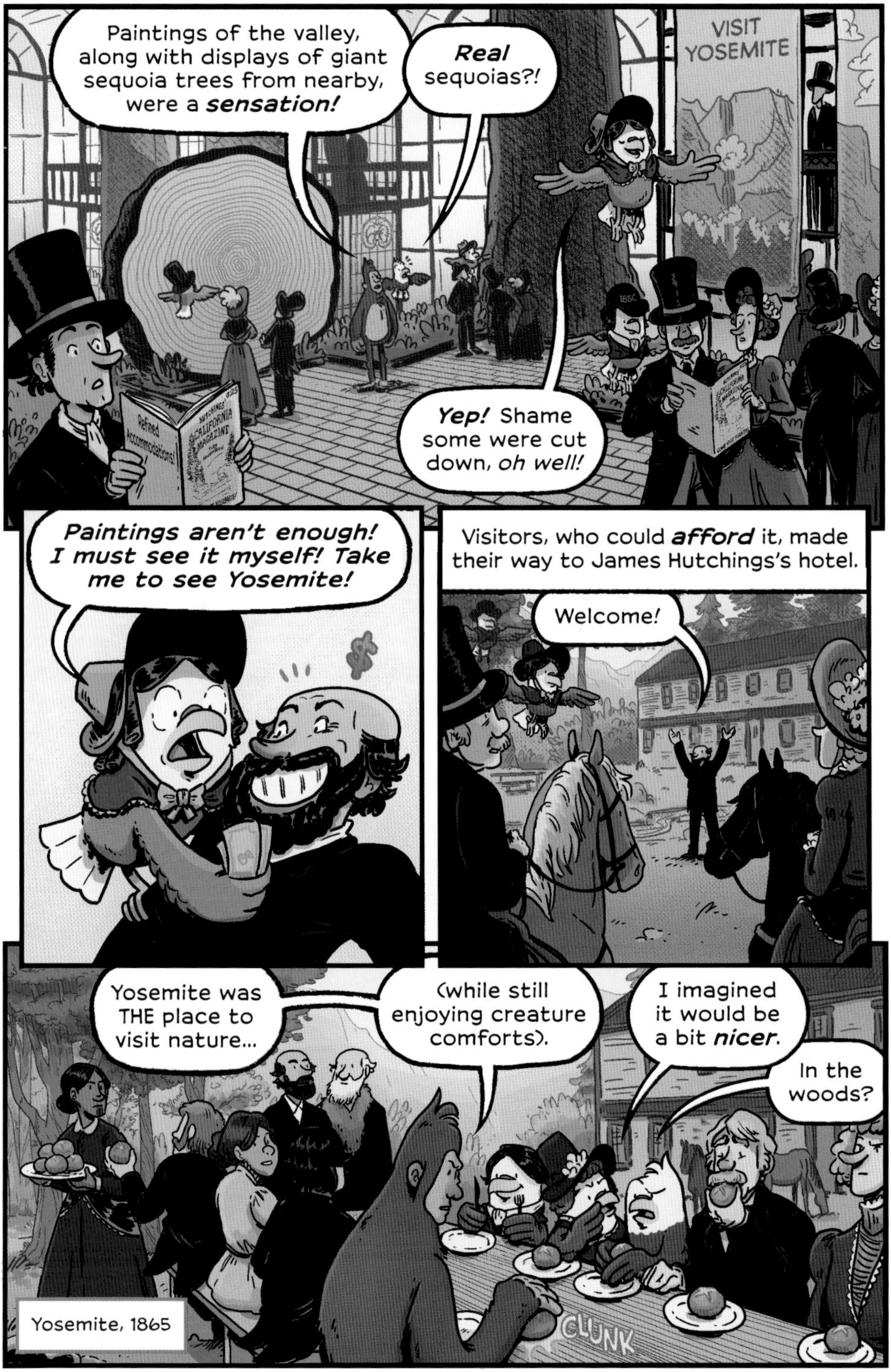
Paintings of the valley, along with displays of giant sequoia trees from nearby, were a ***sensation!***
Real sequoias?!
VISIT YOSEMITE
Refined Accommodations!
HUTCHINGS' CALIFORNIA MAGAZINE
Yep! Shame some were cut down, *oh well!*
Paintings aren't enough! I must see it myself! Take me to see Yosemite!
Visitors, who could ***afford*** it, made their way to James Hutchings's hotel.
Welcome!
Yosemite was THE place to visit nature...
(while still enjoying creature comforts).
I imagined it would be a bit ***nicer***.
In the woods?
Yosemite, 1865
CLUNK

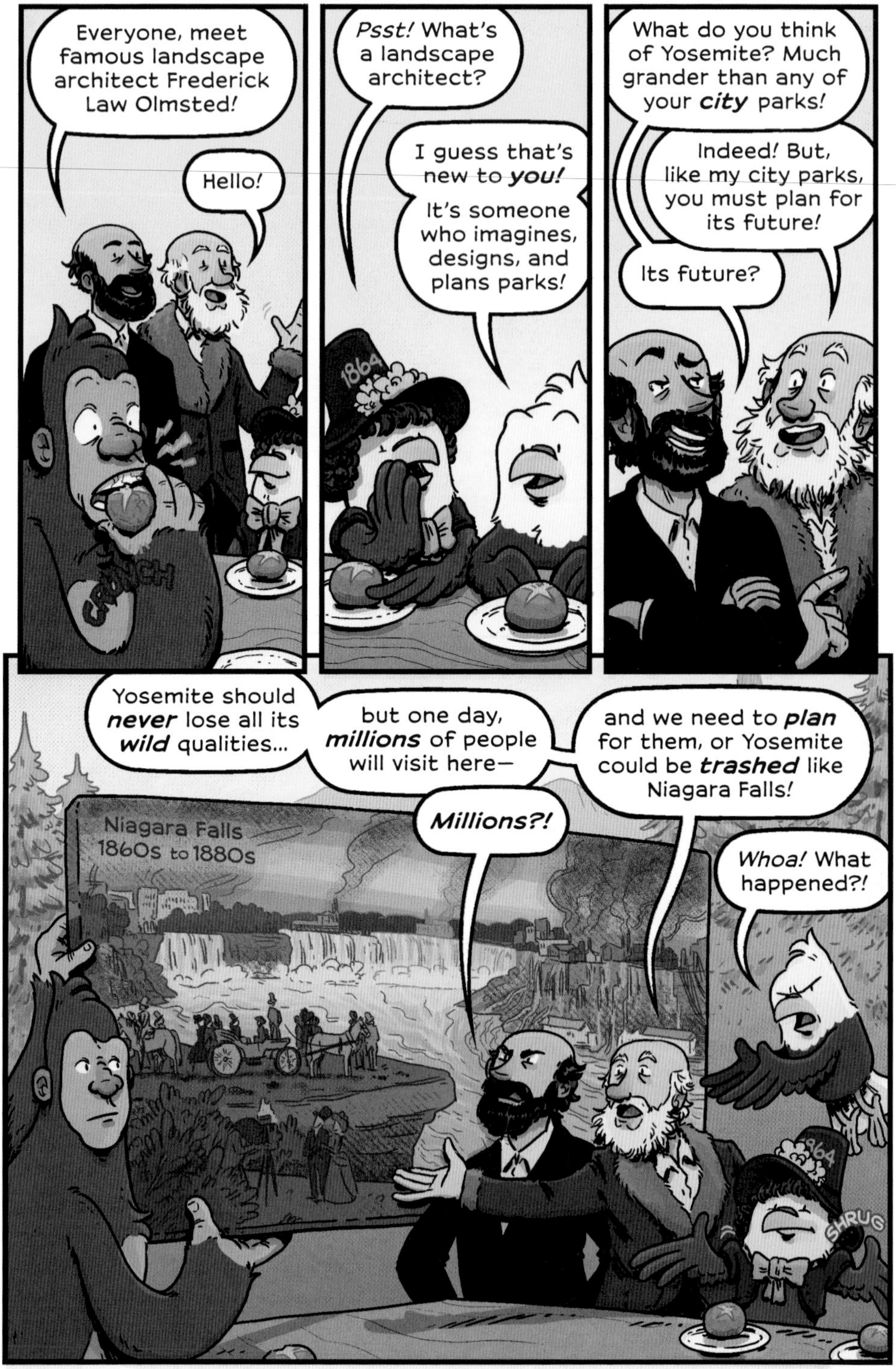
Everyone, meet famous landscape architect Frederick Law Olmsted!
Hello!
CRUNCH
Psst! What's a landscape architect?
I guess that's new to you!
It's someone who imagines, designs, and plans parks!
1864
What do you think of Yosemite? Much grander than any of your city parks!
Indeed! But, like my city parks, you must plan for its future!
Its future?
Yosemite should never lose all its wild qualities...
but one day, millions of people will visit here—
and we need to plan for them, or Yosemite could be trashed like Niagara Falls!
Millions?!
Niagara Falls 1860s to 1880s
Whoa! What happened?!
1864
SHRUG

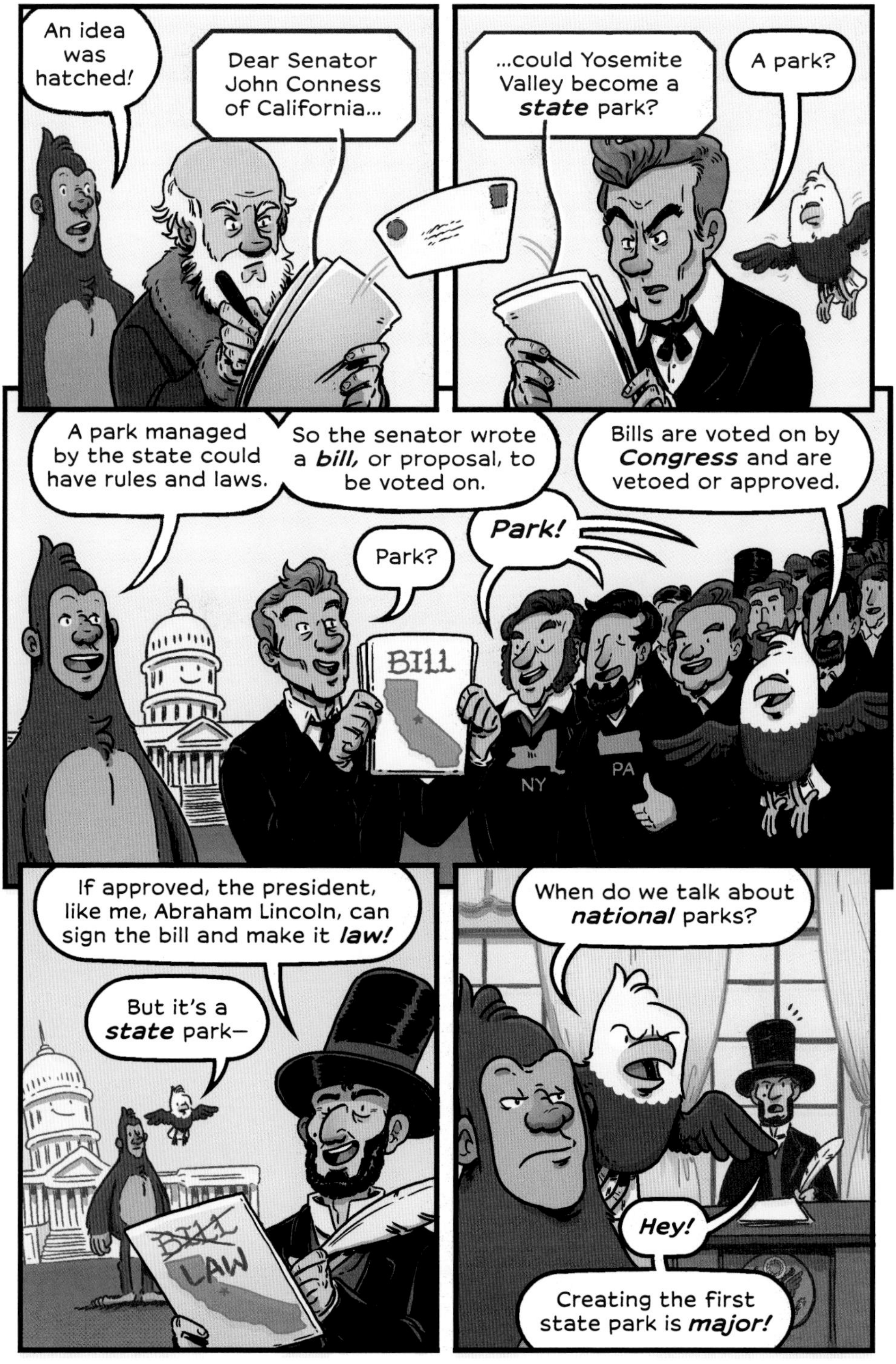
An idea was hatched!
Dear Senator John Conness of California...
...could Yosemite Valley become a *state* park?
A park?
A park managed by the state could have rules and laws.
So the senator wrote a *bill,* or proposal, to be voted on.
Bills are voted on by *Congress* and are vetoed or approved.
Park?
Park!
BILL
NY
PA
If approved, the president, like me, Abraham Lincoln, can sign the bill and make it *law!*
But it's a *state* park—
BILL
LAW
When do we talk about *national* parks?
Hey!
Creating the first state park is *major!*

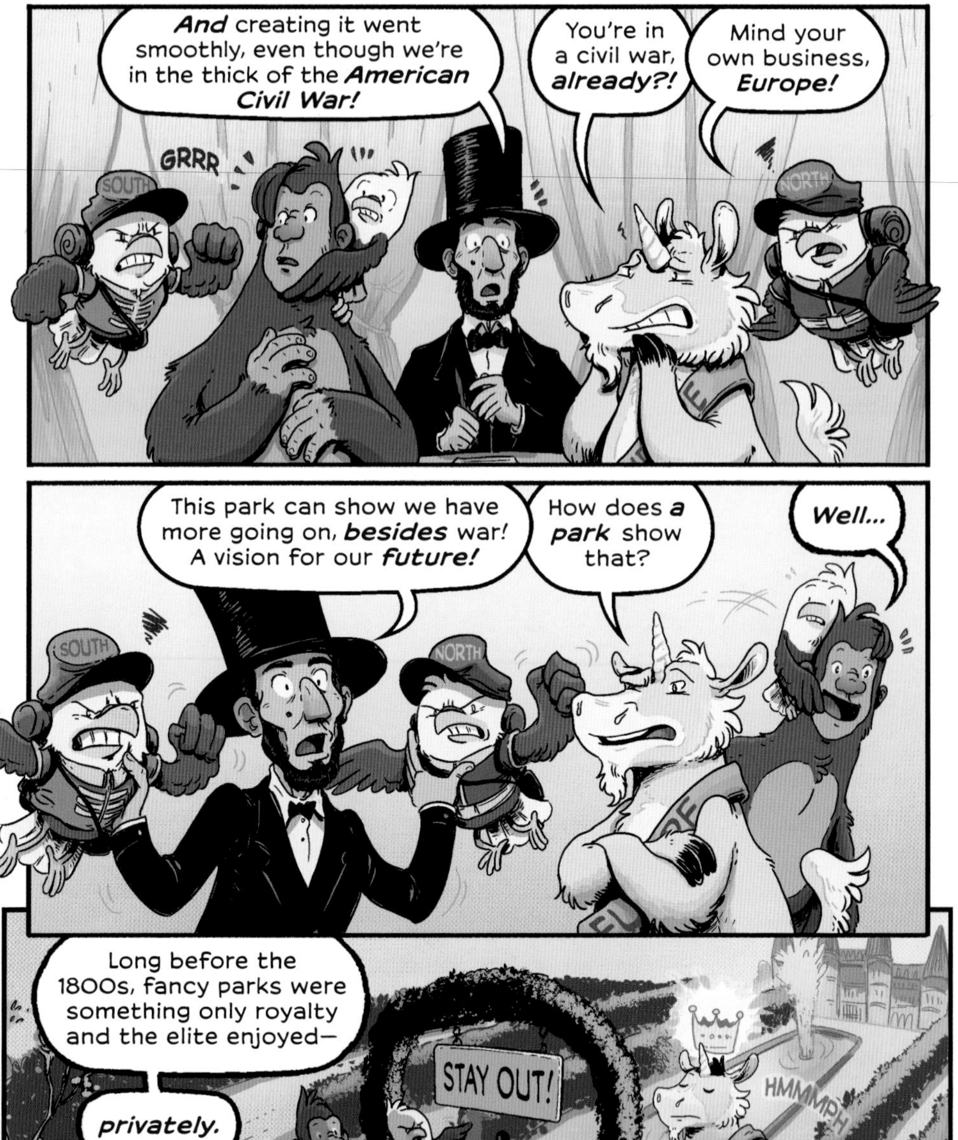

And creating it went smoothly, even though we're in the thick of the ***American Civil War!***
You're in a civil war, ***already?!***
Mind your own business, ***Europe!***
GRRR
SOUTH
NORTH
This park can show we have more going on, ***besides*** war! A vision for our ***future!***
How does ***a park*** show that?
Well...
SOUTH
NORTH
Long before the 1800s, fancy parks were something only royalty and the elite enjoyed—
privately.
STAY OUT!
HMMMPH
GO AW
Rude!
SCRAM!

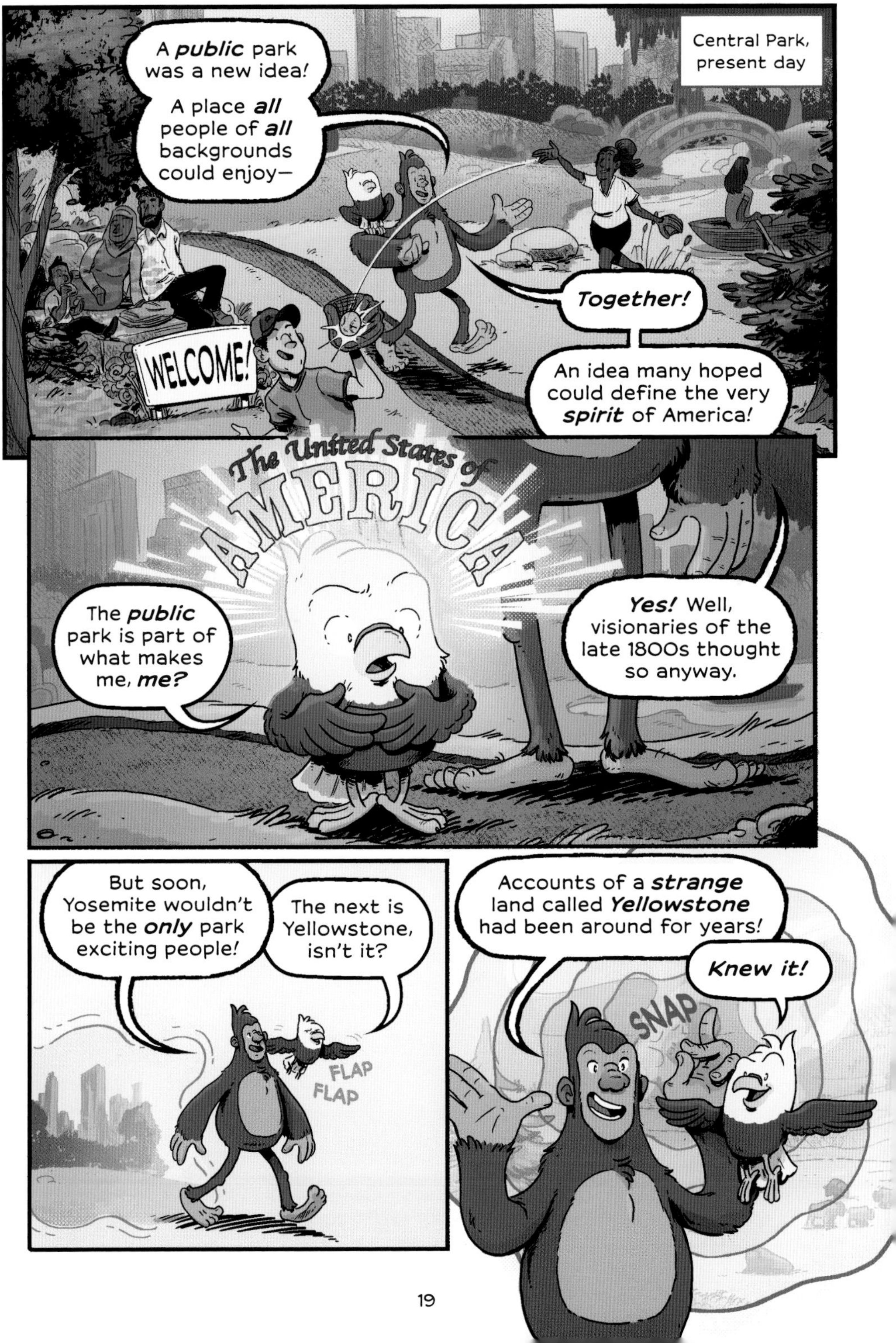
Central Park, present day
A *public* park was a new idea!
A place *all* people of *all* backgrounds could enjoy—
WELCOME!
Together!
An idea many hoped could define the very *spirit* of America!
The United States of AMERICA
The *public* park is part of what makes me, *me?*
Yes! Well, visionaries of the late 1800s thought so anyway.
But soon, Yosemite wouldn't be the *only* park exciting people!
The next is Yellowstone, isn't it?
FLAP FLAP
Accounts of a *strange* land called *Yellowstone* had been around for years!
Knew it!
SNAP

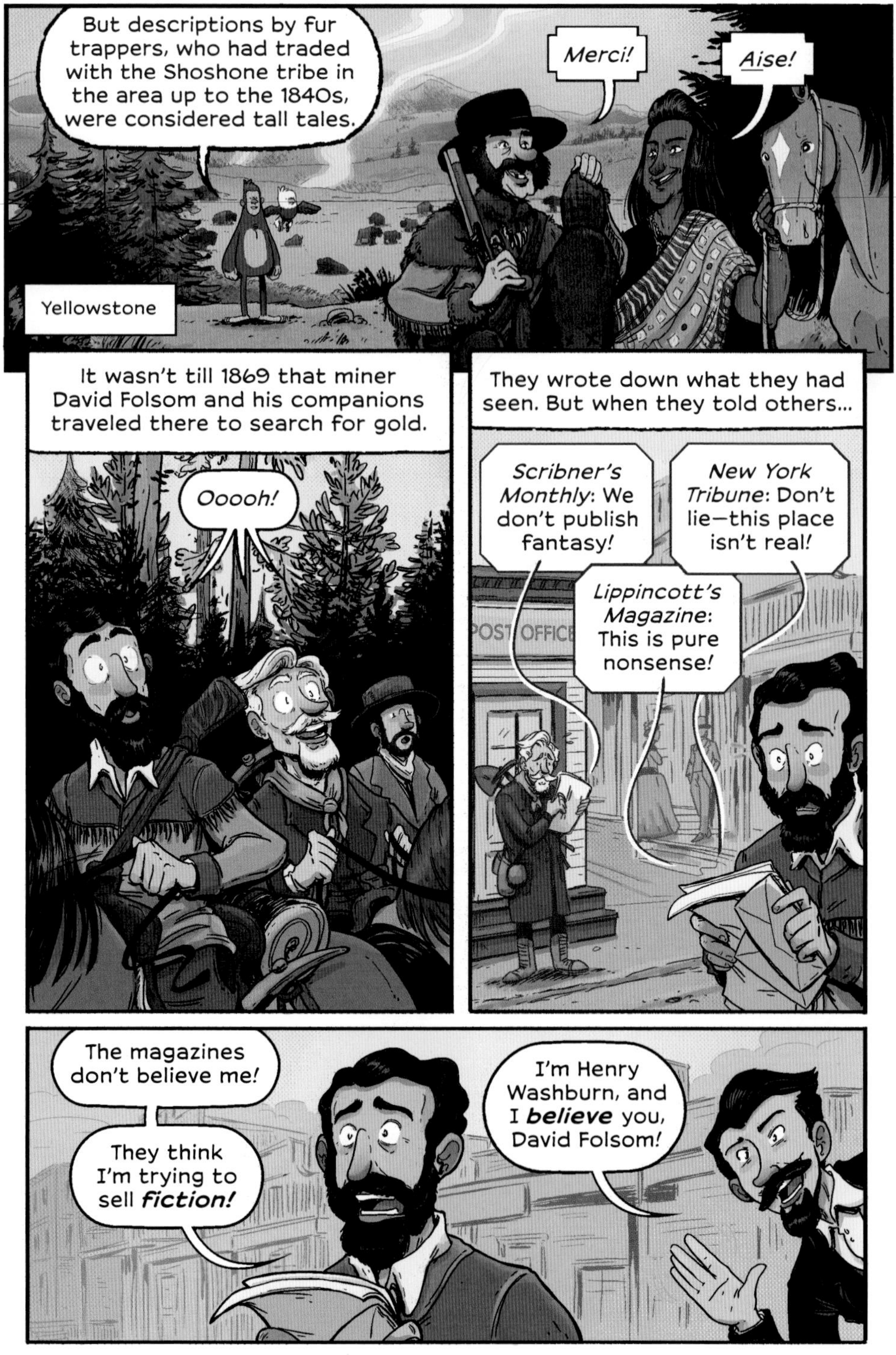
But descriptions by fur trappers, who had traded with the Shoshone tribe in the area up to the 1840s, were considered tall tales.
Merci!
Aise!
Yellowstone
It wasn't till 1869 that miner David Folsom and his companions traveled there to search for gold.
Ooooh!
They wrote down what they had seen. But when they told others...
Scribner's Monthly: We don't publish fantasy!
New York Tribune: Don't lie—this place isn't real!
Lippincott's Magazine: This is pure nonsense!
POST OFFICE
The magazines don't believe me!
They think I'm trying to sell ***fiction!***
I'm Henry Washburn, and I ***believe*** you, David Folsom!

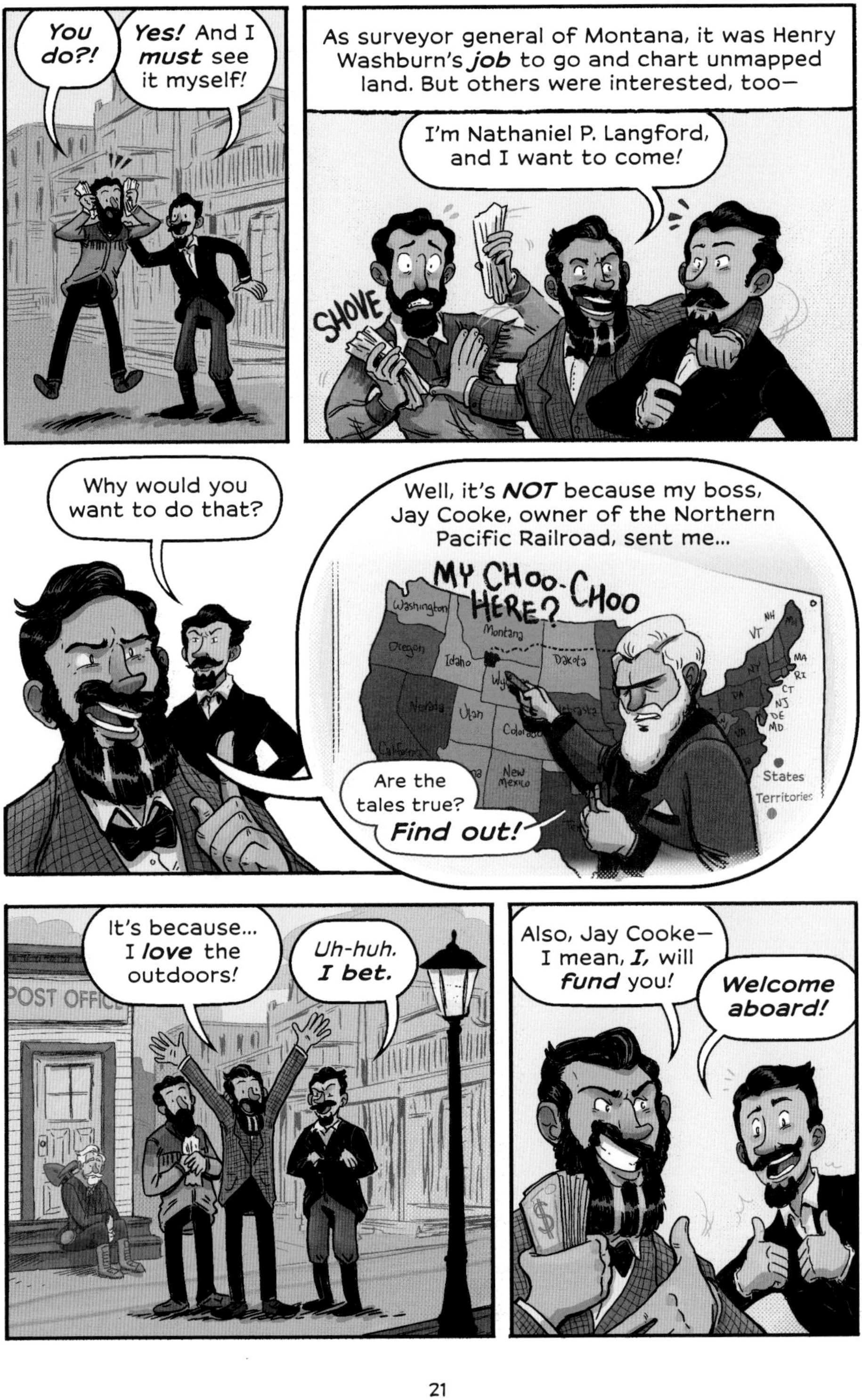

You do?!
Yes! And I must see it myself!
As surveyor general of Montana, it was Henry Washburn's job to go and chart unmapped land. But others were interested, too—
I'm Nathaniel P. Langford, and I want to come!
SHOVE
Why would you want to do that?
Well, it's NOT because my boss, Jay Cooke, owner of the Northern Pacific Railroad, sent me...
MY CHOO-CHOO HERE?
Washington
Oregon
Idaho
Montana
Dakota
Utah
Colorado
New Mexico
NH
VT
MA
RI
CT
NJ
DE
MD
States
Territories
Are the tales true?
Find out!
It's because... I love the outdoors!
Uh-huh. I bet.
POST OFFICE
Also, Jay Cooke— I mean, I, will fund you!
Welcome aboard!

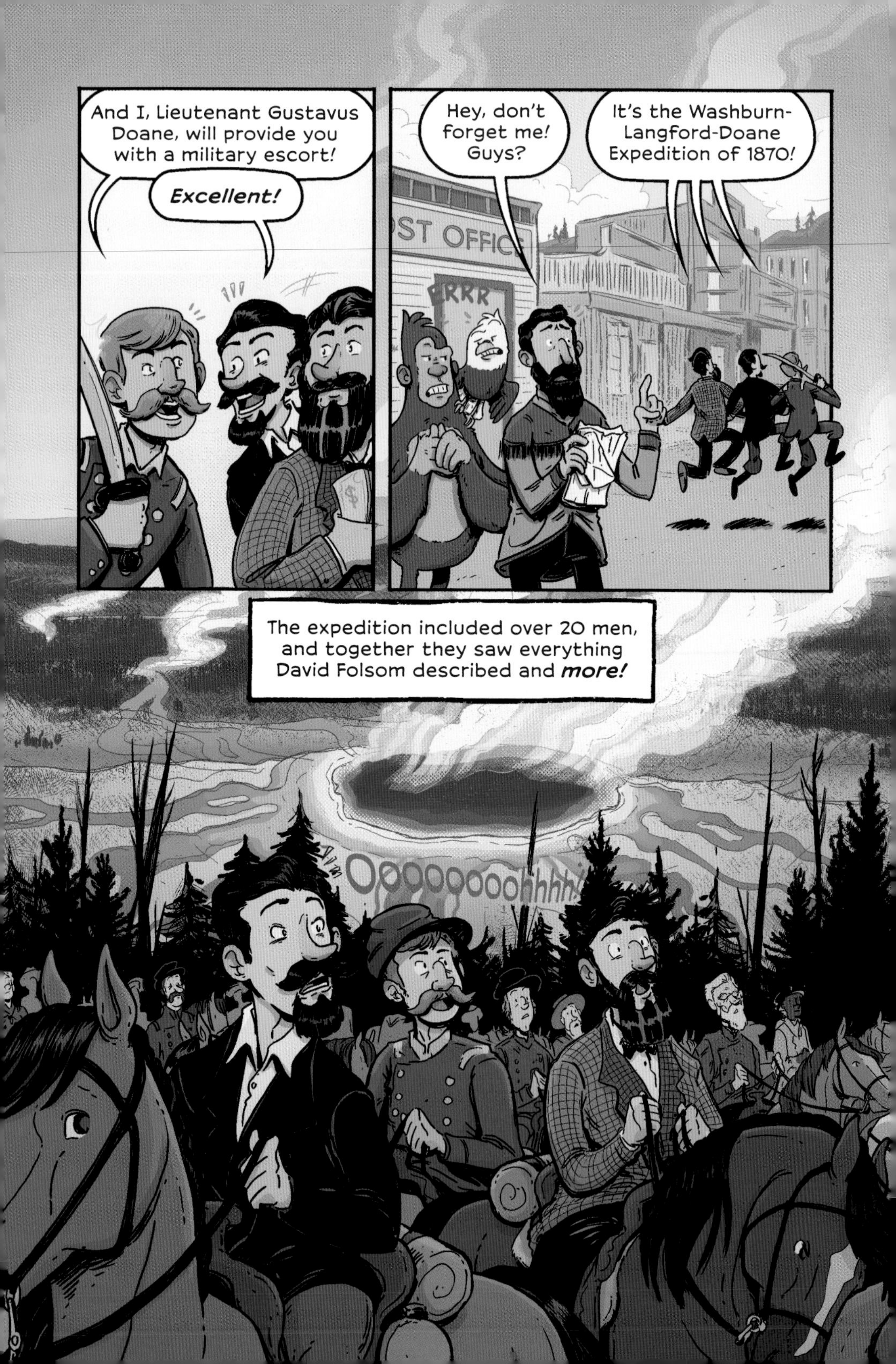
And I, Lieutenant Gustavus Doane, will provide you with a military escort!
Excellent!
Hey, don't forget me! Guys?
It's the Washburn-Langford-Doane Expedition of 1870!
POST OFFICE
ERRR
The expedition included over 20 men, and together they saw everything David Folsom described and more!
Oooooooohhhh!

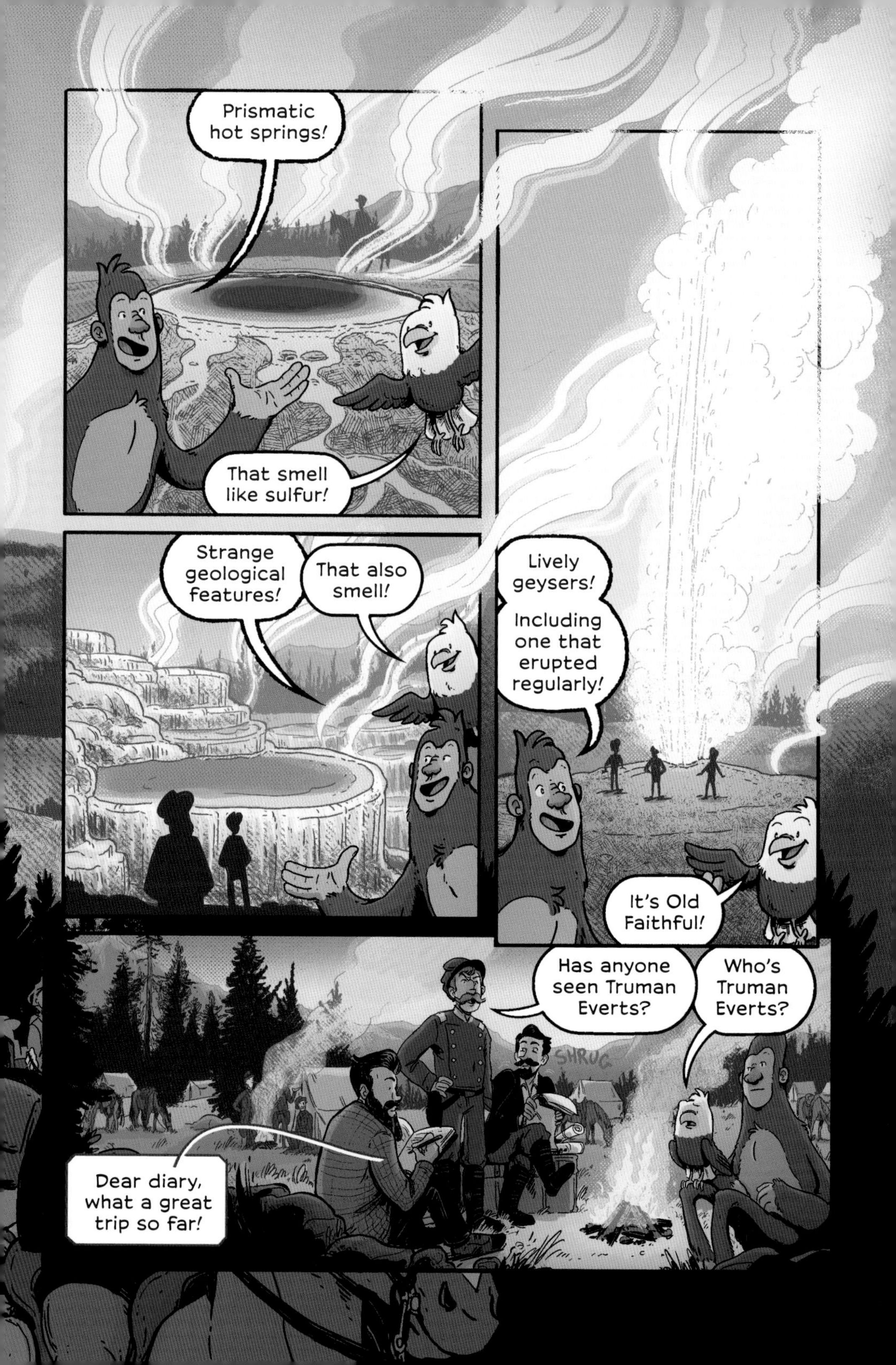
Prismatic hot springs!
That smell like sulfur!
Strange geological features!
That also smell!
Lively geysers!
Including one that erupted regularly!
It's Old Faithful!
Has anyone seen Truman Everts?
Who's Truman Everts?
SHRUG
Dear diary, what a great trip so far!

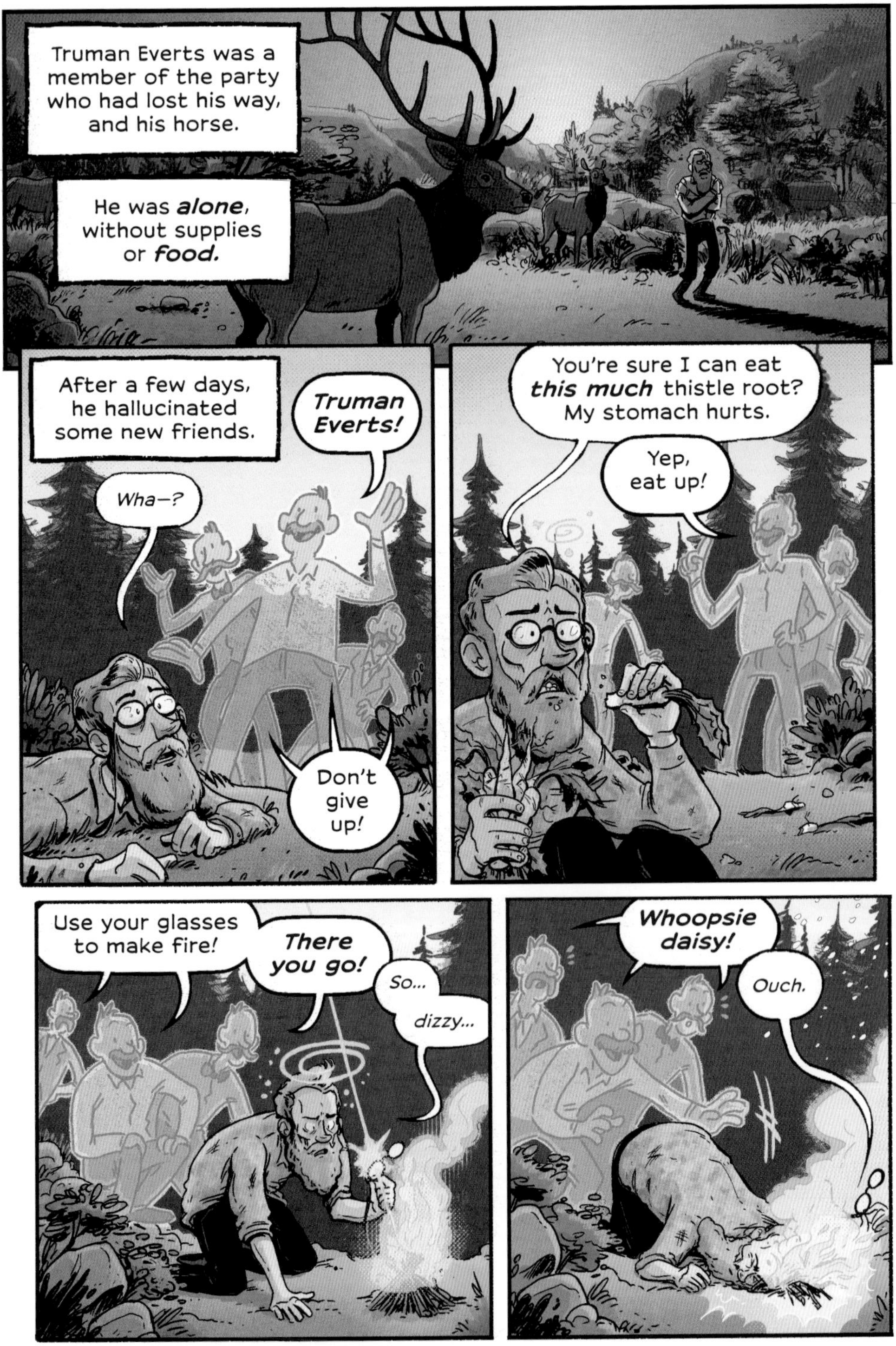

Truman Everts was a member of the party who had lost his way, and his horse.
He was **alone**, without supplies or **food.**
After a few days, he hallucinated some new friends.
Truman Everts!
Wha–?
Don't give up!
You're sure I can eat **this much** thistle root? My stomach hurts.
Yep, eat up!
Use your glasses to make fire!
There you go!
So... dizzy...
Whoopsie daisy!
Ouch.

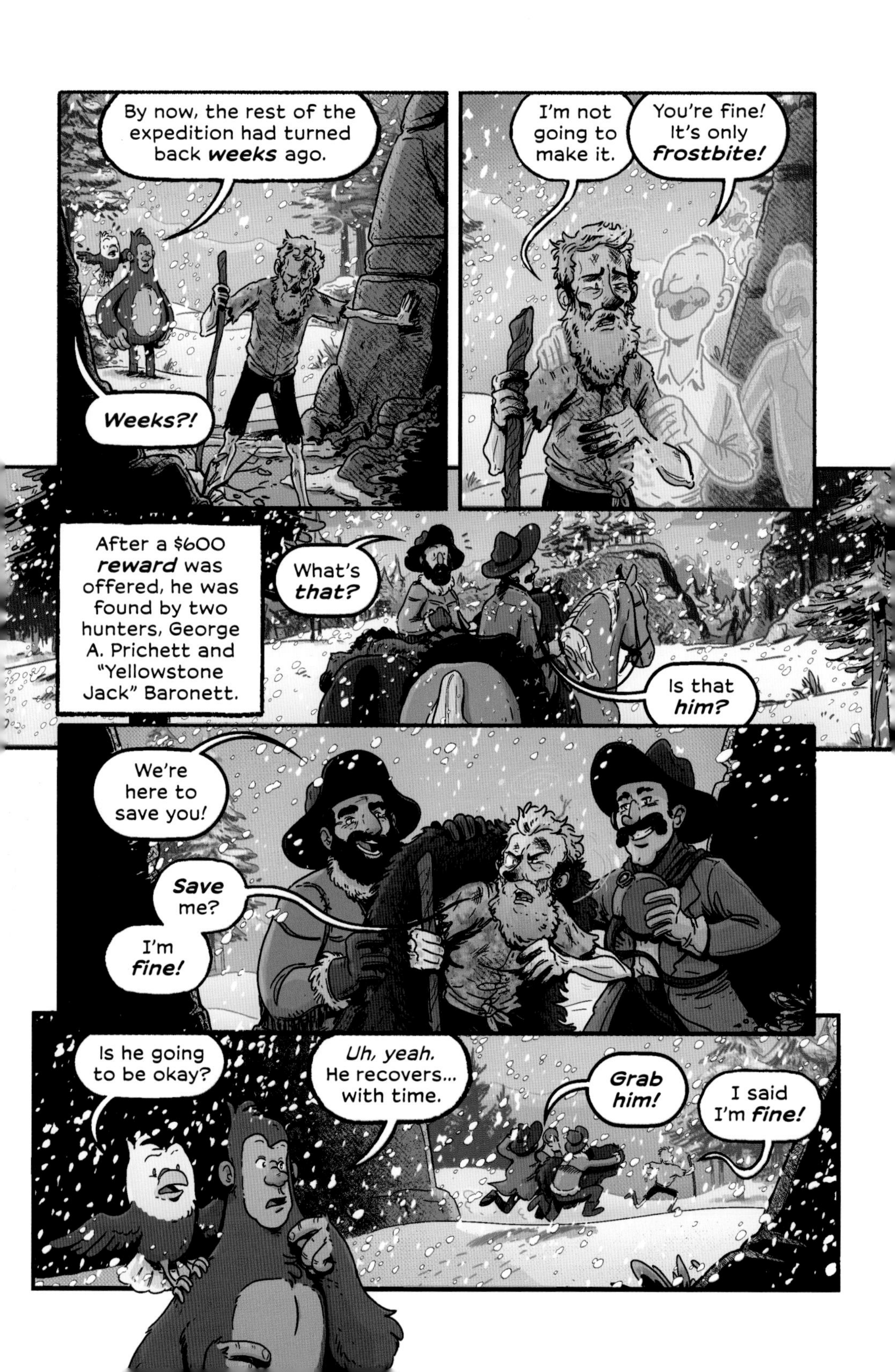

By now, the rest of the expedition had turned back *weeks* ago.
Weeks?!
I'm not going to make it.
You're fine! It's only *frostbite!*
After a $600 *reward* was offered, he was found by two hunters, George A. Prichett and "Yellowstone Jack" Baronett.
What's *that?*
Is that *him?*
We're here to save you!
Save me?
I'm *fine!*
Is he going to be okay?
Uh, yeah. He recovers... with time.
Grab him!
I said I'm *fine!*

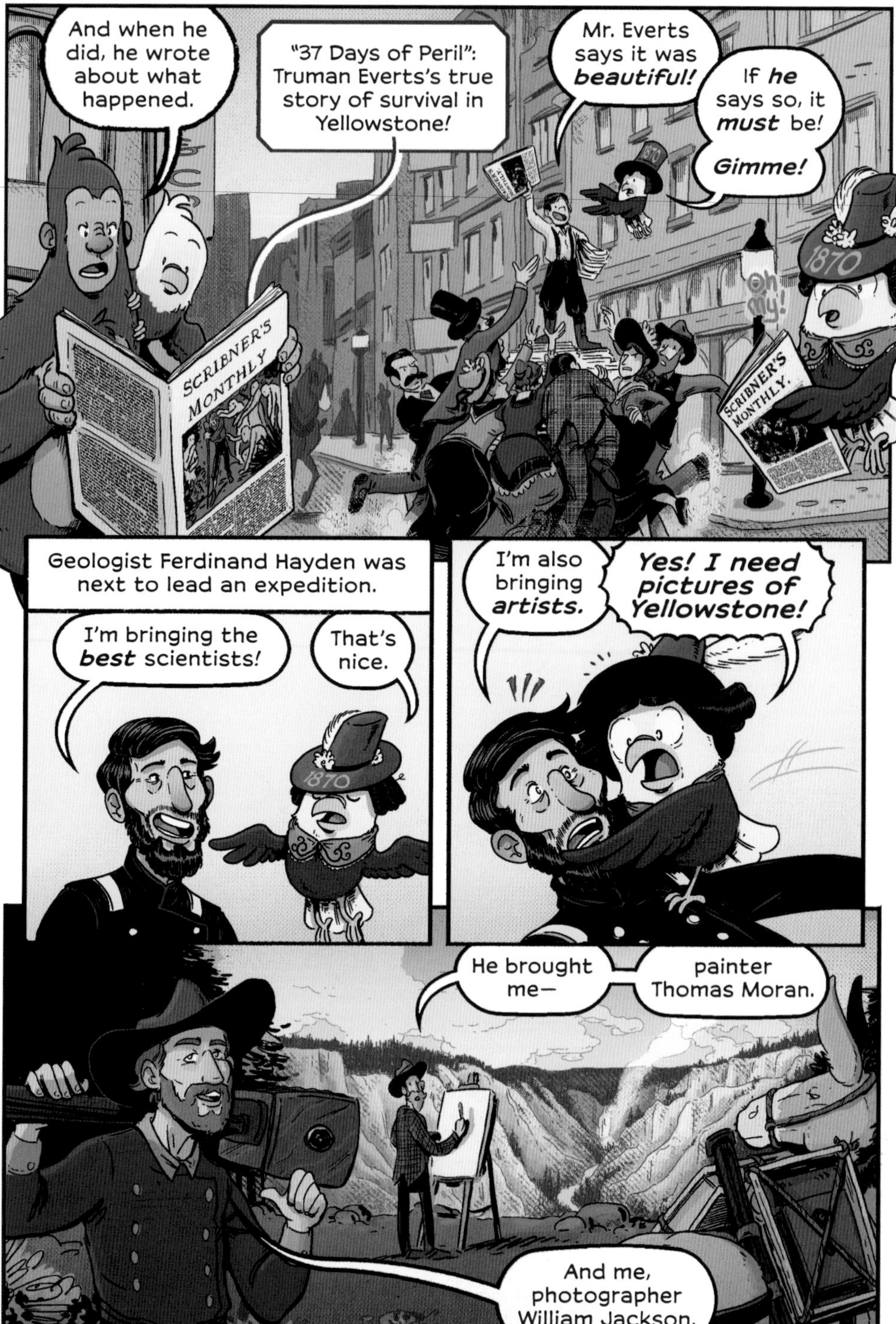
And when he did, he wrote about what happened.
"37 Days of Peril": Truman Everts's true story of survival in Yellowstone!
Mr. Everts says it was **beautiful!**
If **he** says so, it **must** be!
Gimme!
SCRIBNER'S MONTHLY
1870
Oh my!
SCRIBNER'S MONTHLY.
Geologist Ferdinand Hayden was next to lead an expedition.
I'm bringing the **best** scientists!
That's nice.
1870
I'm also bringing **artists.**
Yes! I need pictures of Yellowstone!
He brought me—
painter Thomas Moran.
And me, photographer William Jackson.

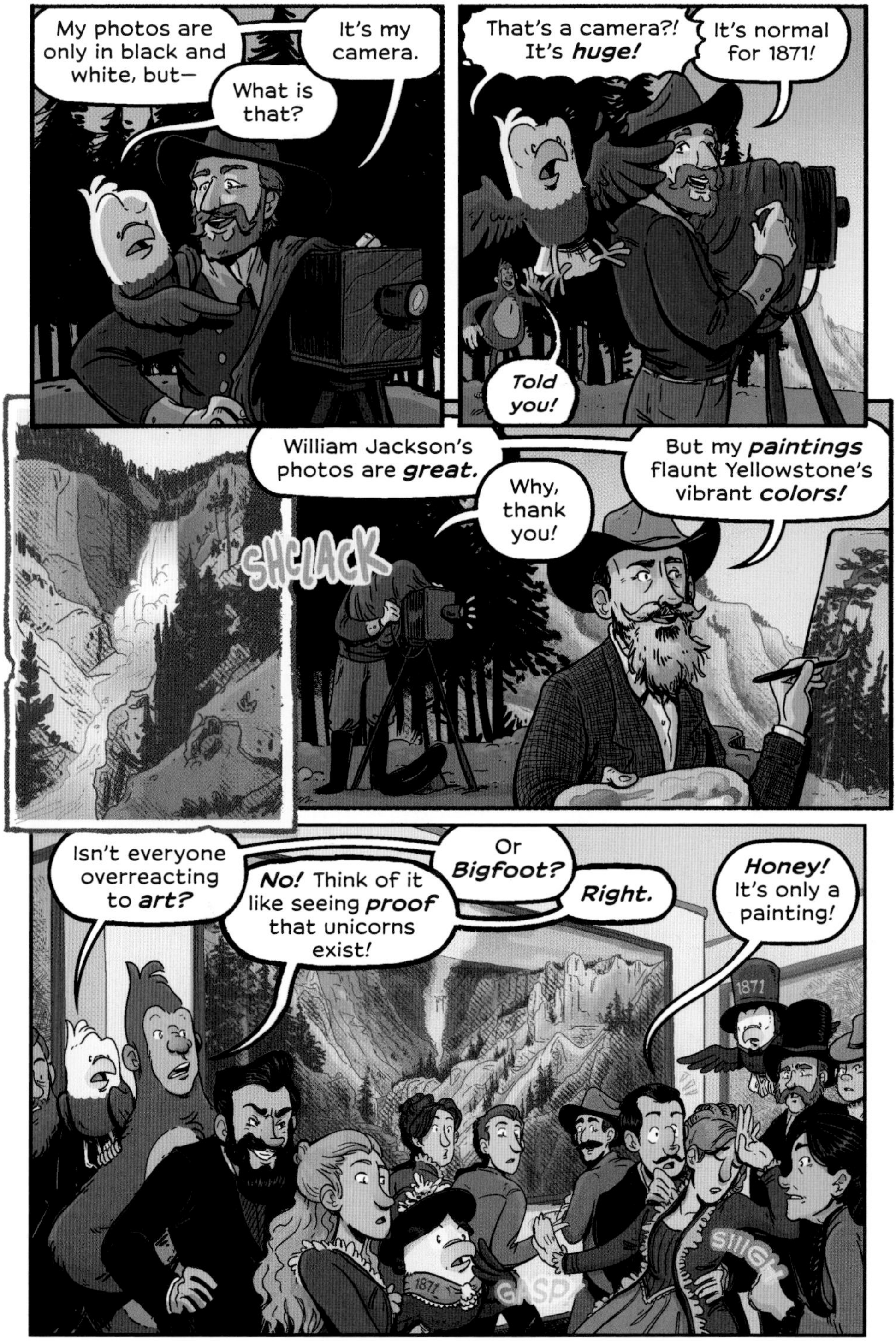
My photos are only in black and white, but—
What is that?
It's my camera.
That's a camera?! It's *huge!*
It's normal for 1871!
Told you!
William Jackson's photos are *great.*
Why, thank you!
But my *paintings* flaunt Yellowstone's vibrant *colors!*
SHCLACK
Isn't everyone overreacting to *art?*
No! Think of it like seeing *proof* that unicorns exist!
Or *Bigfoot?*
Right.
Honey! It's only a painting!
1871
1871
GASP
SIIGH

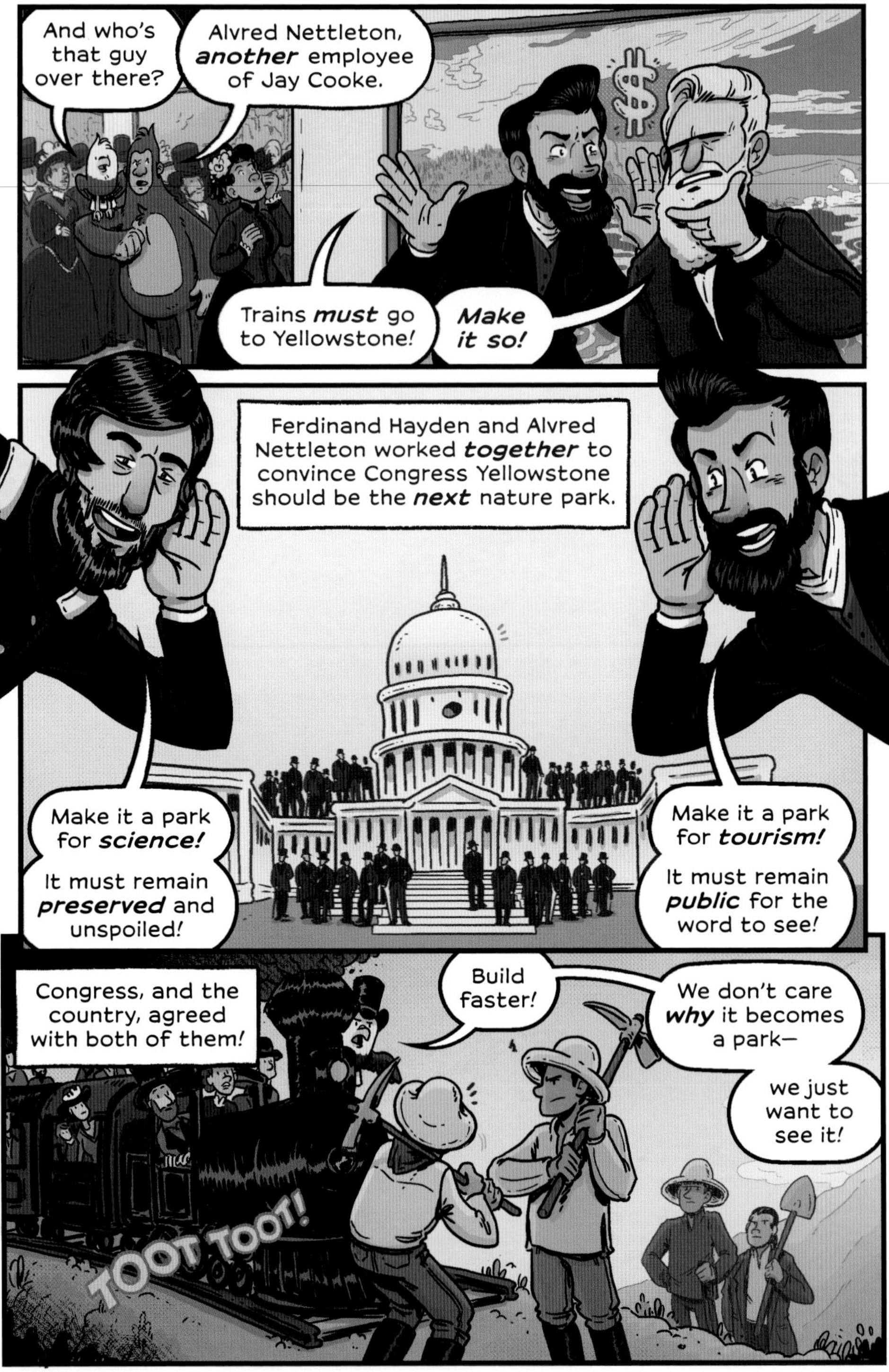
And who's that guy over there?
Alvred Nettleton, *another* employee of Jay Cooke.
Trains *must* go to Yellowstone!
Make it so!
Ferdinand Hayden and Alvred Nettleton worked *together* to convince Congress Yellowstone should be the *next* nature park.
Make it a park for *science!*
It must remain *preserved* and unspoiled!
Make it a park for *tourism!*
It must remain *public* for the word to see!
Congress, and the country, agreed with both of them!
Build faster!
We don't care *why* it becomes a park—
we just want to see it!
TOOT TOOT!

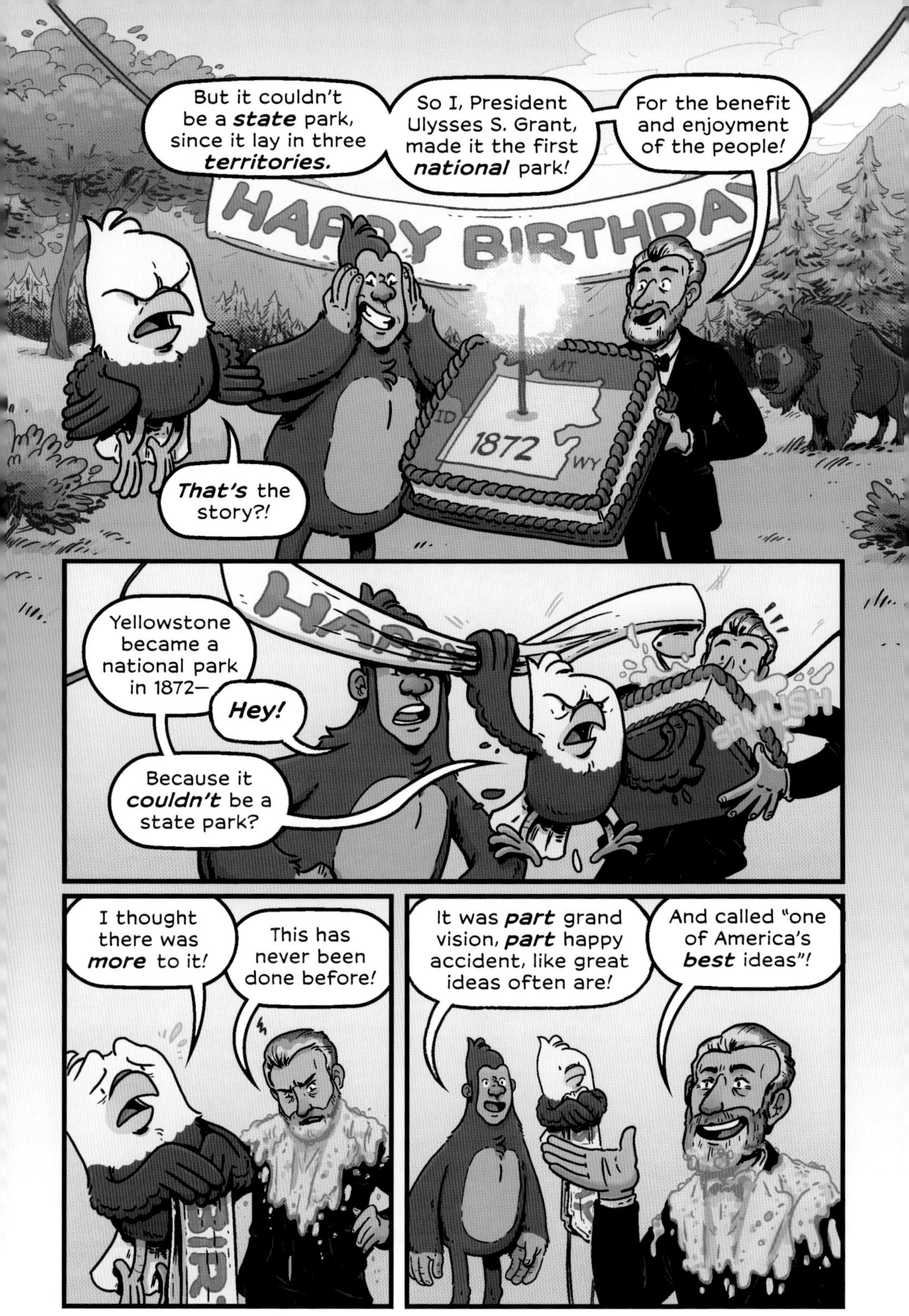
But it couldn't be a ***state*** park, since it lay in three ***territories.***
So I, President Ulysses S. Grant, made it the first ***national*** park!
For the benefit and enjoyment of the people!
HAPPY BIRTHDAY
MT
ID
1872
WY
That's the story?!
Yellowstone became a national park in 1872—
Hey!
Because it ***couldn't*** be a state park?
SMUSH
I thought there was ***more*** to it!
This has never been done before!
It was ***part*** grand vision, ***part*** happy accident, like great ideas often are!
And called "one of America's ***best*** ideas"!

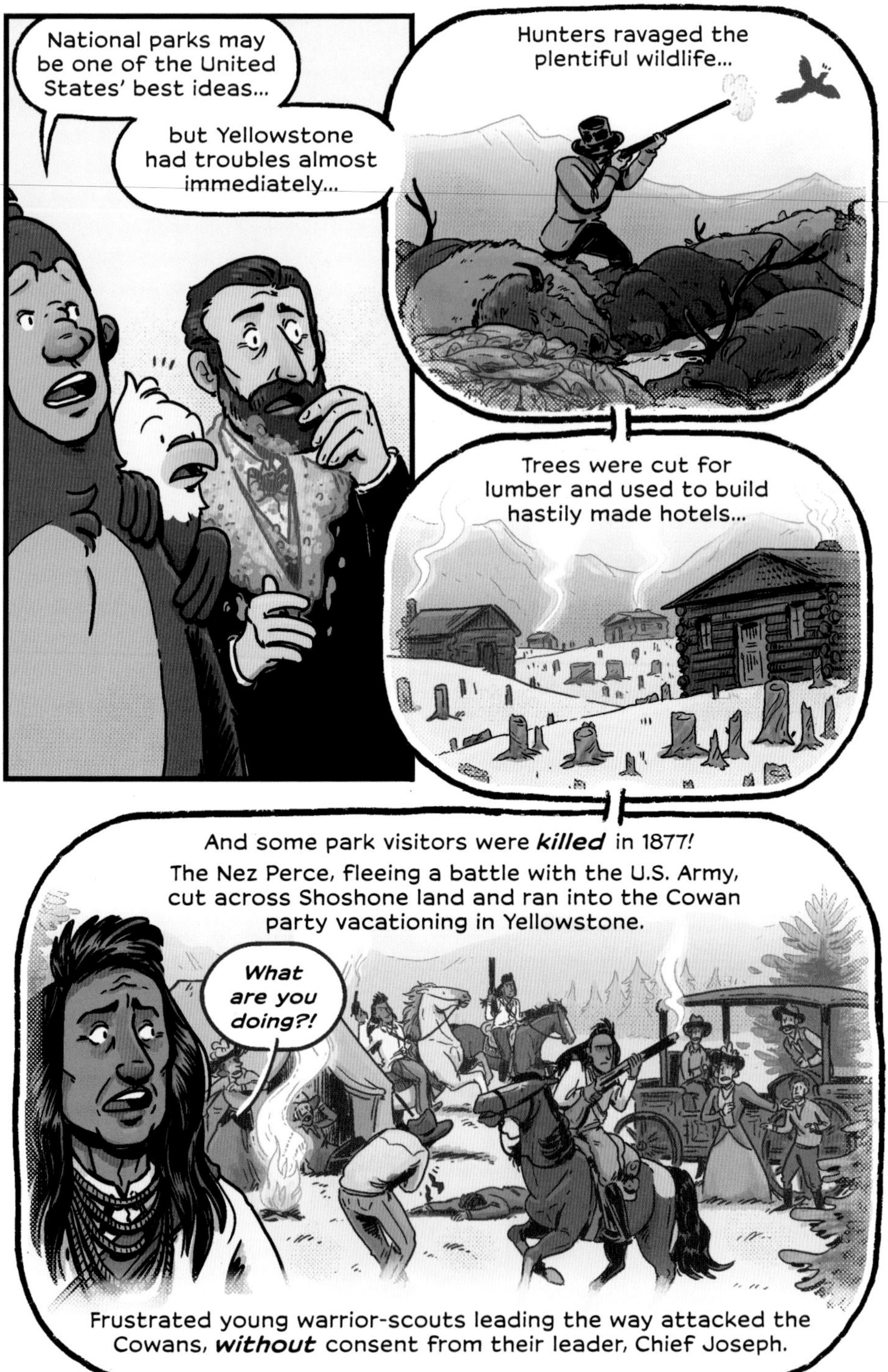
National parks may be one of the United States' best ideas...
but Yellowstone had troubles almost immediately...
Hunters ravaged the plentiful wildlife...
Trees were cut for lumber and used to build hastily made hotels...
And some park visitors were ***killed*** in 1877!
The Nez Perce, fleeing a battle with the U.S. Army, cut across Shoshone land and ran into the Cowan party vacationing in Yellowstone.
What are you doing?!
Frustrated young warrior-scouts leading the way attacked the Cowans, ***without*** consent from their leader, Chief Joseph.

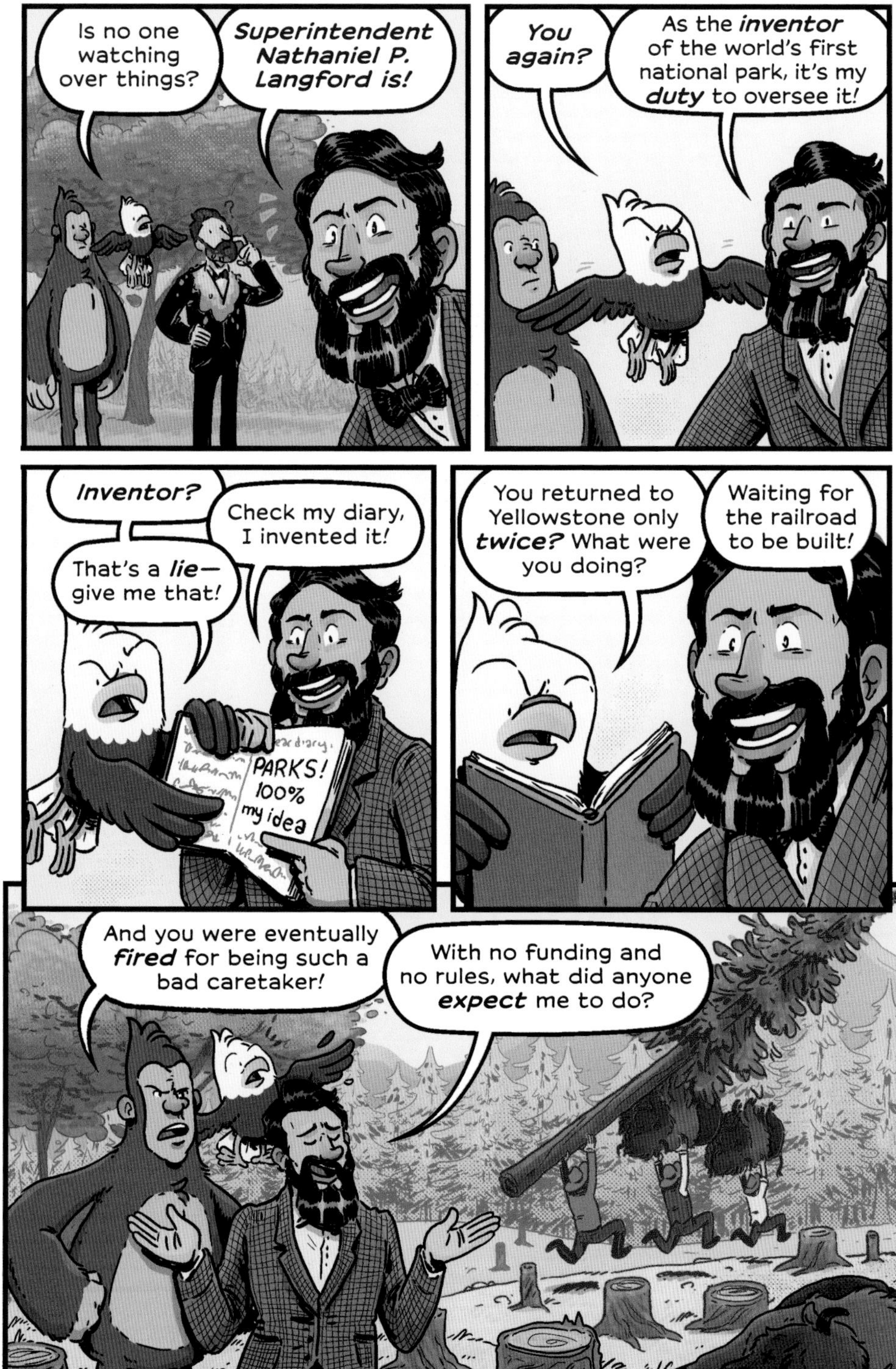
Is no one watching over things?
Superintendent Nathaniel P. Langford is!
You again?
As the *inventor* of the world's first national park, it's my *duty* to oversee it!
Inventor?
Check my diary, I invented it!
That's a *lie*—give me that!
Dear diary,
PARKS! 100% my idea
You returned to Yellowstone only *twice?* What were you doing?
Waiting for the railroad to be built!
And you were eventually *fired* for being such a bad caretaker!
With no funding and no rules, what did anyone *expect* me to do?

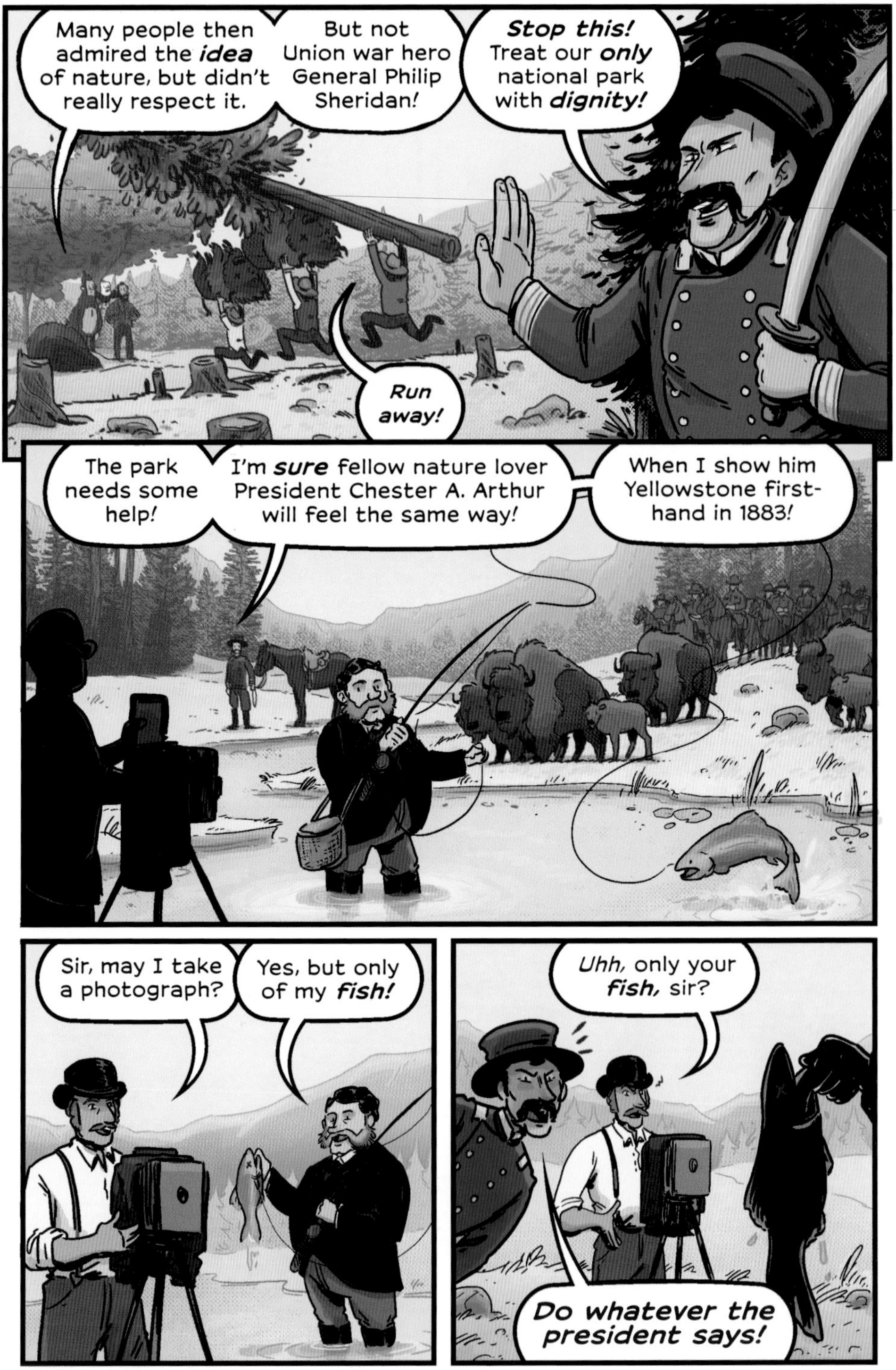

Many people then admired the *idea* of nature, but didn't really respect it.
But not Union war hero General Philip Sheridan!
Stop this! Treat our ***only*** national park with ***dignity!***
Run away!
The park needs some help!
I'm ***sure*** fellow nature lover President Chester A. Arthur will feel the same way!
When I show him Yellowstone first-hand in 1883!
Sir, may I take a photograph?
Yes, but only of my ***fish!***
Uhh, only your ***fish,*** sir?
Do whatever the president says!

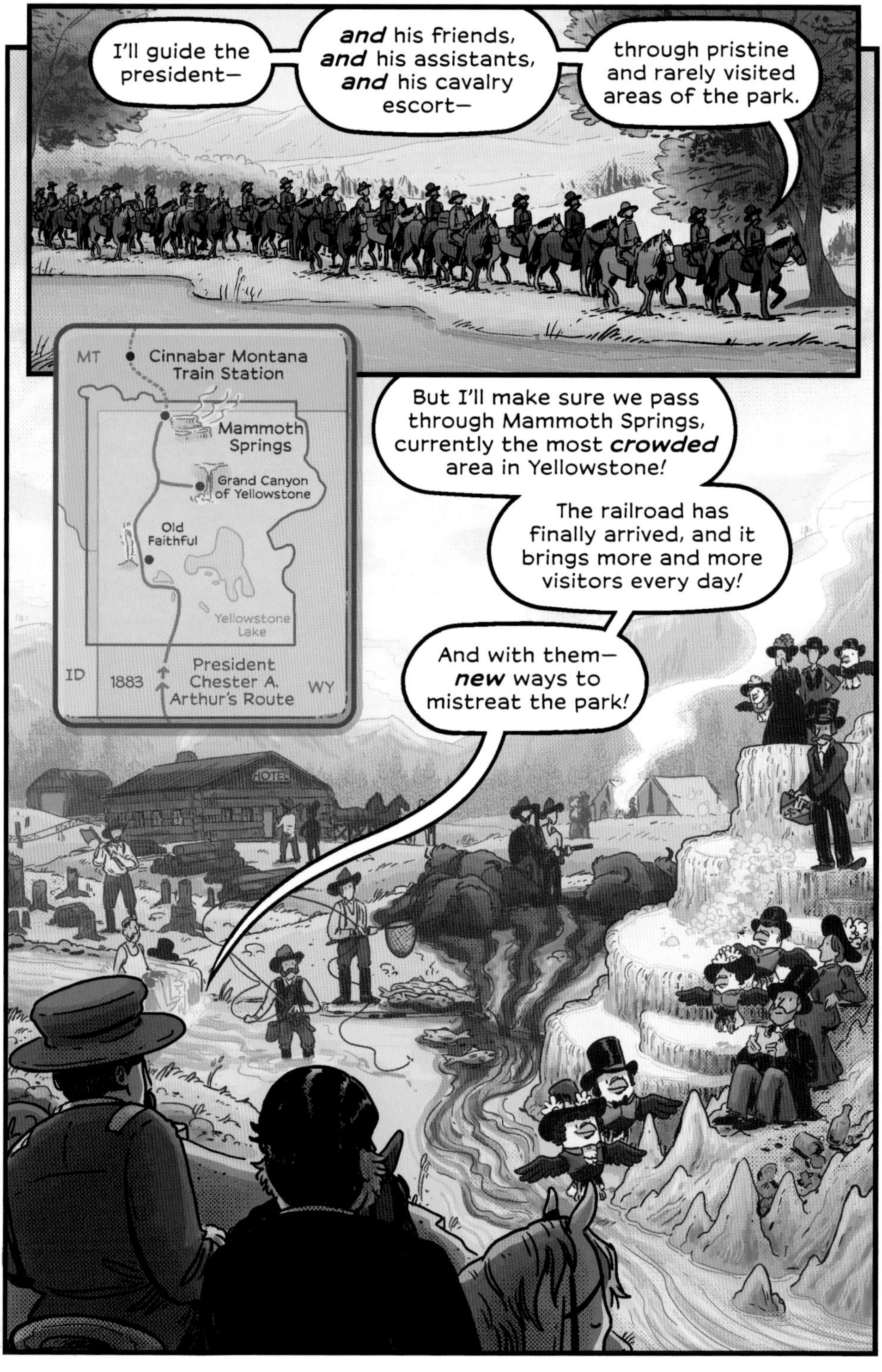

I'll guide the president—
and his friends, *and* his assistants, *and* his cavalry escort—
through pristine and rarely visited areas of the park.
MT
Cinnabar Montana Train Station
Mammoth Springs
Grand Canyon of Yellowstone
Old Faithful
Yellowstone Lake
ID
1883
President Chester A. Arthur's Route
WY
But I'll make sure we pass through Mammoth Springs, currently the most *crowded* area in Yellowstone!
The railroad has finally arrived, and it brings more and more visitors every day!
And with them— *new* ways to mistreat the park!
HOTEL

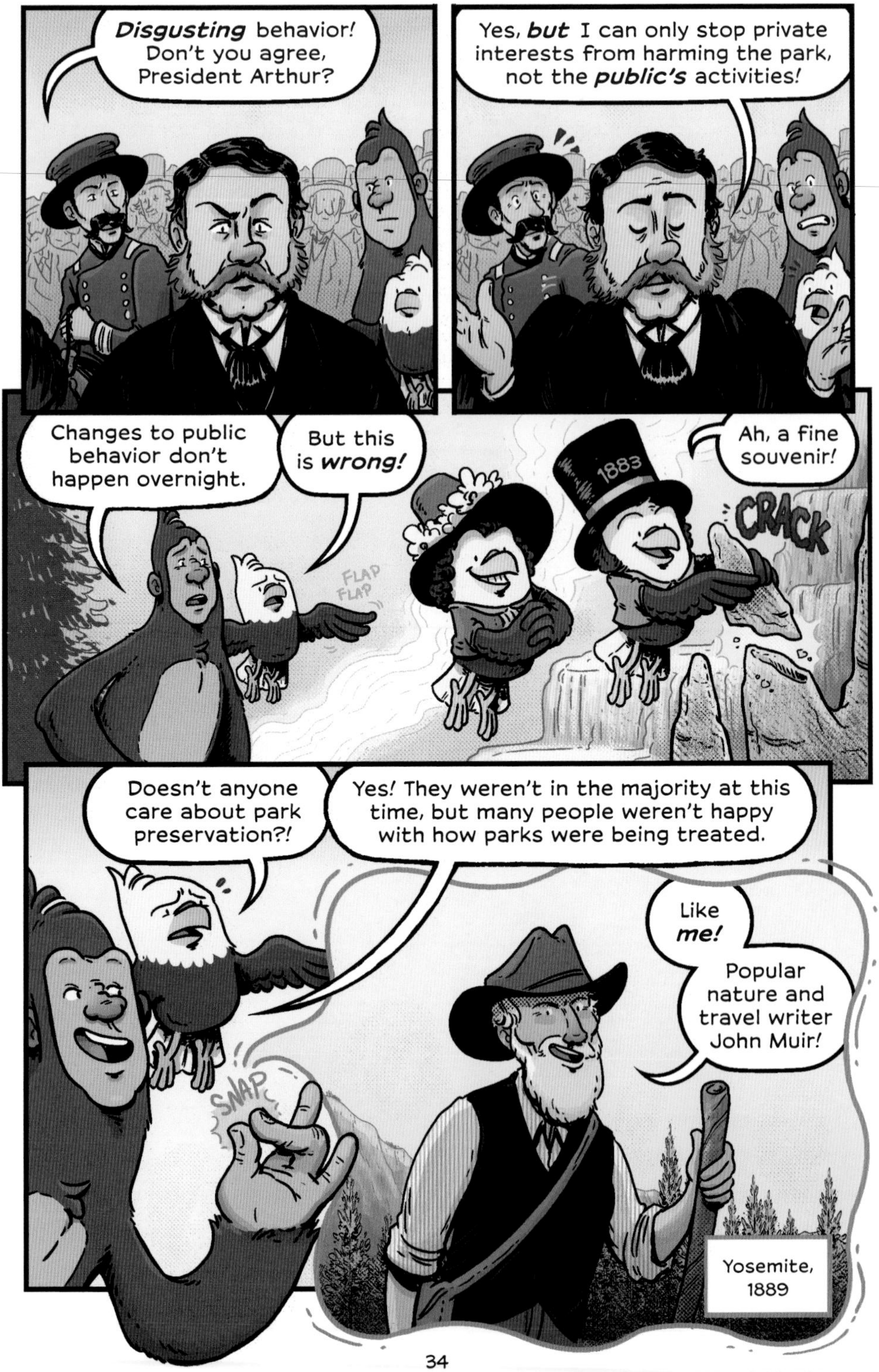

Disguisting behavior! Don't you agree, President Arthur?
Yes, ***but*** I can only stop private interests from harming the park, not the ***public's*** activities!
Changes to public behavior don't happen overnight.
But this is ***wrong!***
FLAP FLAP
1883
Ah, a fine souvenir!
CRACK
Doesn't anyone care about park preservation?!
Yes! They weren't in the majority at this time, but many people weren't happy with how parks were being treated.
Like ***me!***
Popular nature and travel writer John Muir!
SNAP
Yosemite, 1889

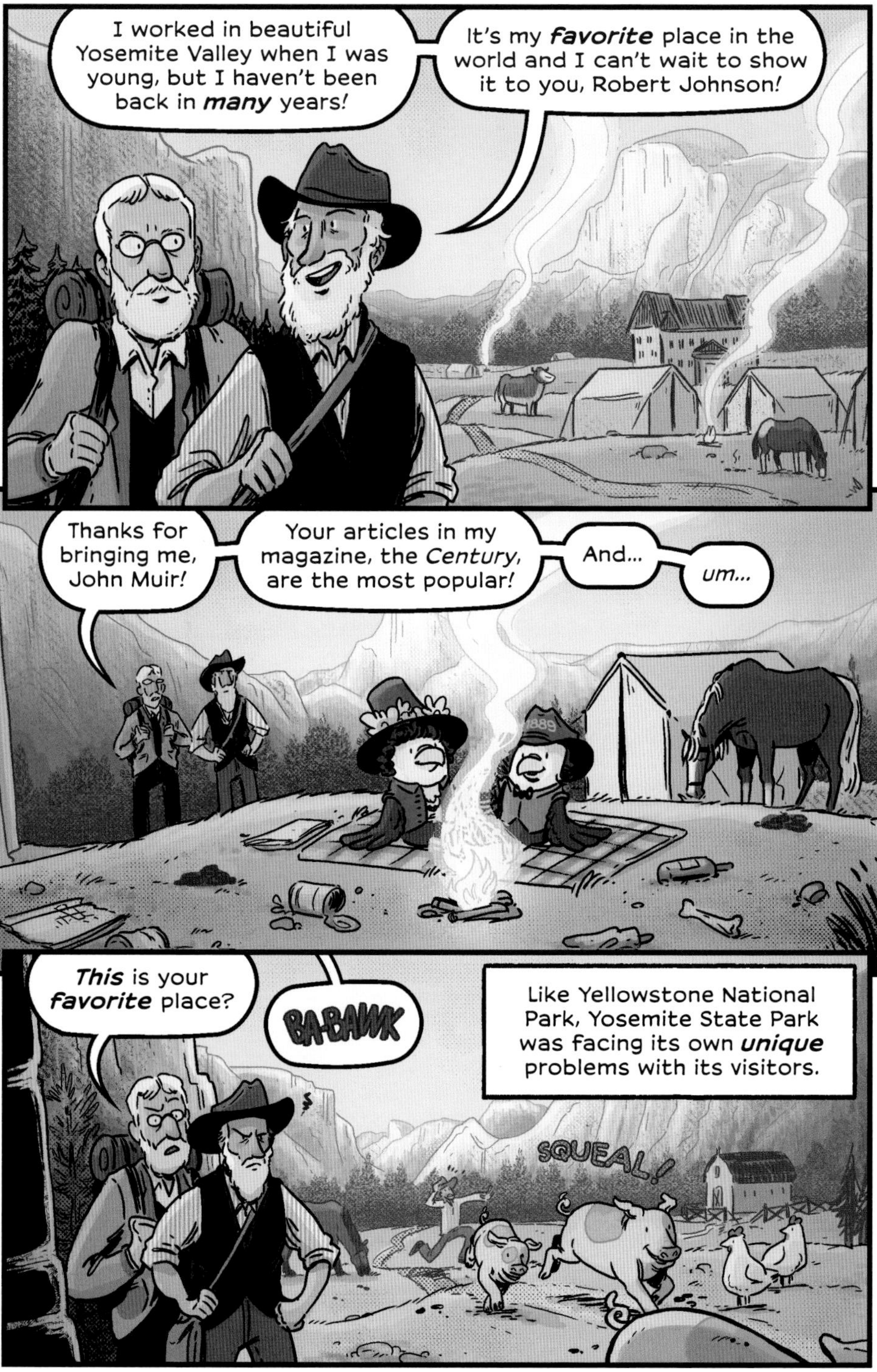
I worked in beautiful Yosemite Valley when I was young, but I haven't been back in ***many*** years!
It's my ***favorite*** place in the world and I can't wait to show it to you, Robert Johnson!
Thanks for bringing me, John Muir!
Your articles in my magazine, the *Century*, are the most popular!
And...
um...
1889
This is your ***favorite*** place?
BA-BAWK
Like Yellowstone National Park, Yosemite State Park was facing its own ***unique*** problems with its visitors.
SQUEAL!

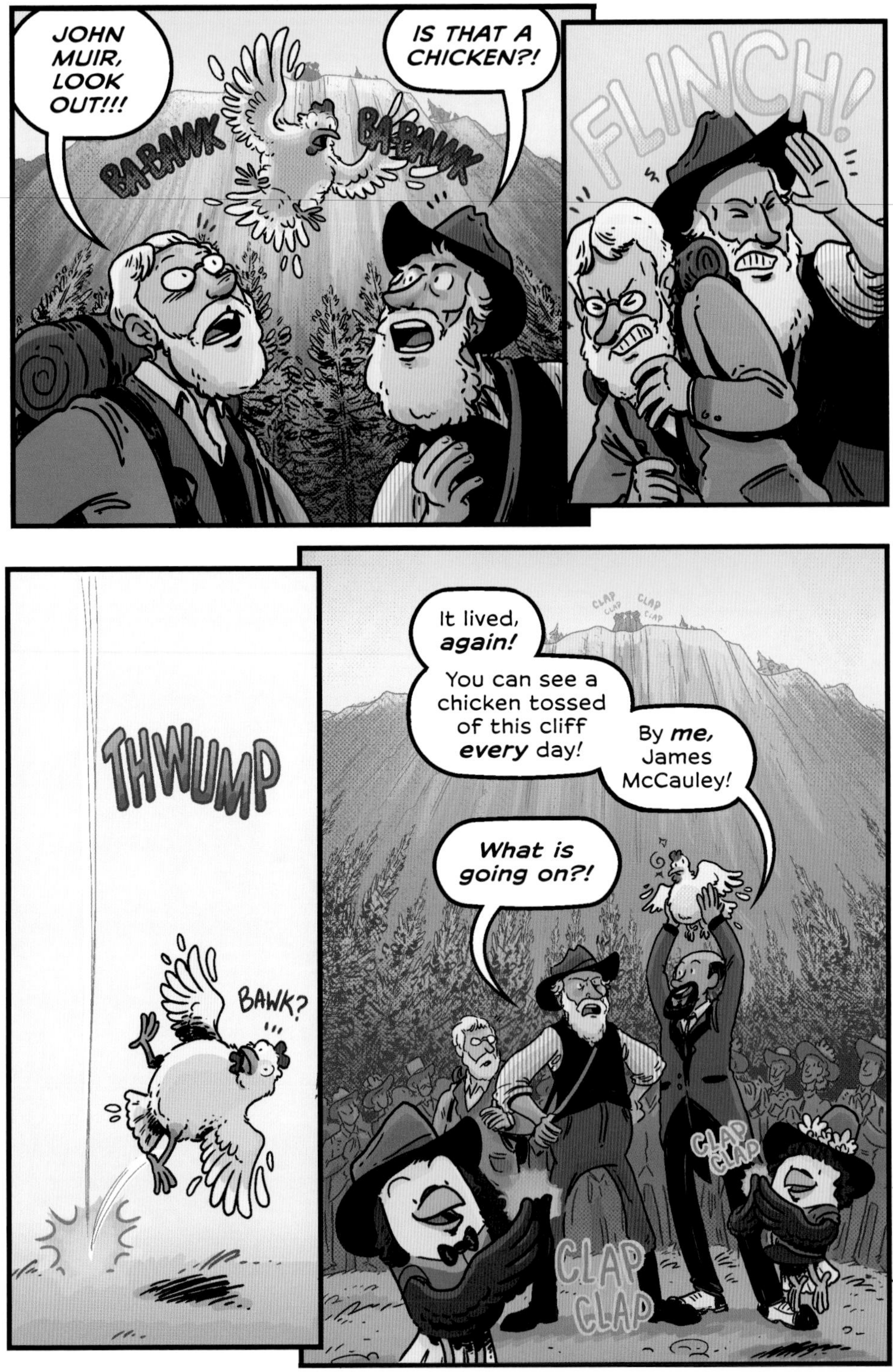
JOHN MUIR, LOOK OUT!!!
BA-BAWK
BA-BAWK
IS THAT A CHICKEN?!
FLINCH!
THWUMP
BAWK?
CLAP CLAP
It lived, again!
You can see a chicken tossed of this cliff every day!
By me, James McCauley!
What is going on?!
CLAP CLAP
CLAP CLAP

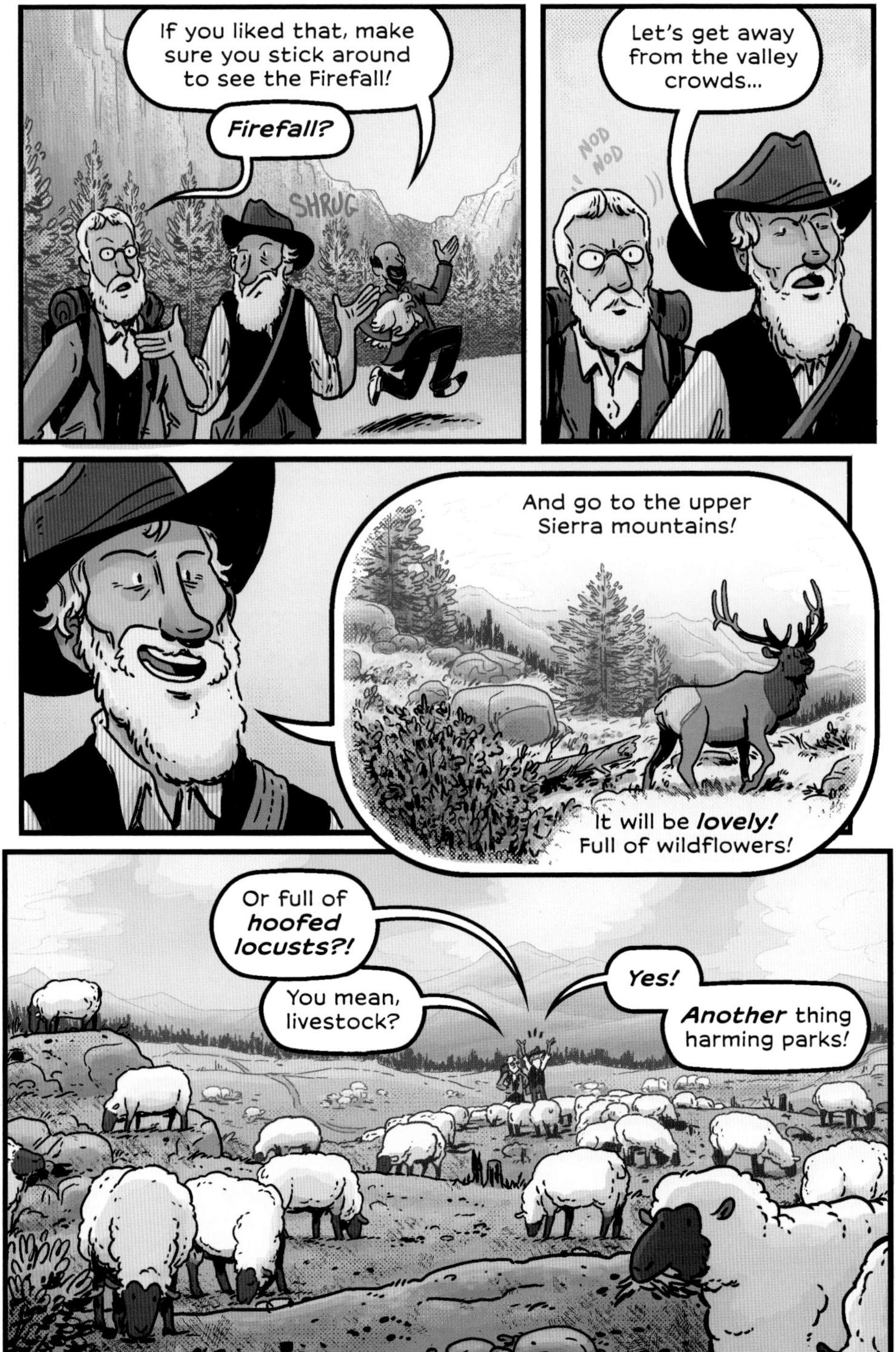
If you liked that, make sure you stick around to see the Firefall!
Firefall?
SHRUG
Let's get away from the valley crowds...
NOD NOD
And go to the upper Sierra mountains!
It will be *lovely!* Full of wildflowers!
Or full of *hoofed locusts?!*
You mean, livestock?
Yes!
Another thing harming parks!

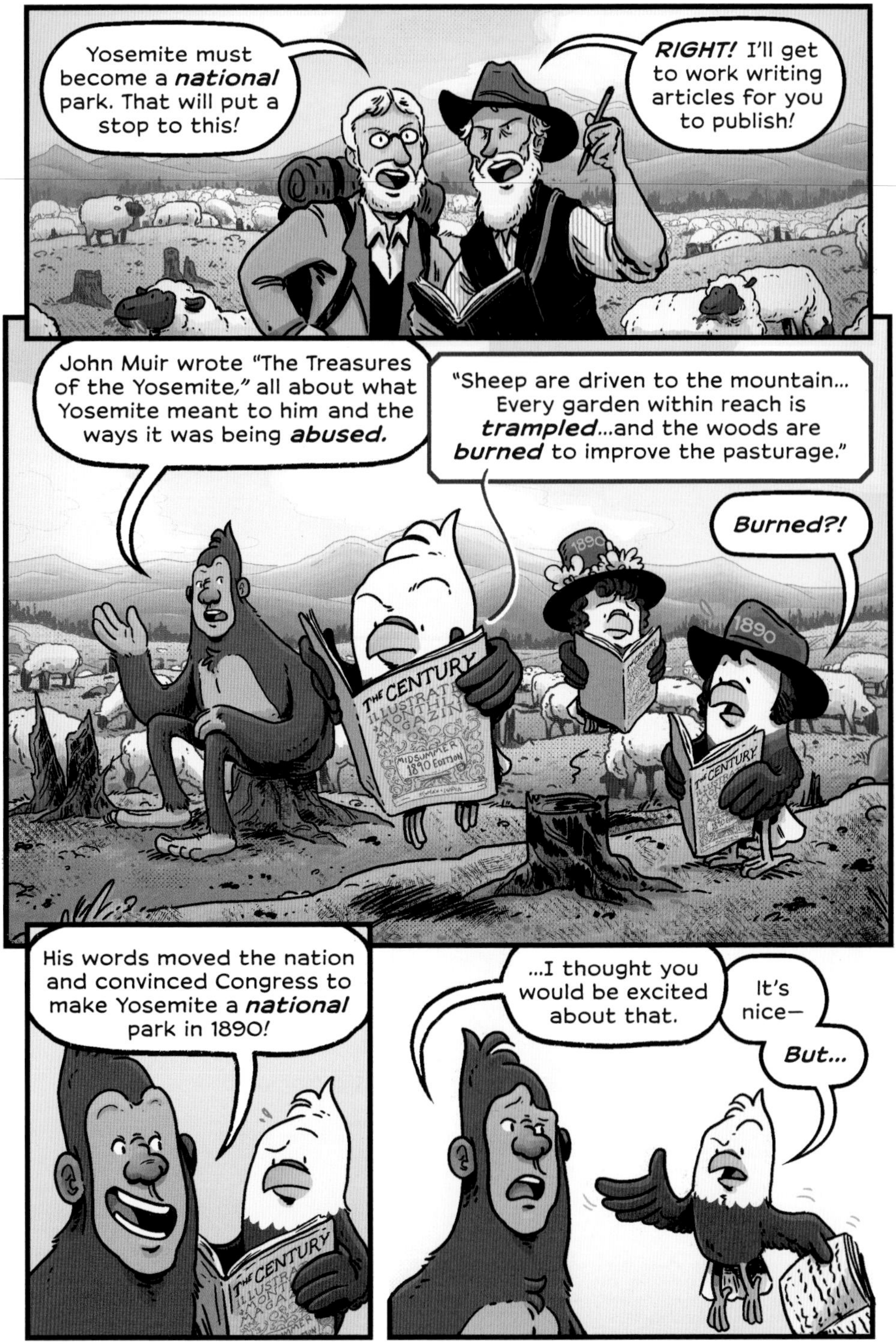
Yosemite must become a ***national*** park. That will put a stop to this!
RIGHT! I'll get to work writing articles for you to publish!
John Muir wrote "The Treasures of the Yosemite," all about what Yosemite meant to him and the ways it was being ***abused.***
"Sheep are driven to the mountain... Every garden within reach is ***trampled***...and the woods are ***burned*** to improve the pasturage."
Burned?!
THE CENTURY ILLUSTRATED MONTHLY MAGAZINE
MIDSUMMER 1890 EDITION
1890
His words moved the nation and convinced Congress to make Yosemite a ***national*** park in 1890!
...I thought you would be excited about that.
It's nice—
But...

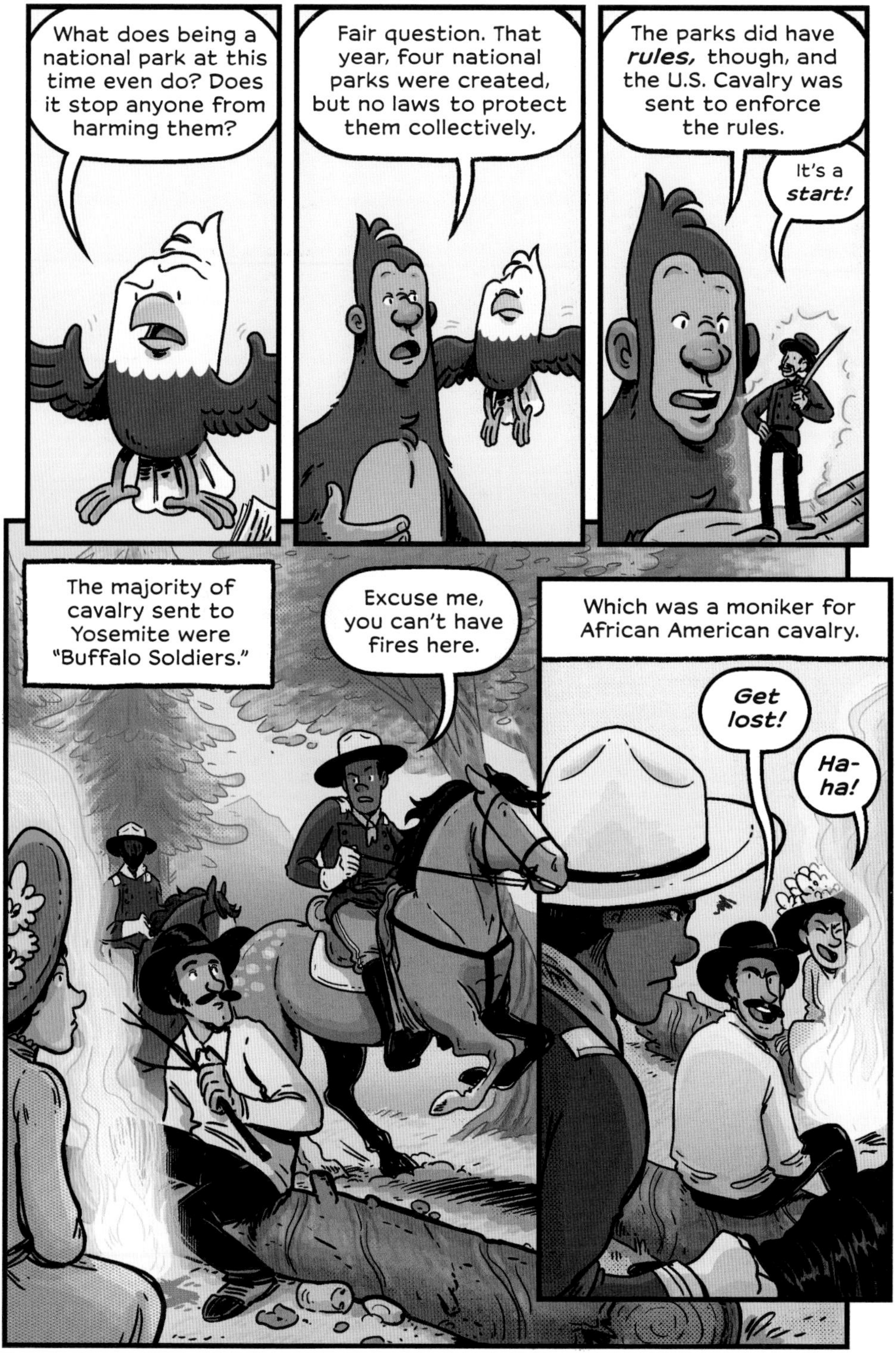
What does being a national park at this time even do? Does it stop anyone from harming them?
Fair question. That year, four national parks were created, but no laws to protect them collectively.
The parks did have *rules,* though, and the U.S. Cavalry was sent to enforce the rules.
It's a *start!*
The majority of cavalry sent to Yosemite were "Buffalo Soldiers."
Excuse me, you can't have fires here.
Which was a moniker for African American cavalry.
Get lost!
Ha-ha!

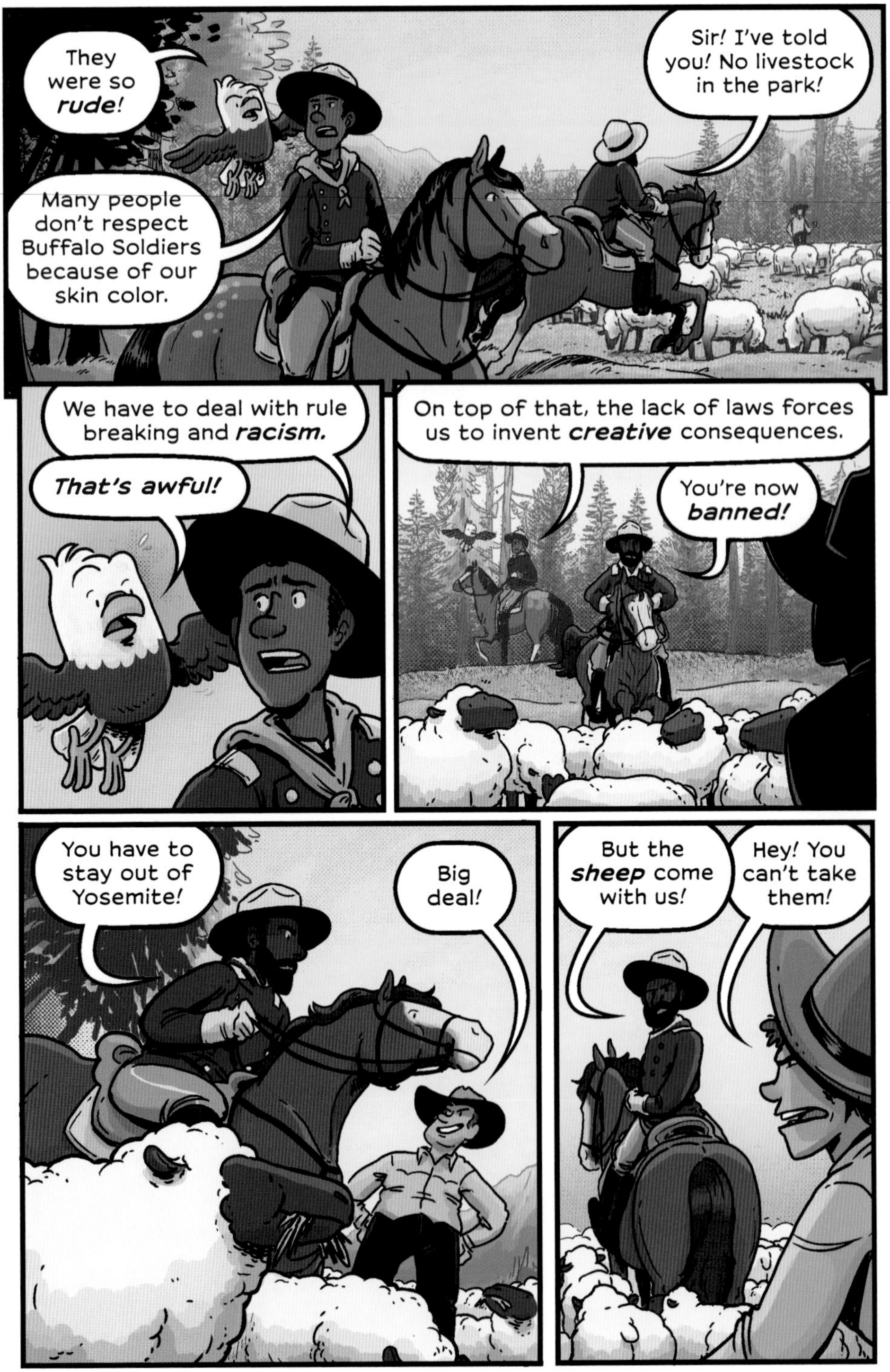
They were so *rude*!
Many people don't respect Buffalo Soldiers because of our skin color.
Sir! I've told you! No livestock in the park!
We have to deal with rule breaking and *racism.*
That's awful!
On top of that, the lack of laws forces us to invent *creative* consequences.
You're now *banned!*
You have to stay out of Yosemite!
Big deal!
But the *sheep* come with us!
Hey! You can't take them!

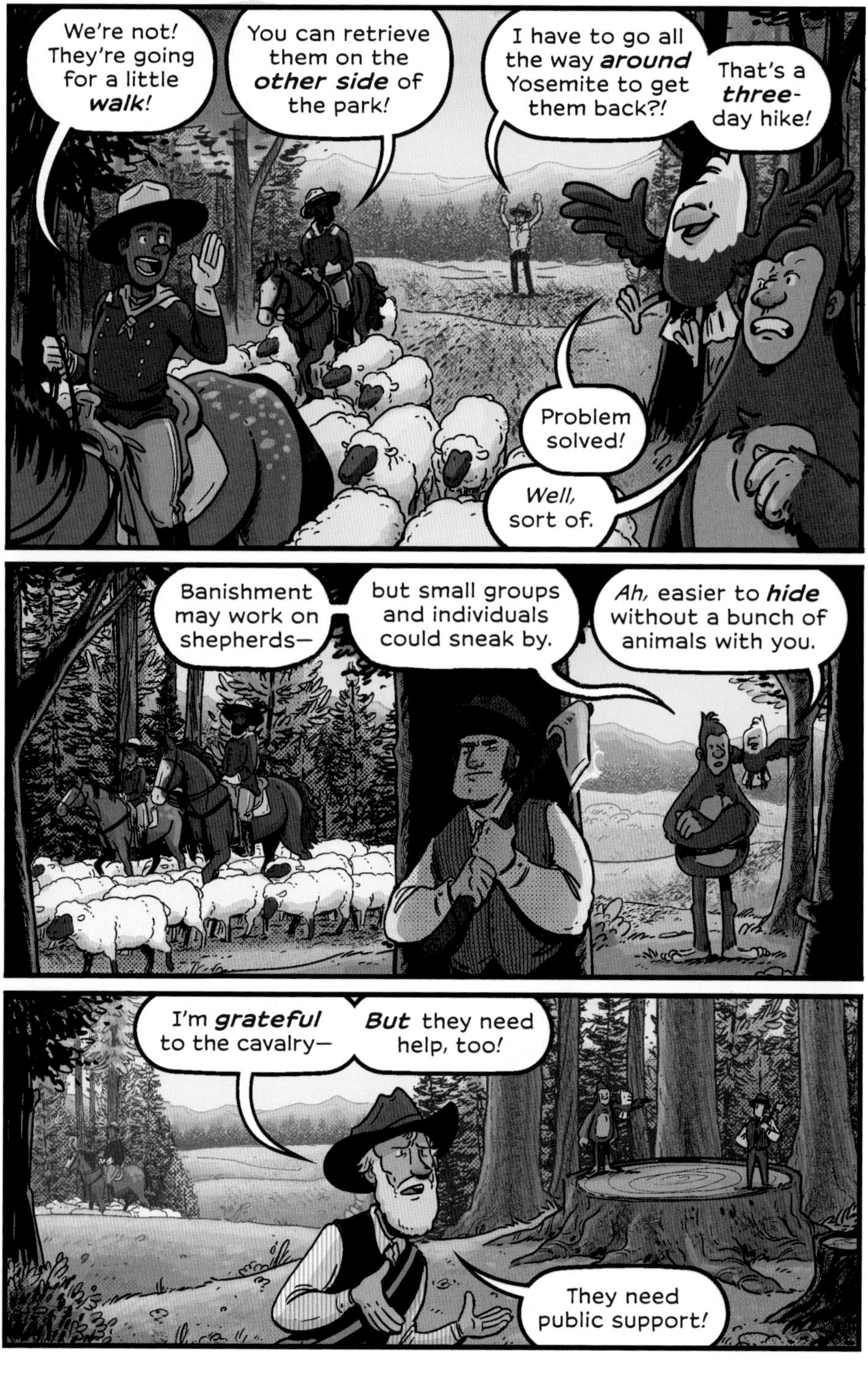
We're not! They're going for a little **walk**!
You can retrieve them on the **other side** of the park!
I have to go all the way **around** Yosemite to get them back?!
That's a **three**-day hike!
Problem solved!
Well, sort of.
Banishment may work on shepherds—
but small groups and individuals could sneak by.
Ah, easier to **hide** without a bunch of animals with you.
I'm **grateful** to the cavalry—
But they need help, too!
They need public support!

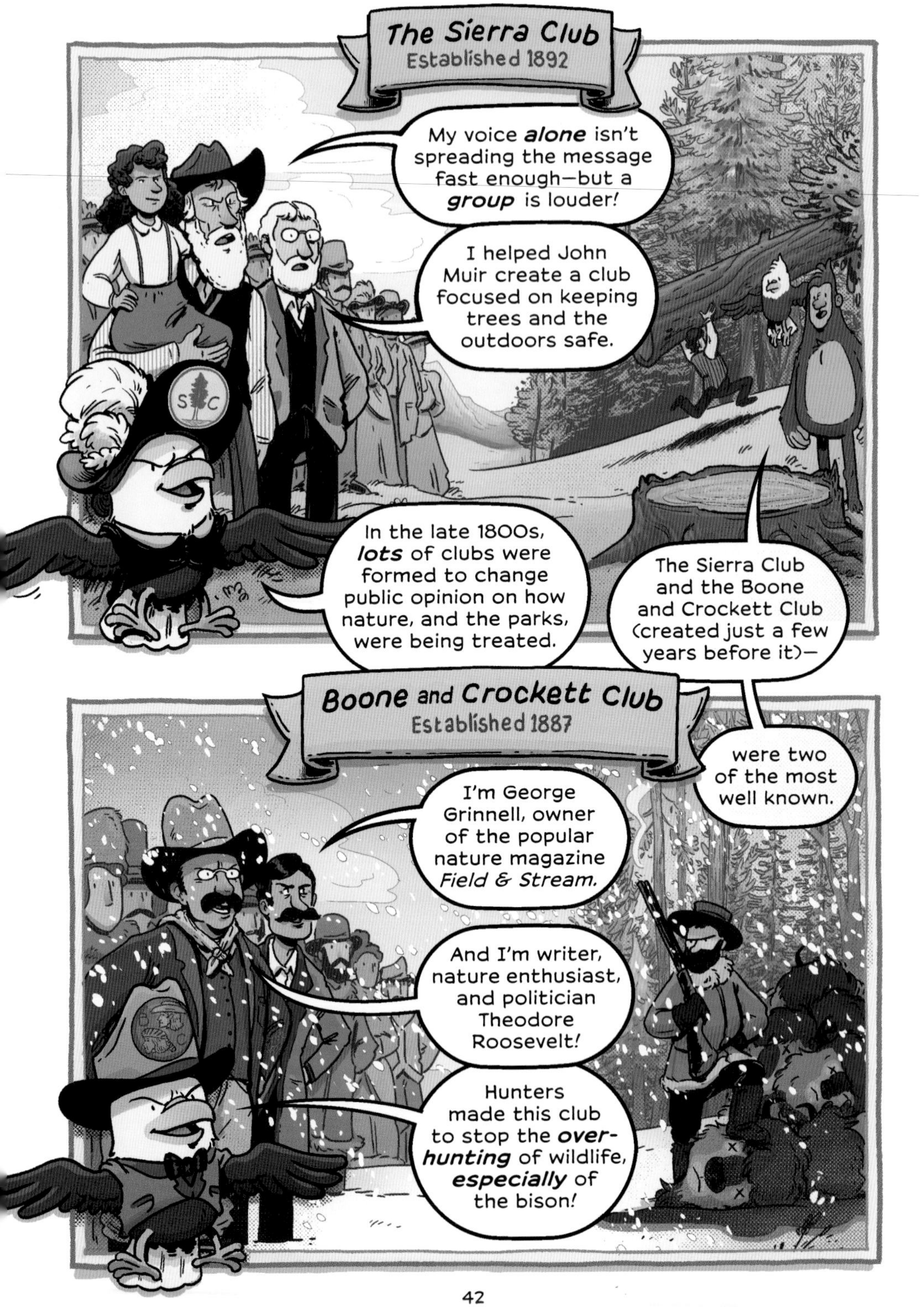
The Sierra Club
Established 1892
My voice *alone* isn't spreading the message fast enough—but a *group* is louder!
I helped John Muir create a club focused on keeping trees and the outdoors safe.
In the late 1800s, *lots* of clubs were formed to change public opinion on how nature, and the parks, were being treated.
The Sierra Club and the Boone and Crockett Club (created just a few years before it)—
were two of the most well known.
Boone and Crockett Club
Established 1887
I'm George Grinnell, owner of the popular nature magazine *Field & Stream*.
And I'm writer, nature enthusiast, and politician Theodore Roosevelt!
Hunters made this club to stop the *over-hunting* of wildlife, *especially* of the bison!

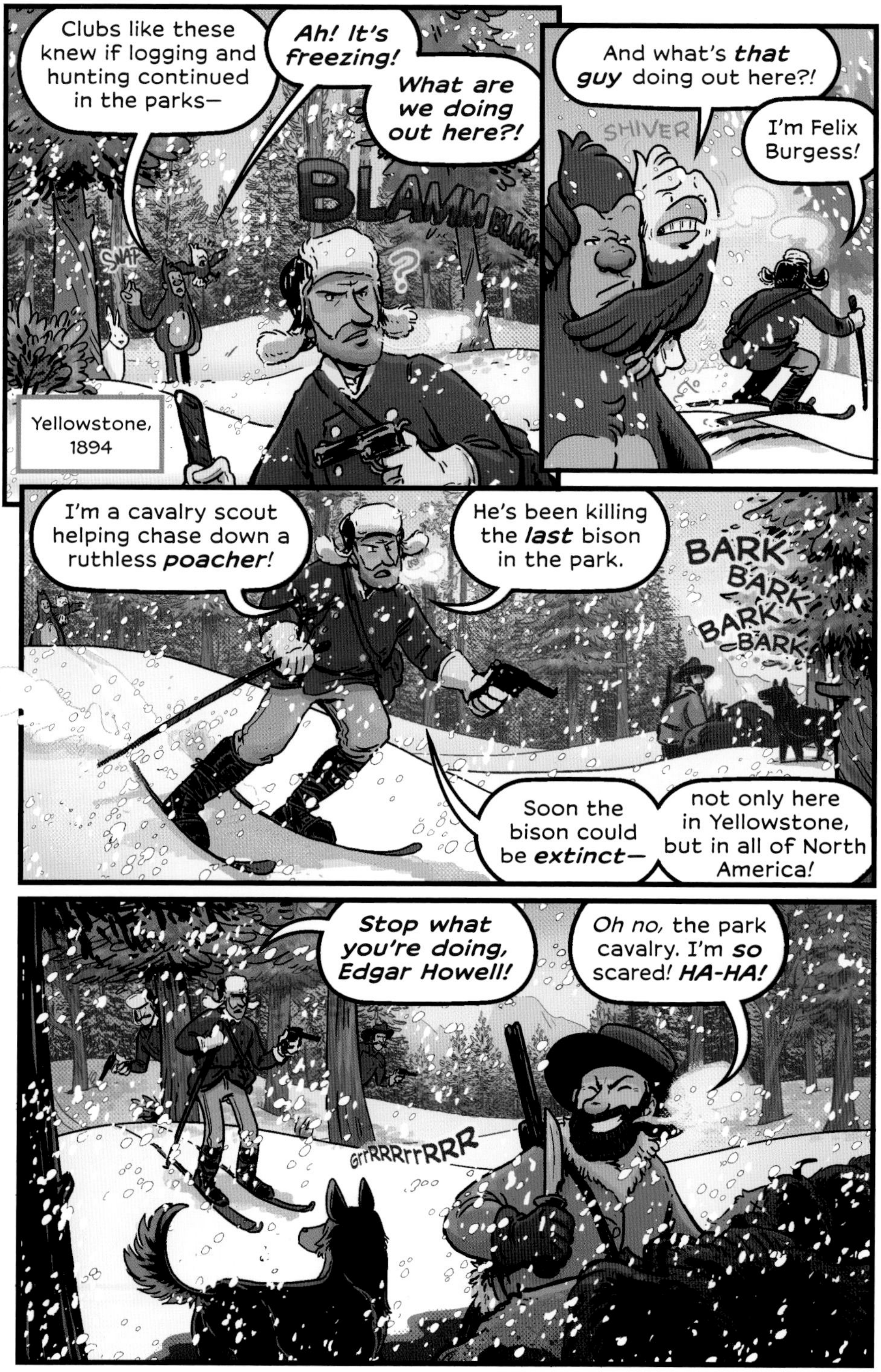
Clubs like these knew if logging and hunting continued in the parks—
Ah! It's freezing!
What are we doing out here?!
BLAMM
BLAMM
SNAP
Yellowstone, 1894
And what's ***that guy*** doing out here?!
SHIVER
I'm Felix Burgess!
I'm a cavalry scout helping chase down a ruthless ***poacher***!
He's been killing the ***last*** bison in the park.
BARK BARK BARK BARK
Soon the bison could be ***extinct***—
not only here in Yellowstone, but in all of North America!
Stop what you're doing, Edgar Howell!
Oh no, the park cavalry. I'm ***so*** scared! ***HA-HA!***
GrrRRRrrRRR

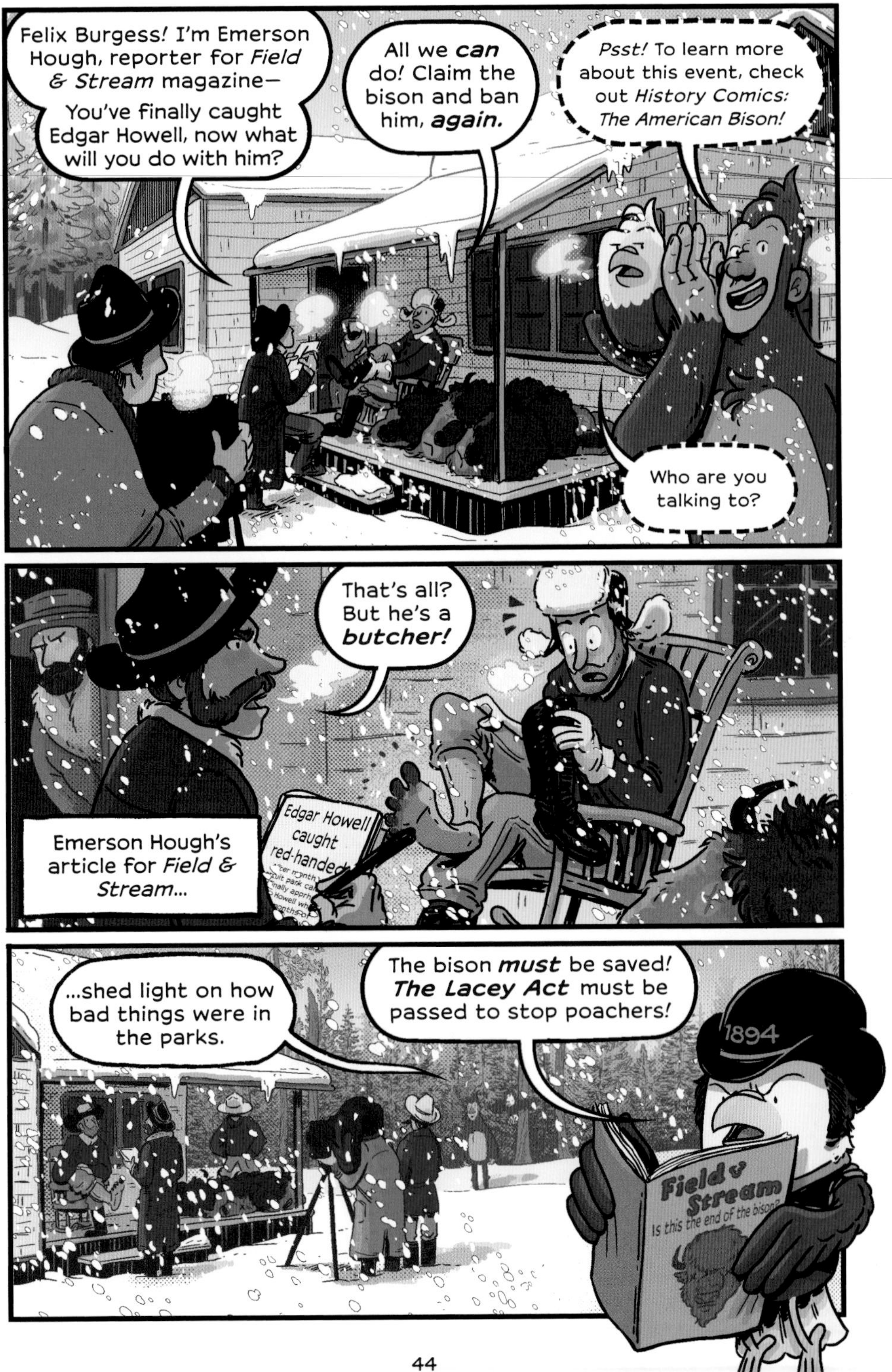
Felix Burgess! I'm Emerson Hough, reporter for *Field & Stream* magazine—
You've finally caught Edgar Howell, now what will you do with him?
All we ***can*** do! Claim the bison and ban him, ***again.***
Psst! To learn more about this event, check out *History Comics: The American Bison!*
Who are you talking to?
That's all? But he's a ***butcher!***
Edgar Howell caught red-handed
Emerson Hough's article for *Field & Stream*...
...shed light on how bad things were in the parks.
The bison ***must*** be saved! ***The Lacey Act*** must be passed to stop poachers!
1894
Field & Stream
Is this the end of the bison?

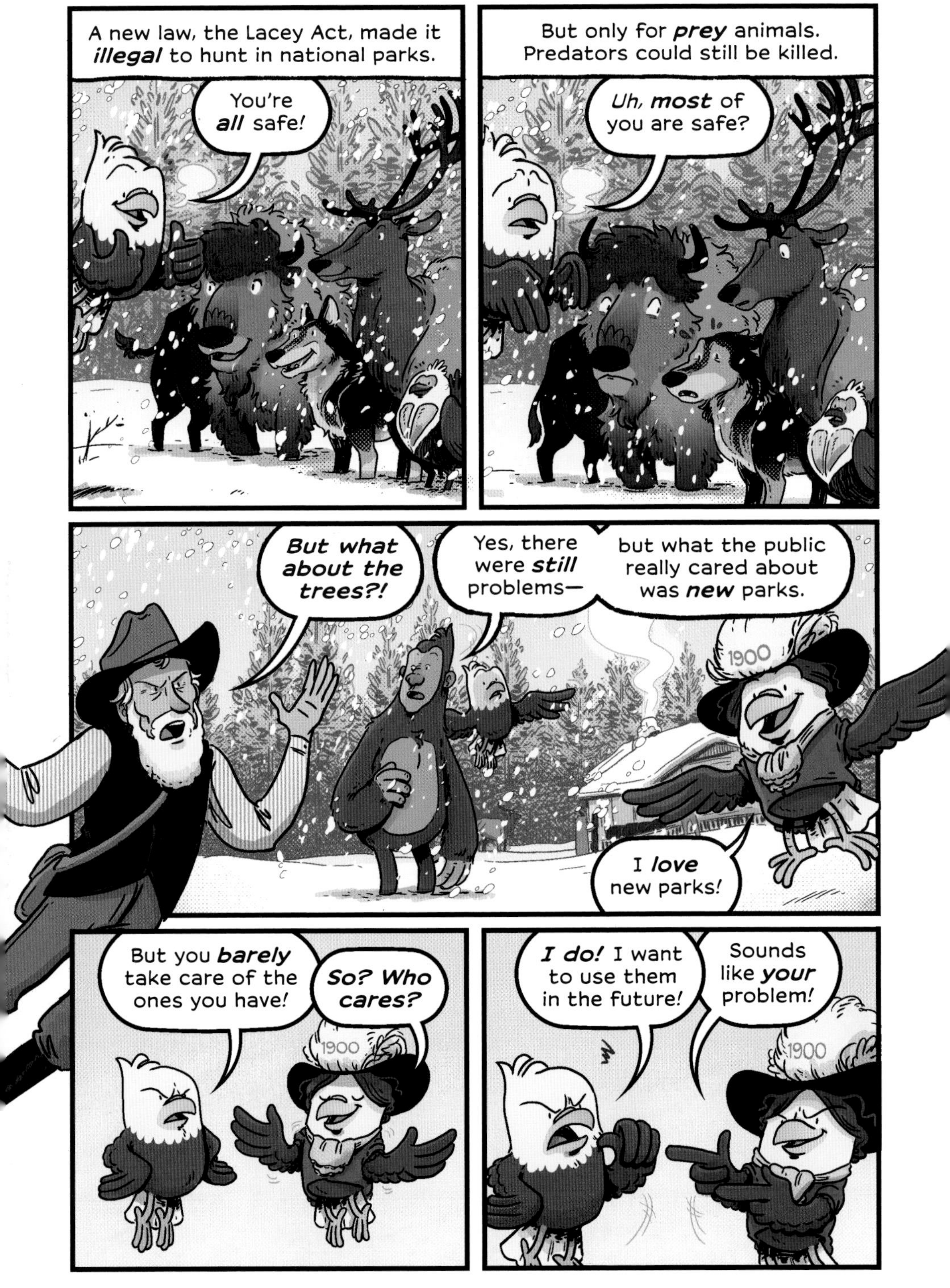
A new law, the Lacey Act, made it *illegal* to hunt in national parks.
You're *all* safe!
But only for *prey* animals. Predators could still be killed.
*Uh, **most** of you are safe?*
But what about the trees?!
Yes, there were ***still*** problems—
but what the public really cared about was ***new*** parks.
1900
I *love* new parks!
But you ***barely*** take care of the ones you have!
1900
So? Who cares?
I do! I want to use them in the future!
Sounds like ***your*** problem!
1900

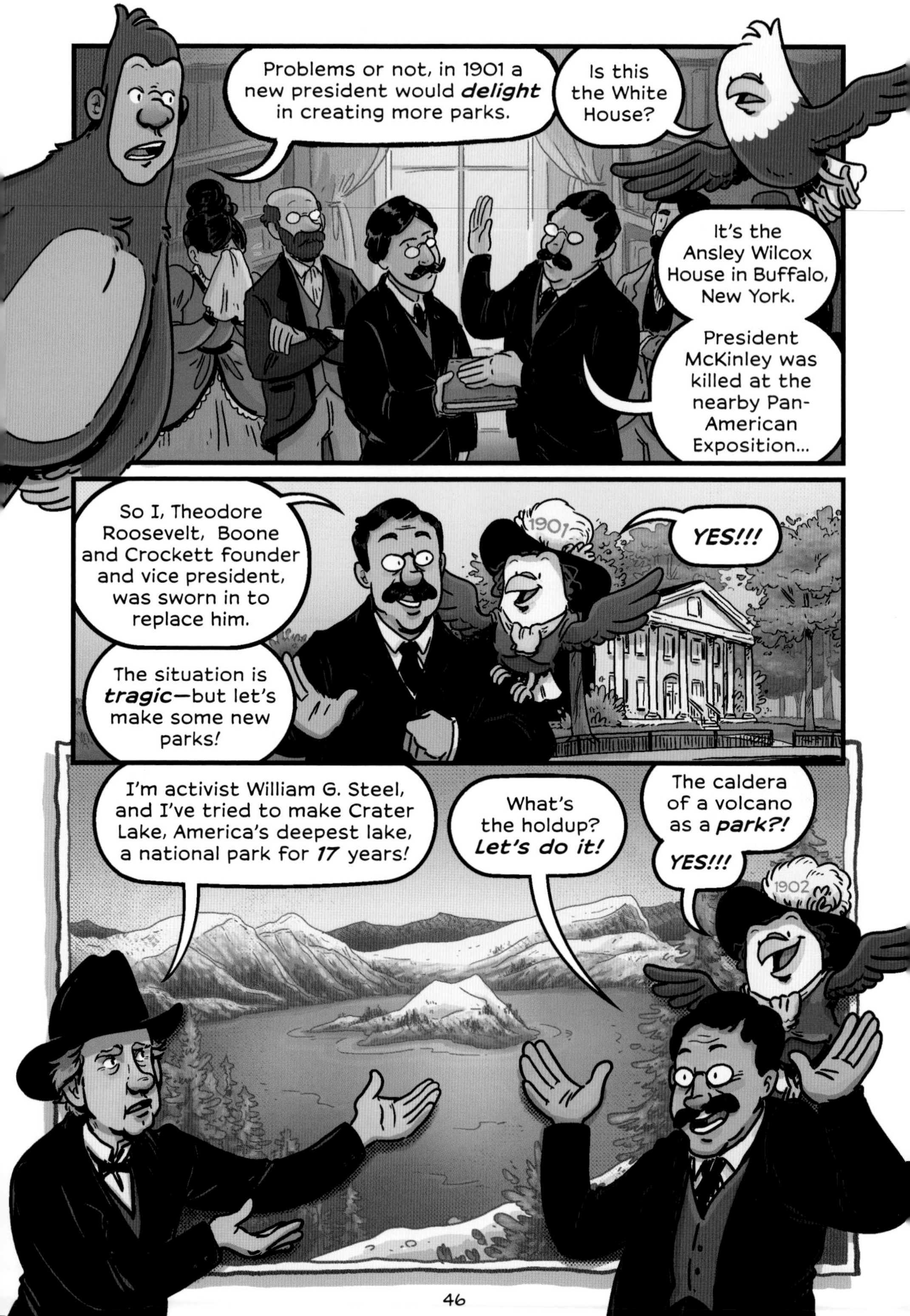
Problems or not, in 1901 a new president would ***delight*** in creating more parks.
Is this the White House?
It's the Ansley Wilcox House in Buffalo, New York.
President McKinley was killed at the nearby Pan-American Exposition...
So I, Theodore Roosevelt, Boone and Crockett founder and vice president, was sworn in to replace him.
1901
YES!!!
The situation is ***tragic***—but let's make some new parks!
I'm activist William G. Steel, and I've tried to make Crater Lake, America's deepest lake, a national park for ***17*** years!
What's the holdup? ***Let's do it!***
The caldera of a volcano as a ***park?!***
YES!!!
1902

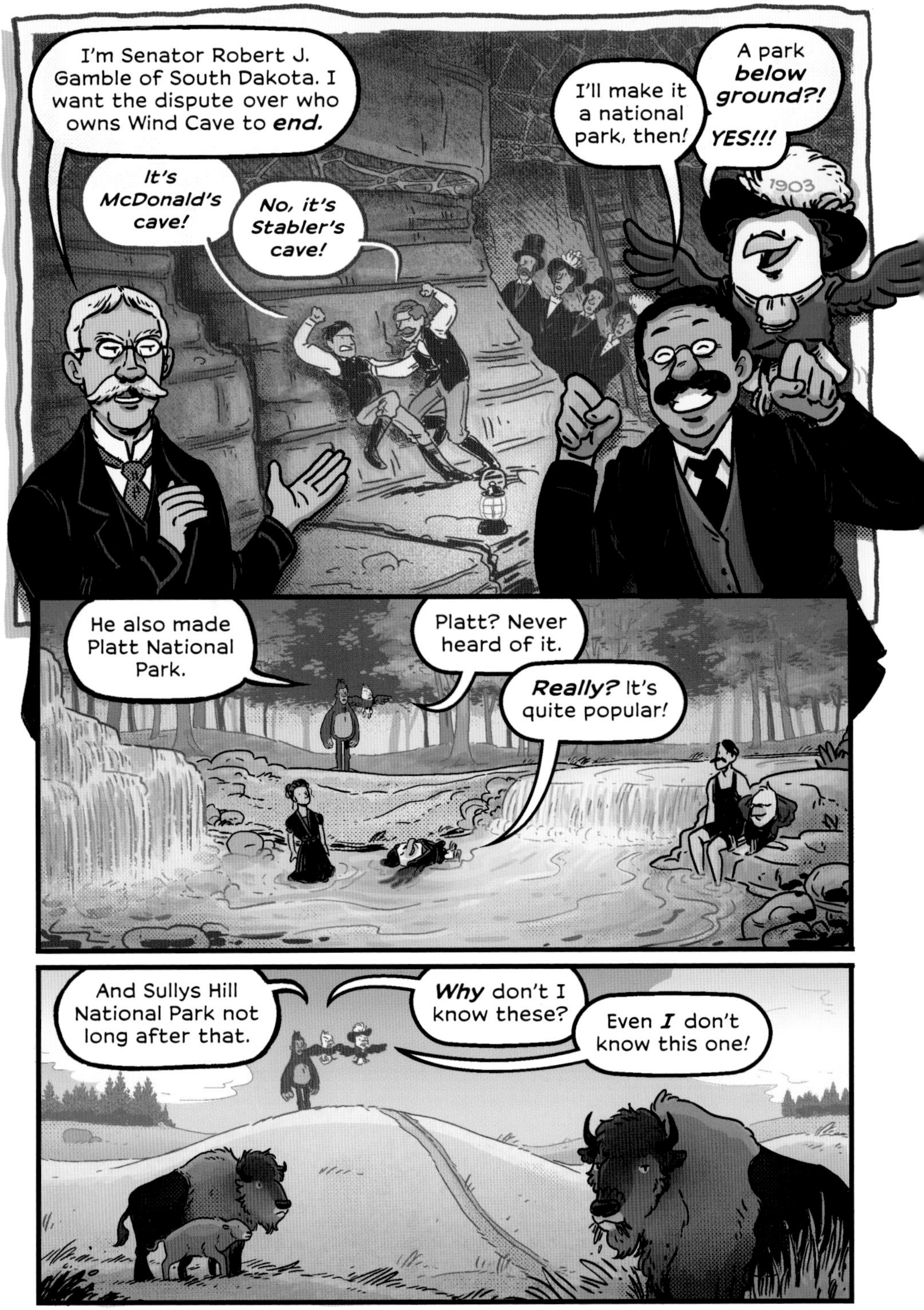
I'm Senator Robert J. Gamble of South Dakota. I want the dispute over who owns Wind Cave to *end.*
It's McDonald's cave!
No, it's Stabler's cave!
I'll make it a national park, then!
A park *below ground?!*
YES!!!
1903
He also made Platt National Park.
Platt? Never heard of it.
Really? It's quite popular!
And Sullys Hill National Park not long after that.
Why don't I know these?
Even *I* don't know this one!

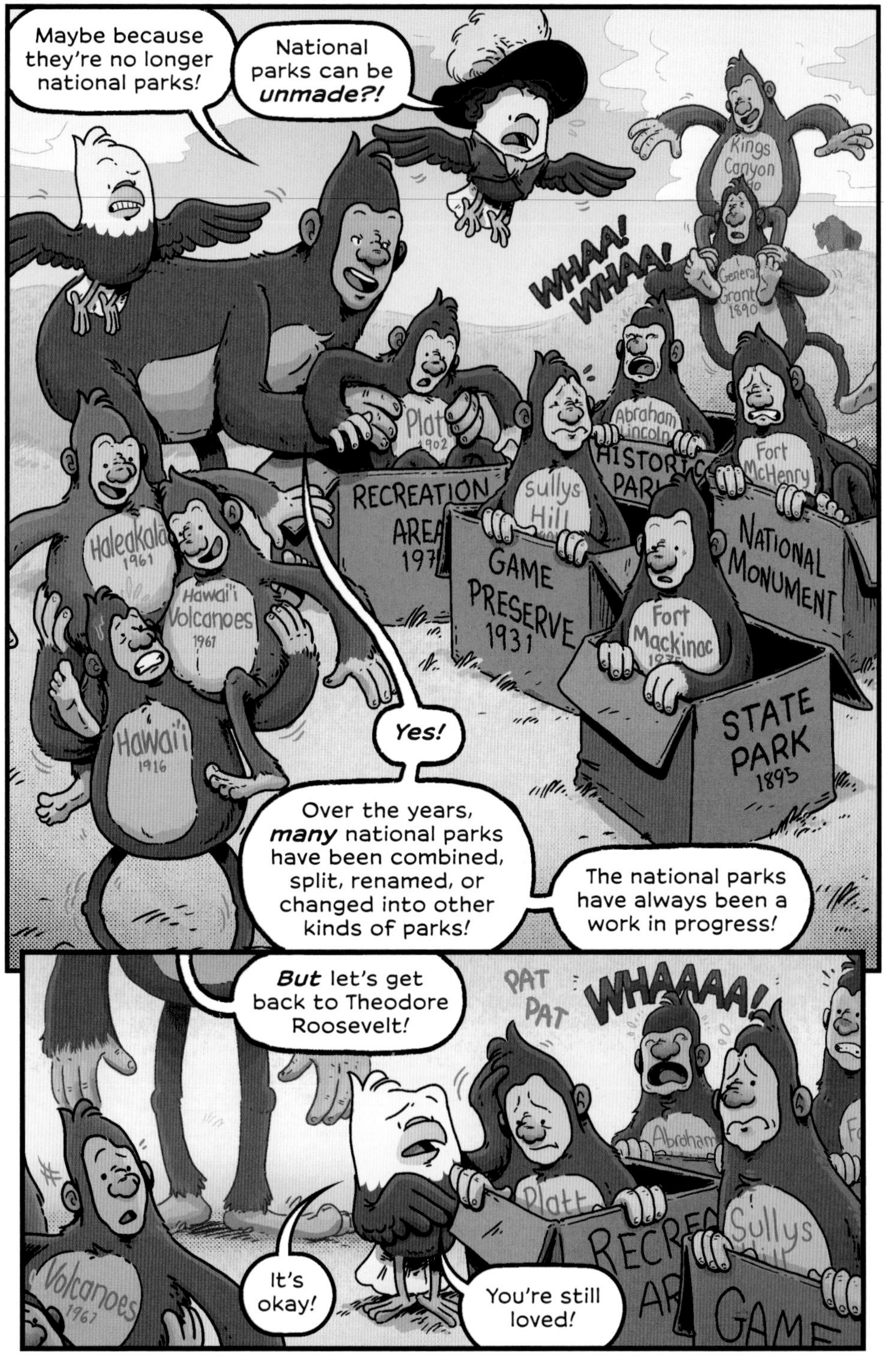

Maybe because they're no longer national parks!
National parks can be *unmade?!*
Kings Canyon
WHAA! WHAA!
General Grant 1890
Platt 1902
Abraham Lincoln
HISTORIC PARK
Fort McHenry
RECREATION AREA 197
Sullys Hill
NATIONAL MONUMENT
Haleakalā 1961
GAME PRESERVE 1931
Hawai'i Volcanoes 1961
Fort Mackinac
STATE PARK 1895
Hawai'i 1916
Yes!
Over the years, *many* national parks have been combined, split, renamed, or changed into other kinds of parks!
The national parks have always been a work in progress!
But let's get back to Theodore Roosevelt!
PAT PAT
WHAAAA!
Abraham
Platt
Sullys
Volcanoes 1967
It's okay!
You're still loved!
GAME

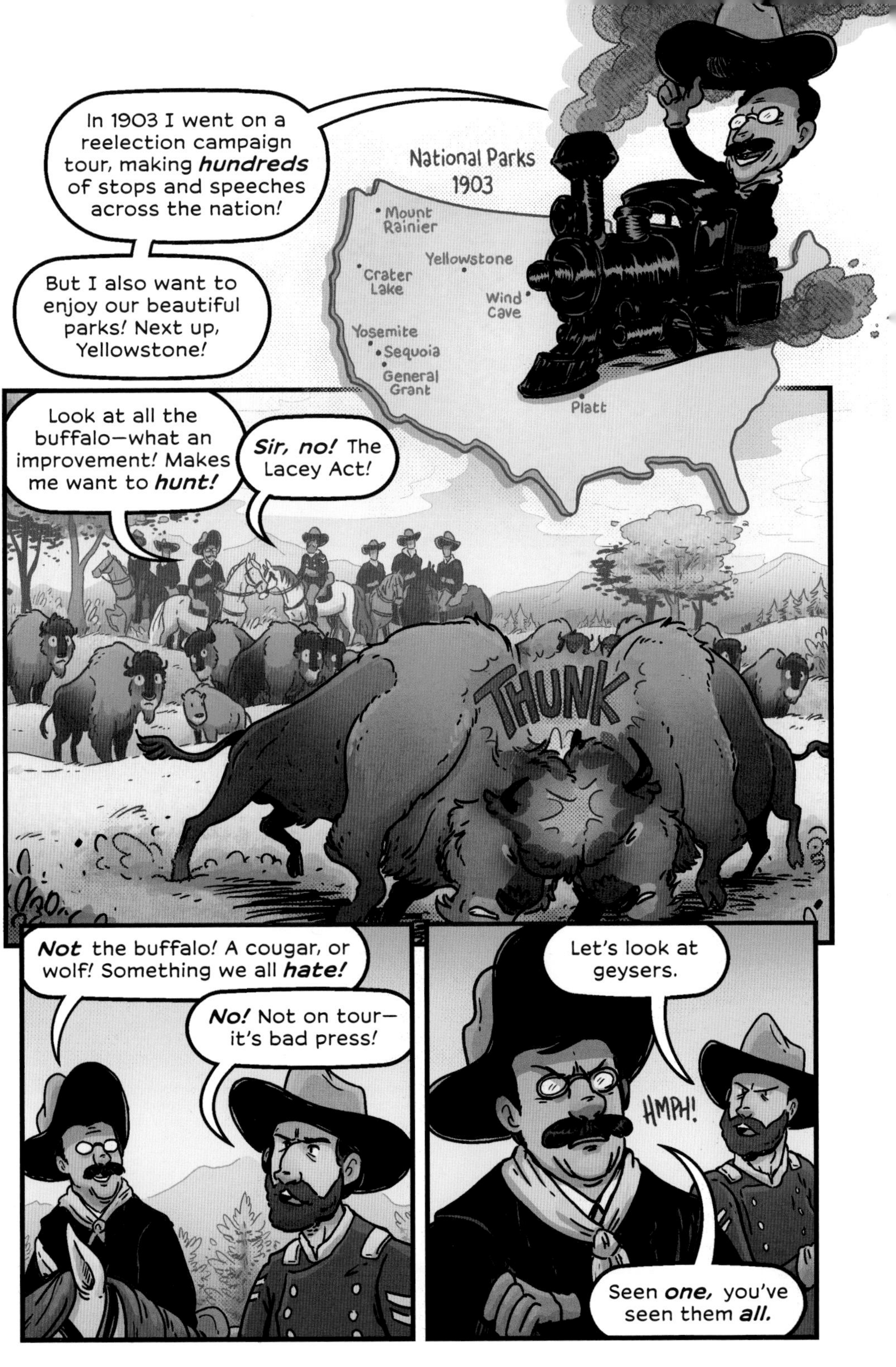
In 1903 I went on a reelection campaign tour, making ***hundreds*** of stops and speeches across the nation!
National Parks 1903
Mount Rainier
Yellowstone
Crater Lake
Wind Cave
Yosemite
Sequoia
General Grant
Platt
But I also want to enjoy our beautiful parks! Next up, Yellowstone!
Look at all the buffalo—what an improvement! Makes me want to ***hunt!***
Sir, no! The Lacey Act!
THUNK
Not the buffalo! A cougar, or wolf! Something we all ***hate!***
No! Not on tour—it's bad press!
Let's look at geysers.
HMPH!
Seen ***one,*** you've seen them ***all.***

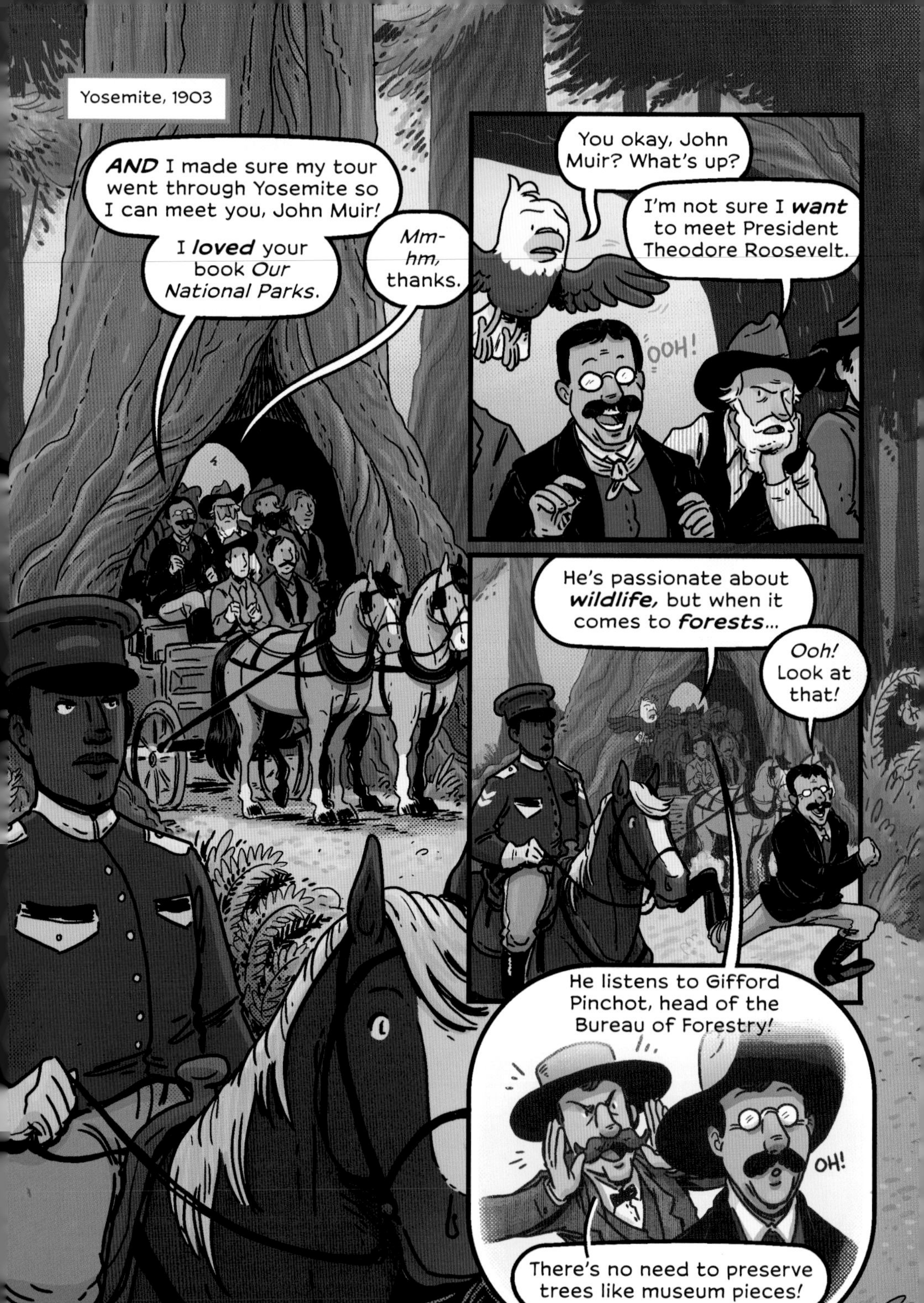
Yosemite, 1903
AND I made sure my tour went through Yosemite so I can meet you, John Muir!
I **loved** your book *Our National Parks.*
Mm-hm, thanks.
You okay, John Muir? What's up?
I'm not sure I ***want*** to meet President Theodore Roosevelt.
OOH!
He's passionate about ***wildlife,*** but when it comes to ***forests***...
Ooh! Look at *that!*
He listens to Gifford Pinchot, head of the Bureau of Forestry!
OH!
There's no need to preserve trees like museum pieces!

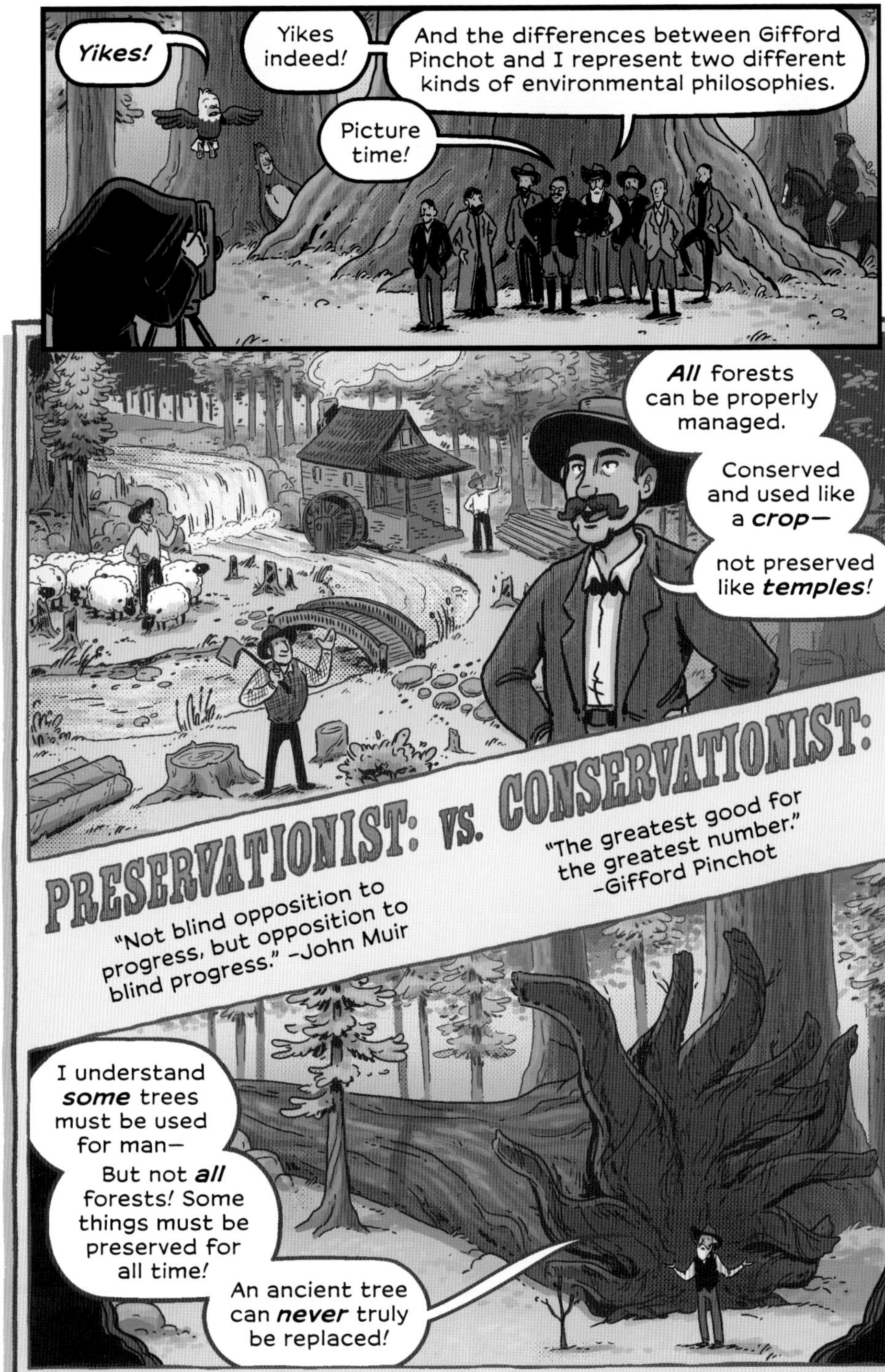
Yikes!
Yikes indeed!
And the differences between Gifford Pinchot and I represent two different kinds of environmental philosophies.
Picture time!
All forests can be properly managed.
Conserved and used like a *crop*—
not preserved like *temples*!
PRESERVATIONIST: VS. CONSERVATIONIST:
"The greatest good for the greatest number." –Gifford Pinchot
"Not blind opposition to progress, but opposition to blind progress." –John Muir
I understand *some* trees must be used for man—
But not *all* forests! Some things must be preserved for all time!
An ancient tree can *never* truly be replaced!

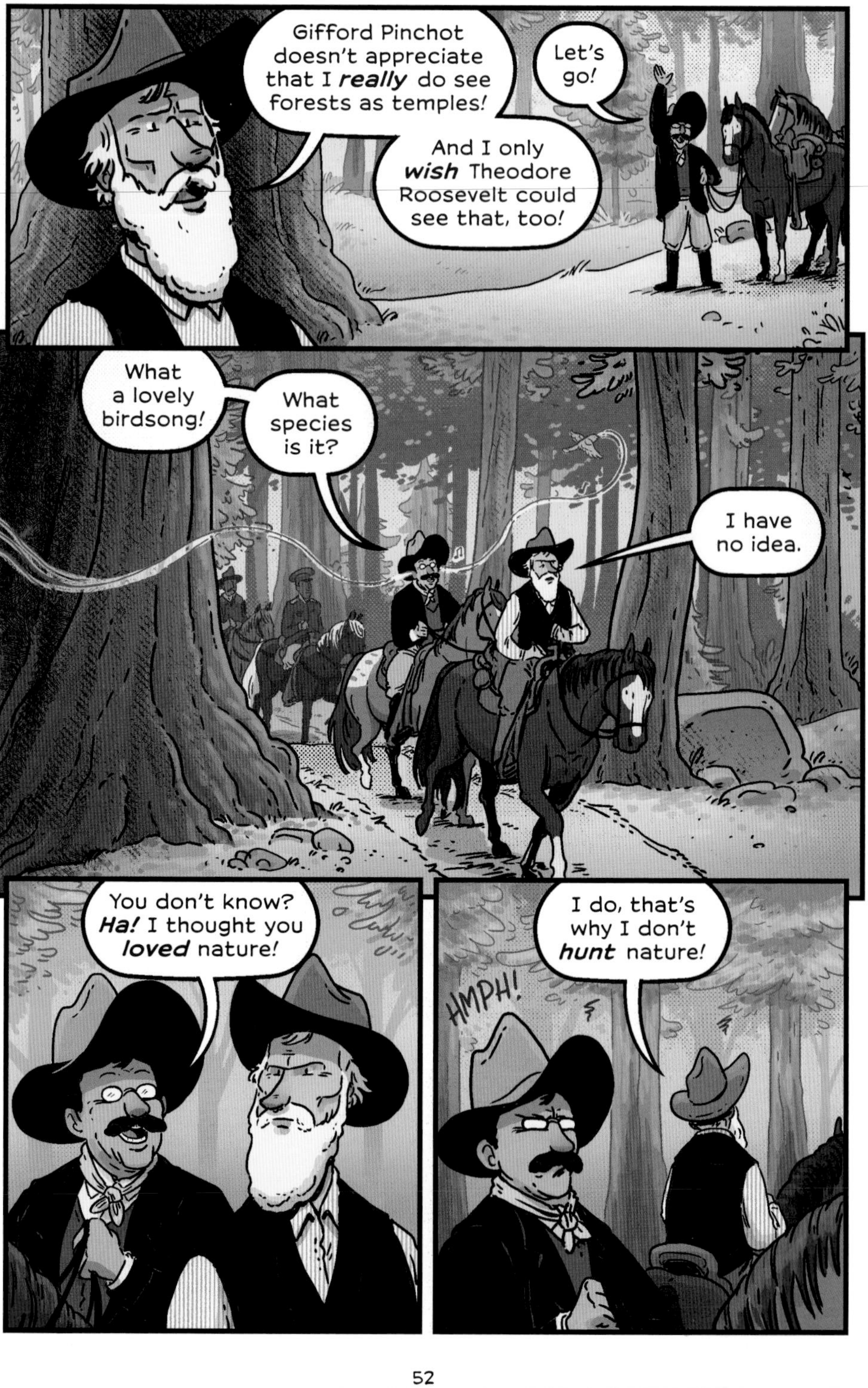
Gifford Pinchot doesn't appreciate that I ***really*** do see forests as temples!
And I only ***wish*** Theodore Roosevelt could see that, too!
Let's go!
What a lovely birdsong!
What species is it?
I have no idea.
You don't know? ***Ha!*** I thought you ***loved*** nature!
I do, that's why I don't ***hunt*** nature!
HMPH!

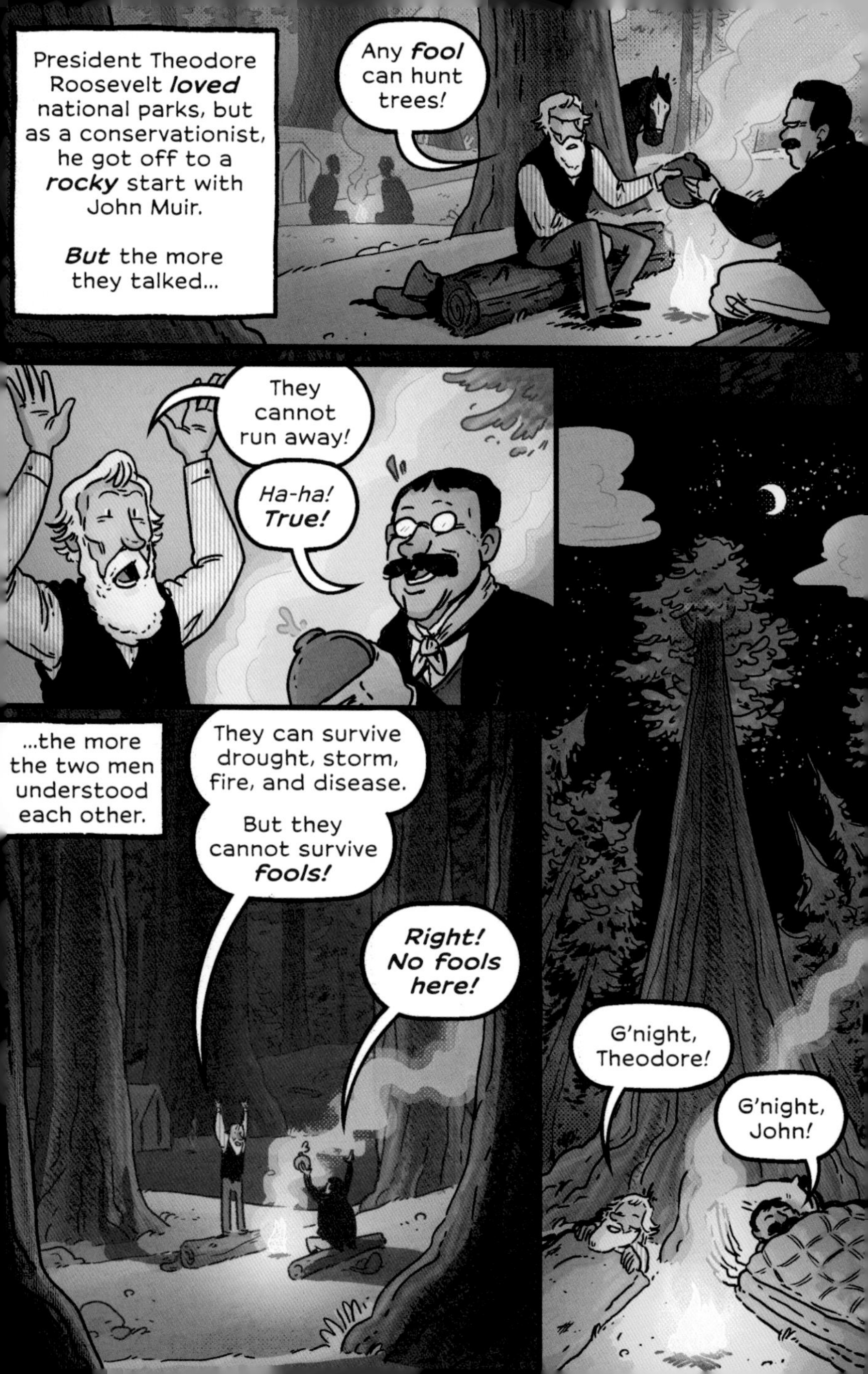
President Theodore Roosevelt *loved* national parks, but as a conservationist, he got off to a *rocky* start with John Muir.
But the more they talked...
Any *fool* can hunt trees!
They cannot run away!
Ha-ha! ***True!***
...the more the two men understood each other.
They can survive drought, storm, fire, and disease.
But they cannot survive ***fools!***
Right! No fools here!
G'night, Theodore!
G'night, John!

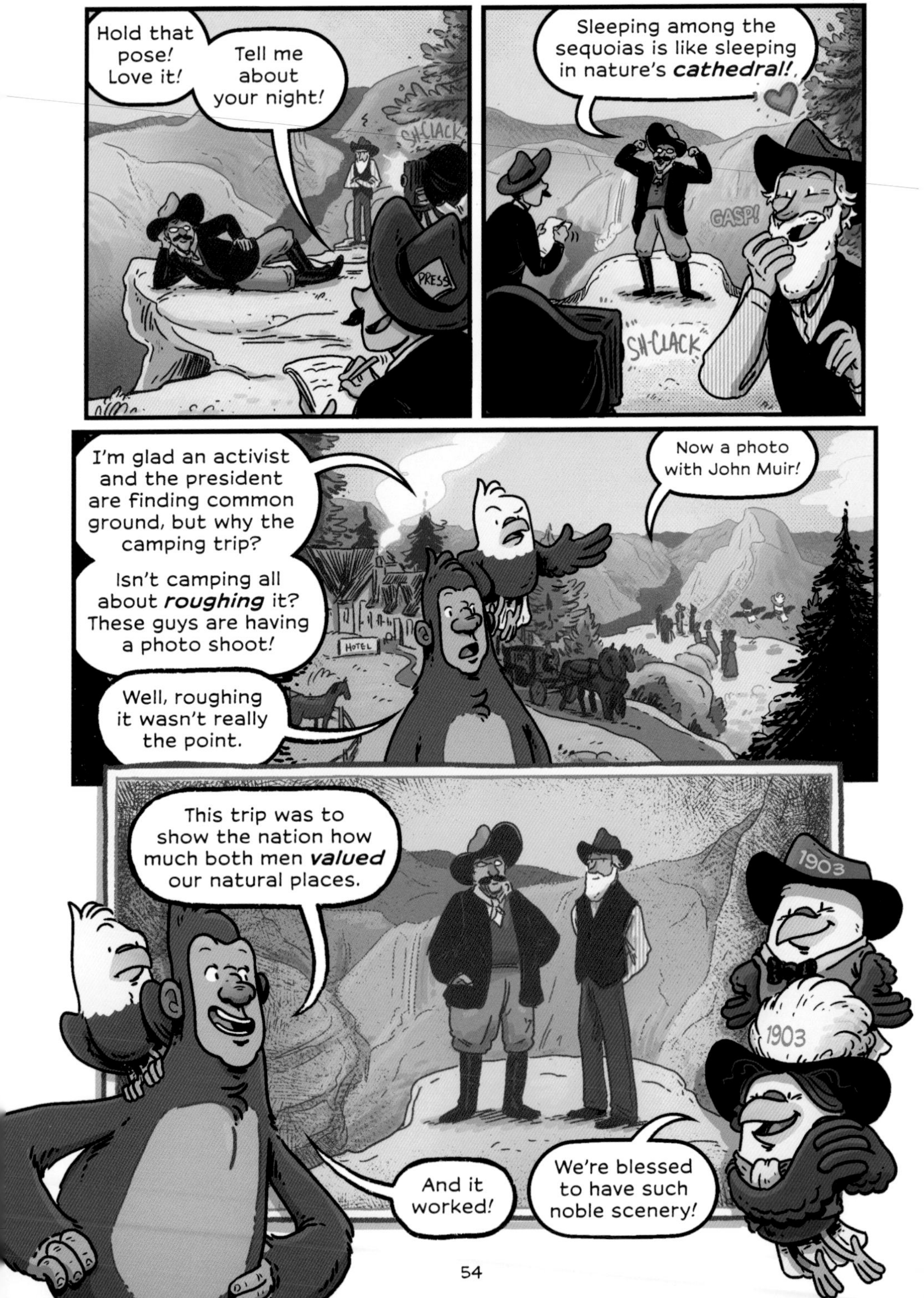
Hold that pose! Love it!
Tell me about your night!
SH-CLACK
Sleeping among the sequoias is like sleeping in nature's ***cathedral!***
GASP!
SH-CLACK
I'm glad an activist and the president are finding common ground, but why the camping trip?
Isn't camping all about ***roughing*** it? These guys are having a photo shoot!
Now a photo with John Muir!
HOTEL
Well, roughing it wasn't really the point.
This trip was to show the nation how much both men ***valued*** our natural places.
1903
1903
And it worked!
We're blessed to have such noble scenery!

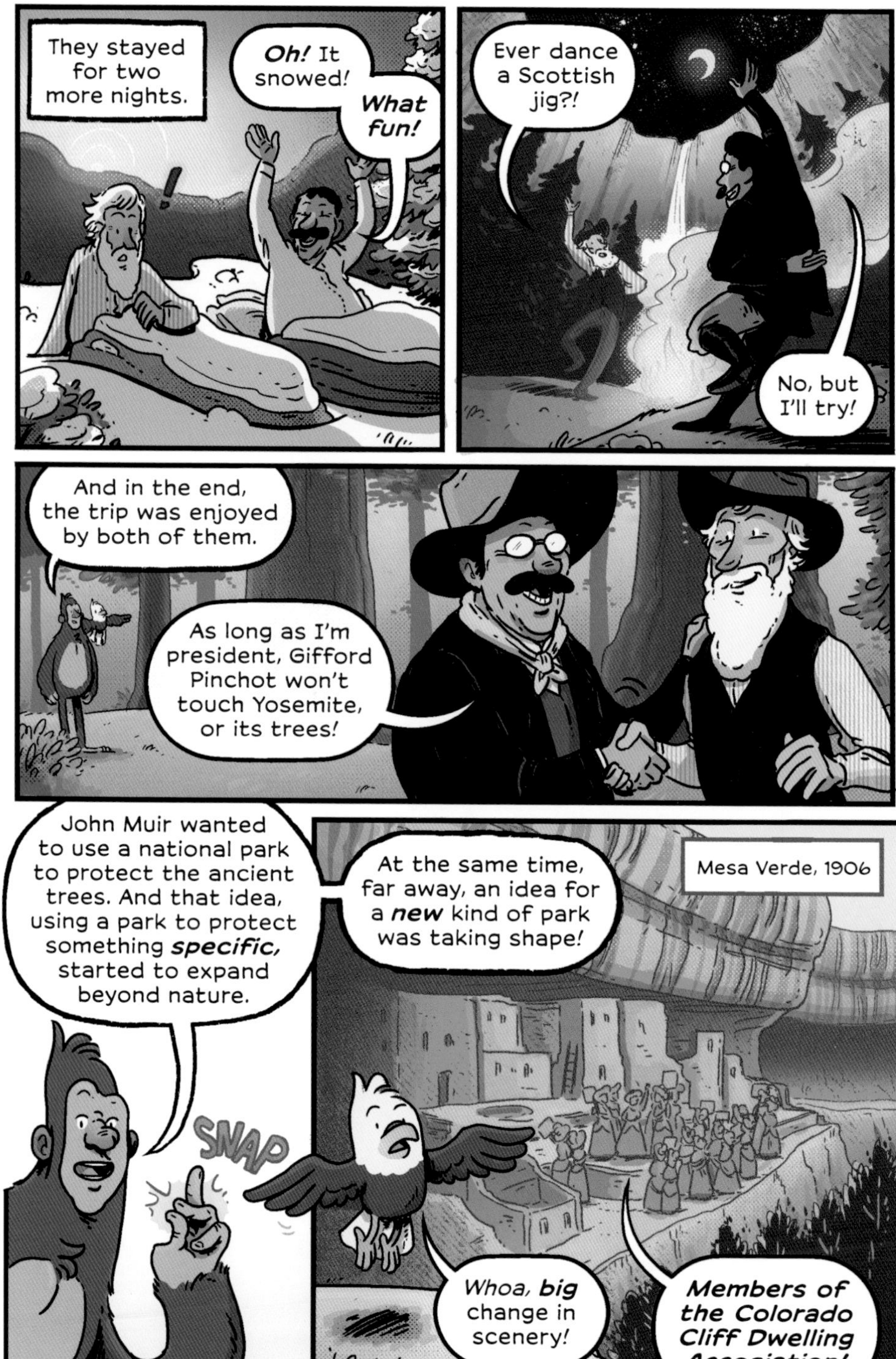
They stayed for two more nights.
Oh! It snowed!
What fun!
Ever dance a Scottish jig?!
No, but I'll try!
And in the end, the trip was enjoyed by both of them.
As long as I'm president, Gifford Pinchot won't touch Yosemite, or its trees!
John Muir wanted to use a national park to protect the ancient trees. And that idea, using a park to protect something ***specific,*** started to expand beyond nature.
SNAP
At the same time, far away, an idea for a ***new*** kind of park was taking shape!
Mesa Verde, 1906
Whoa, ***big*** change in scenery!
Members of the Colorado Cliff Dwelling Association!

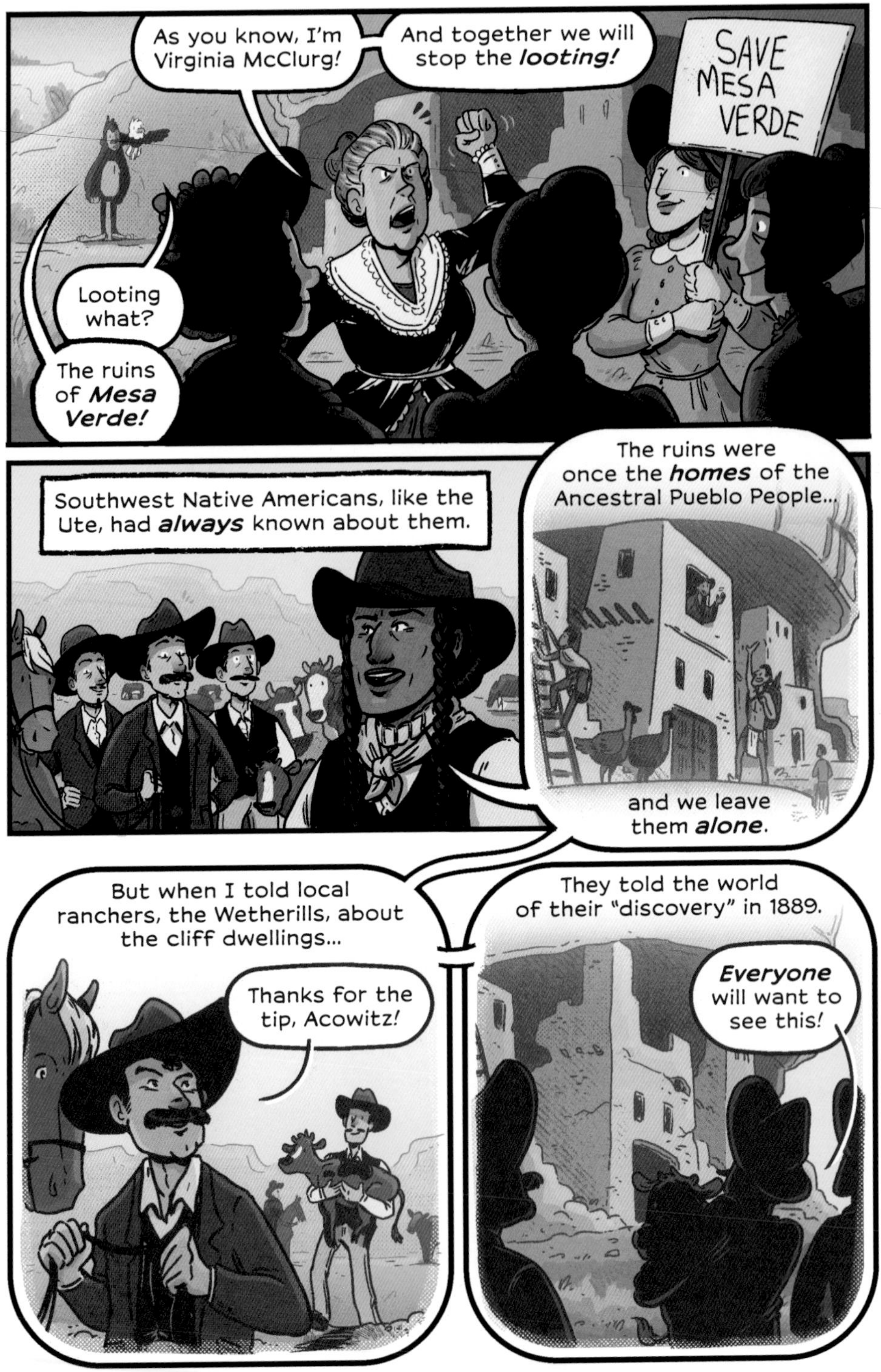
As you know, I'm Virginia McClurg!
And together we will stop the *looting!*
SAVE MESA VERDE
Looting what?
The ruins of *Mesa Verde!*
Southwest Native Americans, like the Ute, had *always* known about them.
The ruins were once the *homes* of the Ancestral Pueblo People...
and we leave them *alone*.
But when I told local ranchers, the Wetherills, about the cliff dwellings...
Thanks for the tip, Acowitz!
They told the world of their "discovery" in 1889.
Everyone will want to see this!

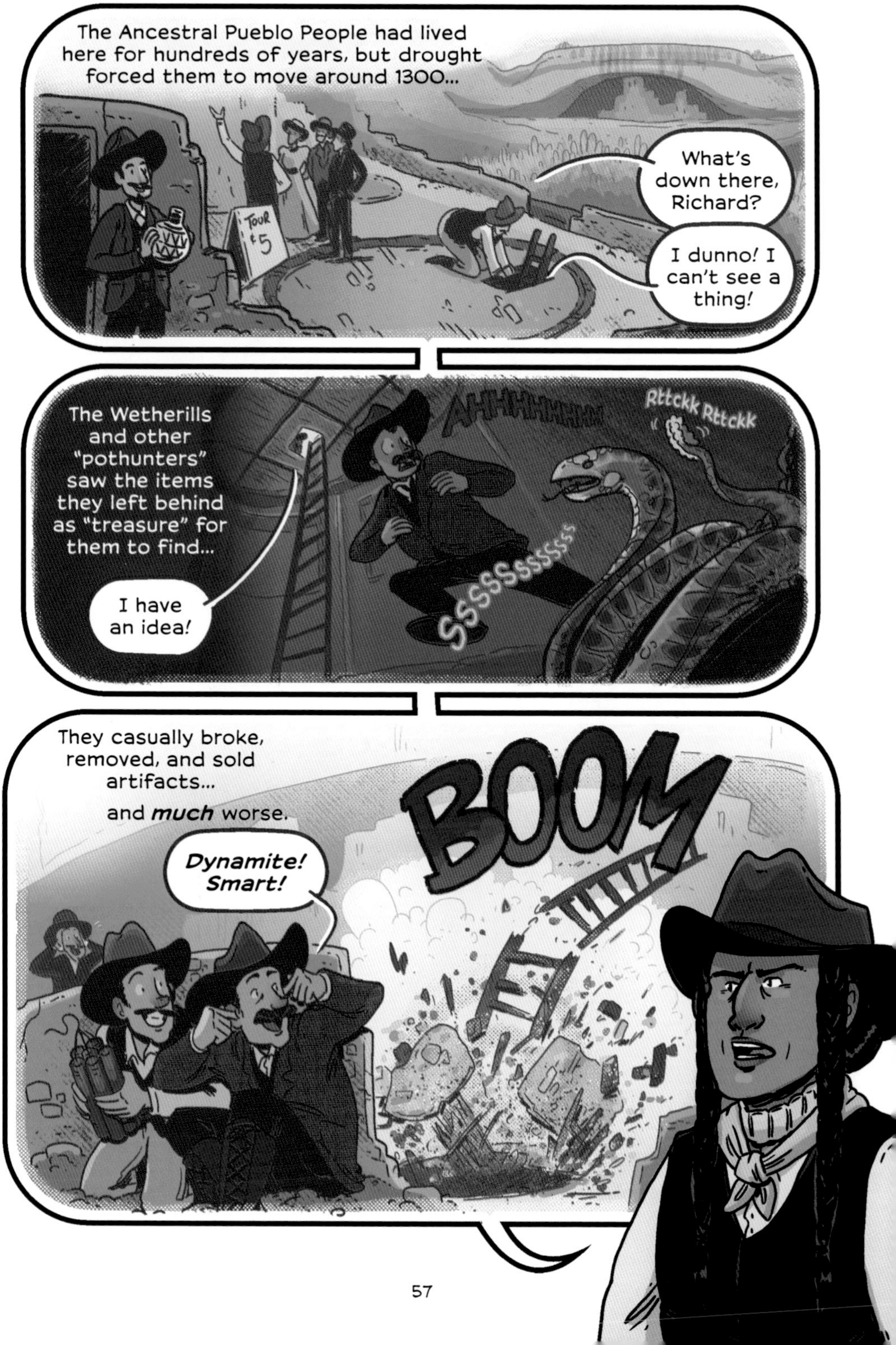
The Ancestral Pueblo People had lived here for hundreds of years, but drought forced them to move around 1300...
TOUR $5
What's down there, Richard?
I dunno! I can't see a thing!
The Wetherills and other "pothunters" saw the items they left behind as "treasure" for them to find...
AHHHHHHHH
Rttckk Rttckk
SSSSSSSSSSSS
I have an idea!
They casually broke, removed, and sold artifacts...
and *much* worse.
BOOM
Dynamite! Smart!

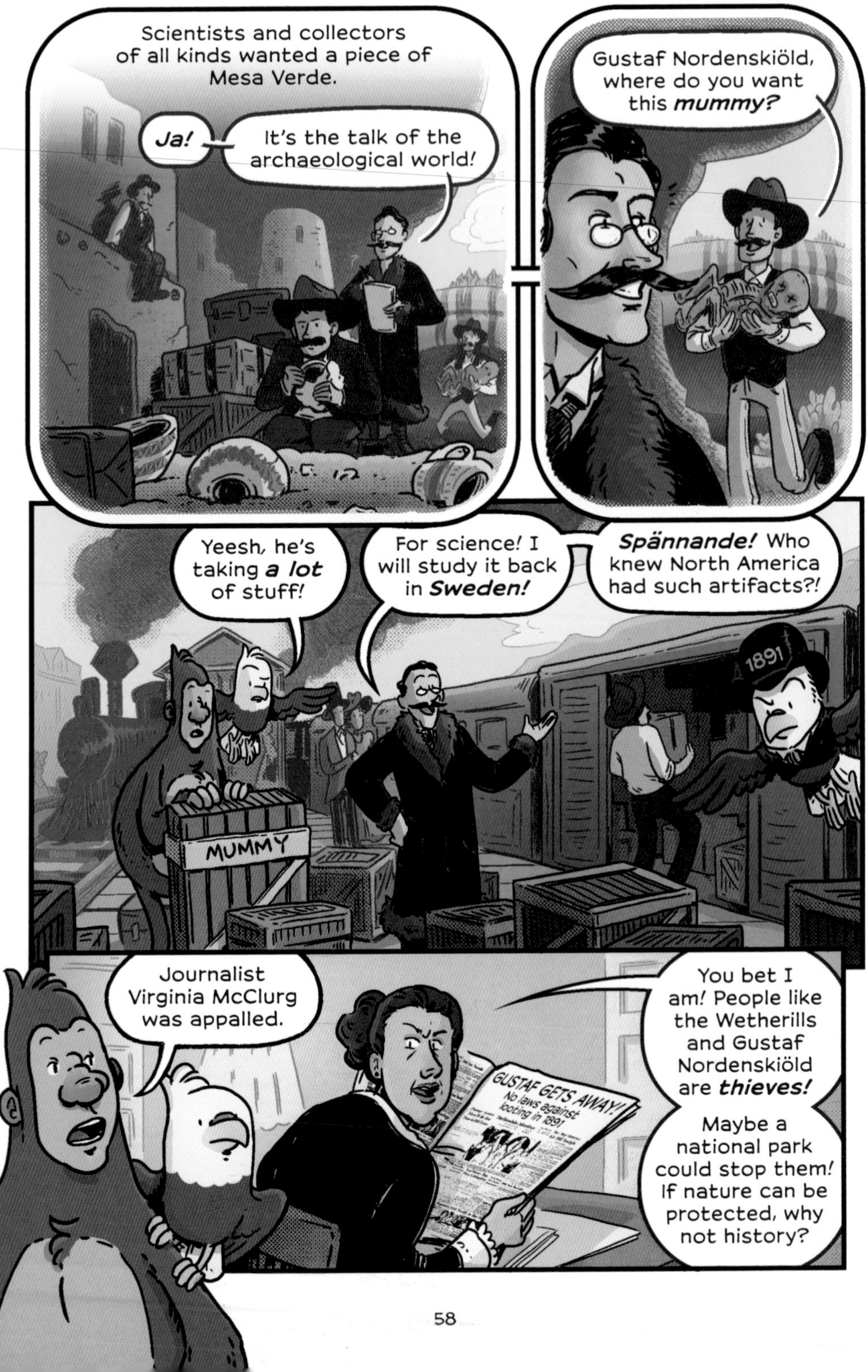

Scientists and collectors of all kinds wanted a piece of Mesa Verde.
Ja!
It's the talk of the archaeological world!
Gustaf Nordenskiöld, where do you want this ***mummy?***
Yeesh, he's taking ***a lot*** of stuff!
For science! I will study it back in ***Sweden!***
Spännande! Who knew North America had such artifacts?!
MUMMY
1891
Journalist Virginia McClurg was appalled.
GUSTAF GETS AWAY! No laws against looting in 1891
You bet I am! People like the Wetherills and Gustaf Nordenskiöld are ***thieves!***
Maybe a national park could stop them! If nature can be protected, why not history?

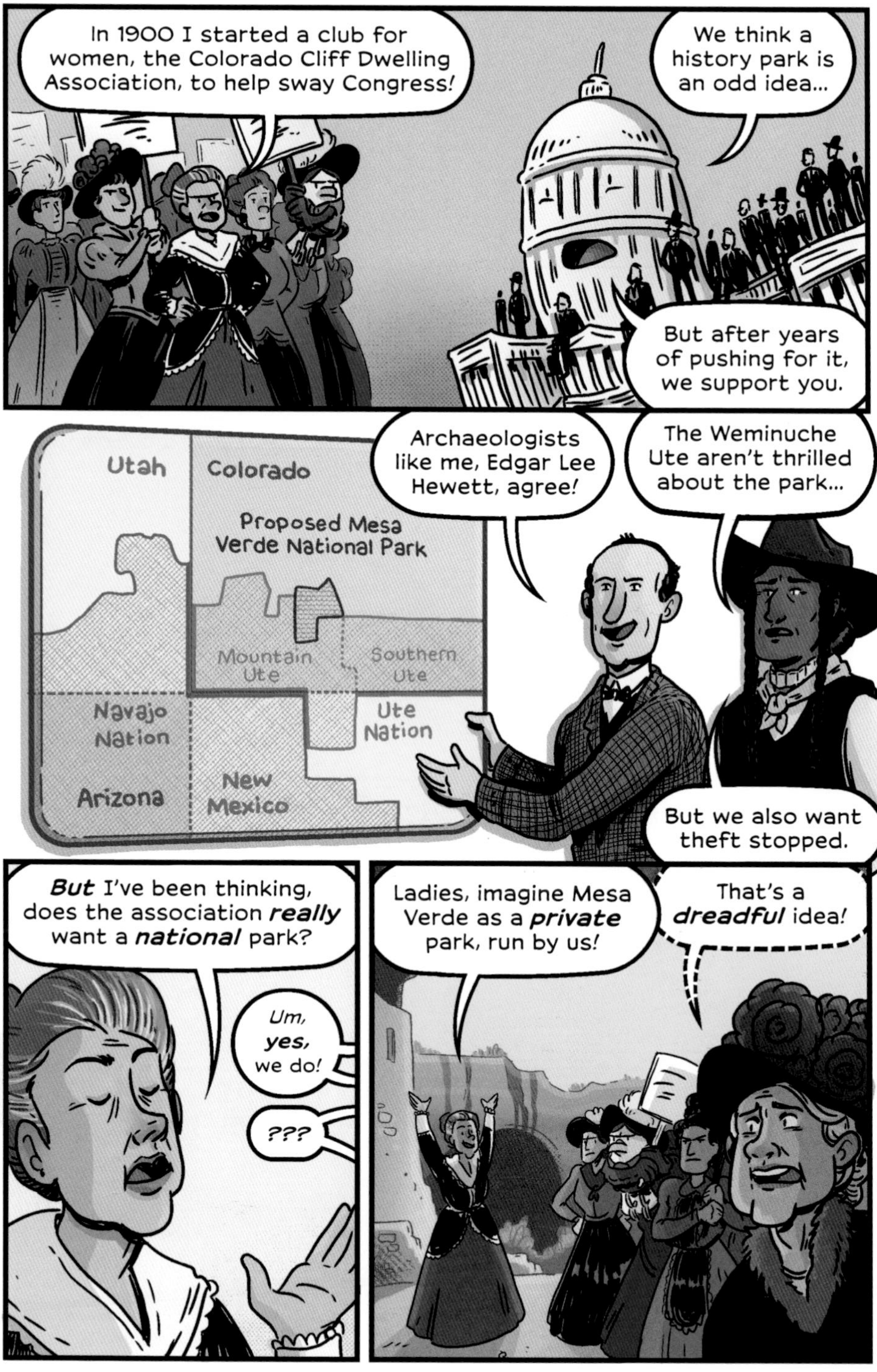
In 1900 I started a club for women, the Colorado Cliff Dwelling Association, to help sway Congress!
We think a history park is an odd idea...
But after years of pushing for it, we support you.
Utah
Colorado
Proposed Mesa Verde National Park
Mountain Ute
Southern Ute
Navajo Nation
Ute Nation
Arizona
New Mexico
Archaeologists like me, Edgar Lee Hewett, agree!
The Weminuche Ute aren't thrilled about the park...
But we also want theft stopped.
But I've been thinking, does the association ***really*** want a ***national*** park?
*Um, **yes,** we do!*
???
Ladies, imagine Mesa Verde as a ***private*** park, run by us!
That's a ***dreadful*** idea!

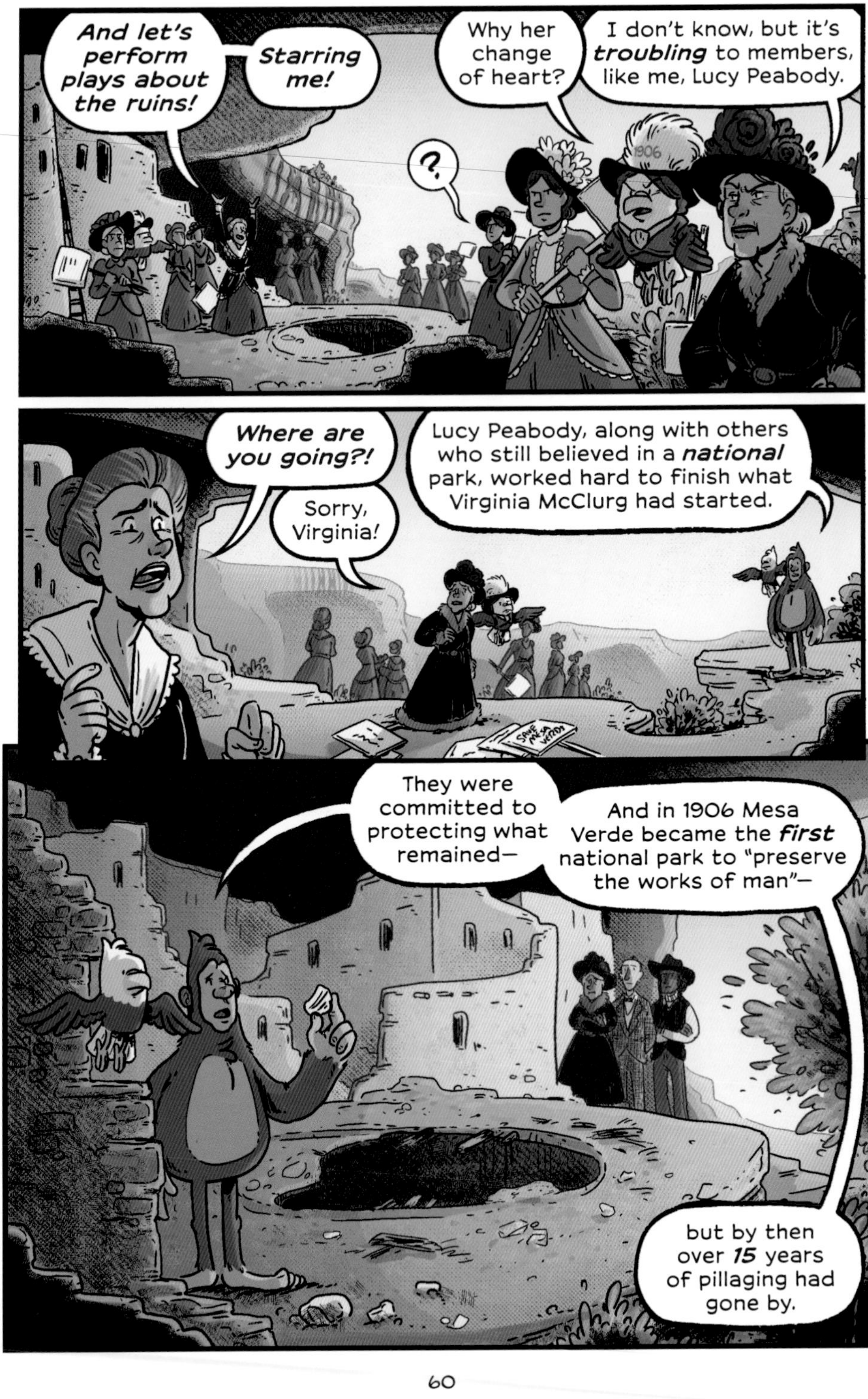

And let's perform plays about the ruins!
Starring me!
Why her change of heart?
I don't know, but it's ***troubling*** to members, like me, Lucy Peabody.
?
1906
Where are you going?!
Sorry, Virginia!
Lucy Peabody, along with others who still believed in a ***national*** park, worked hard to finish what Virginia McClurg had started.
SAVE MESA VERDE
They were committed to protecting what remained—
And in 1906 Mesa Verde became the ***first*** national park to "preserve the works of man"—
but by then over ***15*** years of pillaging had gone by.

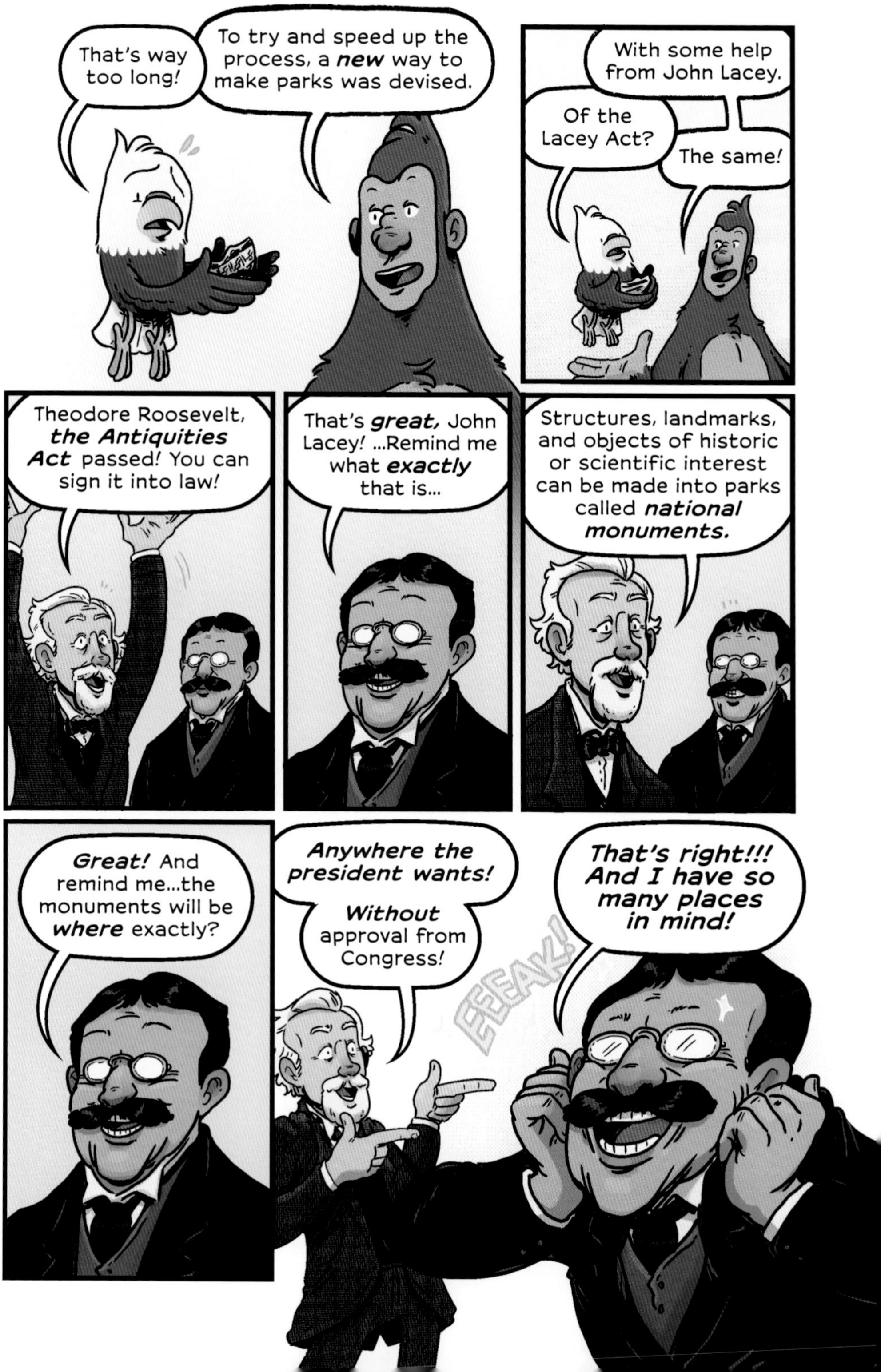
That's way too long!
To try and speed up the process, a ***new*** way to make parks was devised.
With some help from John Lacey.
Of the Lacey Act?
The same!
Theodore Roosevelt, ***the Antiquities Act*** passed! You can sign it into law!
That's ***great,*** John Lacey! ...Remind me what ***exactly*** that is...
Structures, landmarks, and objects of historic or scientific interest can be made into parks called ***national monuments.***
Great! And remind me...the monuments will be ***where*** exactly?
Anywhere the president wants!
Without approval from Congress!
FEEAK!
That's right!!! And I have so many places in mind!

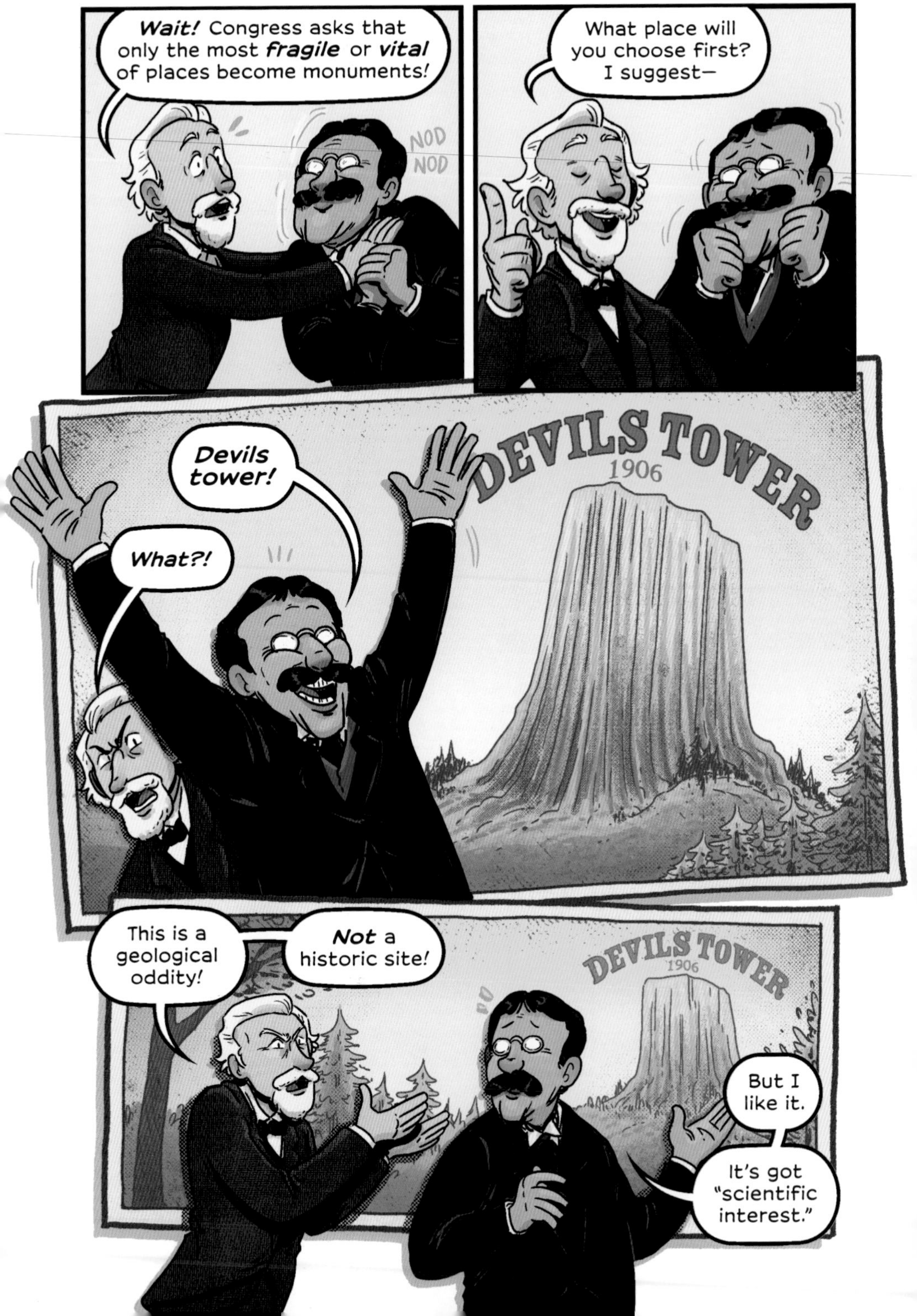
Wait! Congress asks that only the most ***fragile*** or ***vital*** of places become monuments!
NOD NOD
What place will you choose first? I suggest—
Devils tower!
DEVILS TOWER 1906
What?!
This is a geological oddity!
Not a historic site!
DEVILS TOWER 1906
But I like it.
It's got "scientific interest."

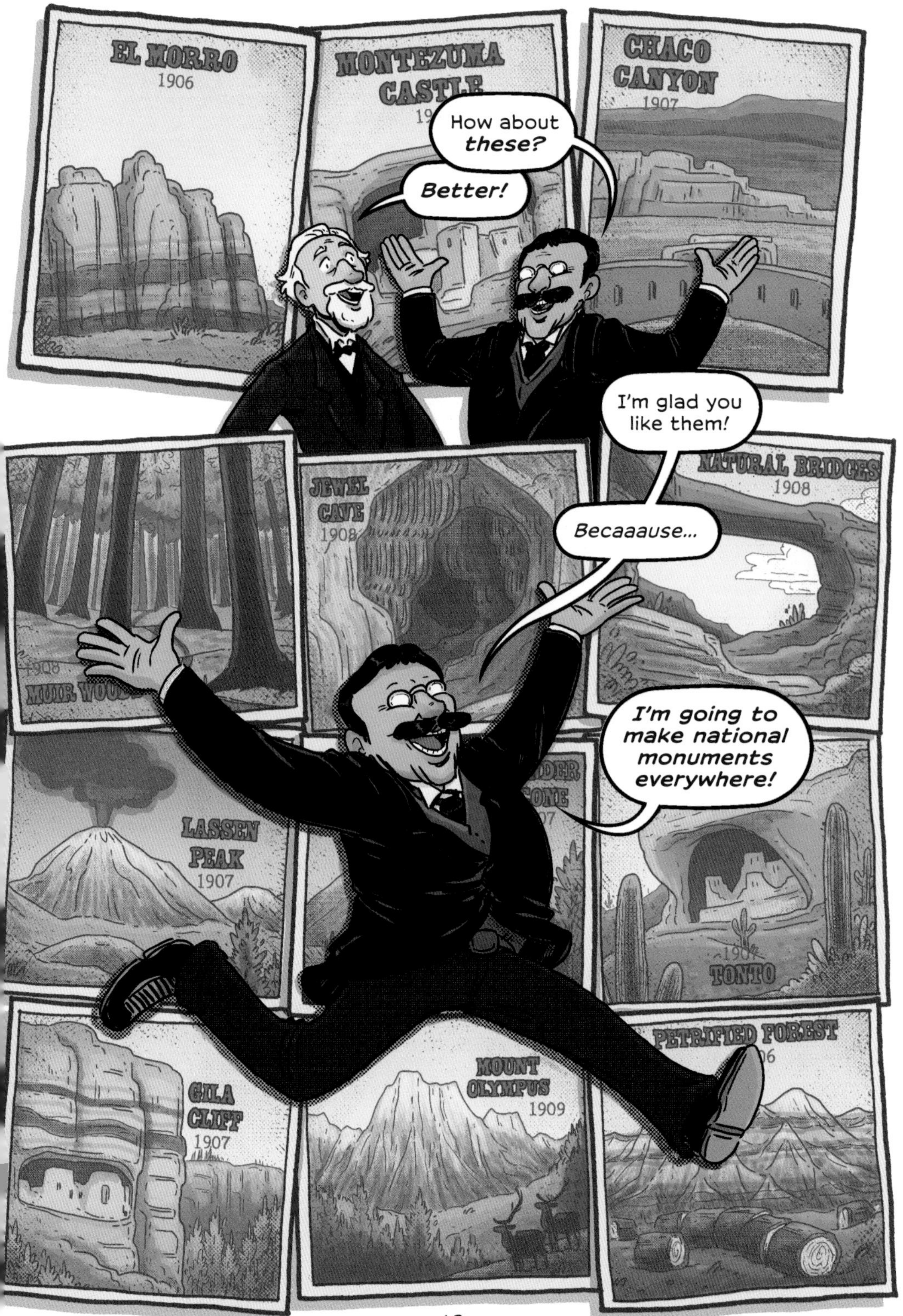
EL MORRO
1906
MONTEZUMA
CASTLE
CHACO
CANYON
1907
How about *these?*
Better!
I'm glad you like them!
JEWEL
CAVE
1908
NATURAL BRIDGES
1908
Becaaause...
I'm going to make national monuments everywhere!
LASSEN
PEAK
1907
TONTO
GILA
CLIFF
1907
MOUNT
OLYMPUS
1909
PETRIFIED FOREST

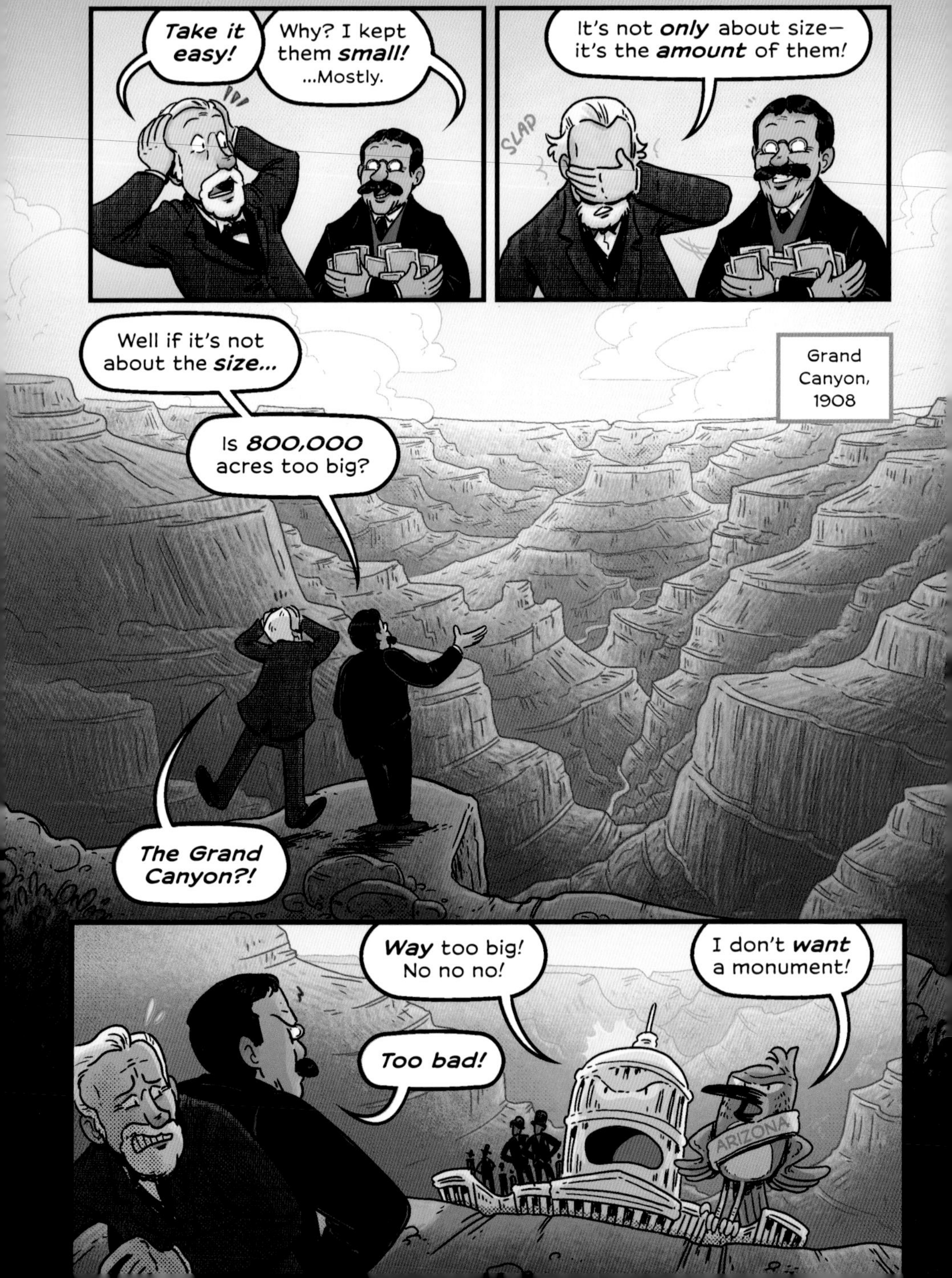

Take it easy!
Why? I kept them small! ...Mostly.
SLAP
It's not only about size—it's the amount of them!
Grand Canyon, 1908
Well if it's not about the size...
Is 800,000 acres too big?
The Grand Canyon?!
Way too big! No no no!
I don't want a monument!
Too bad!
ARIZONA

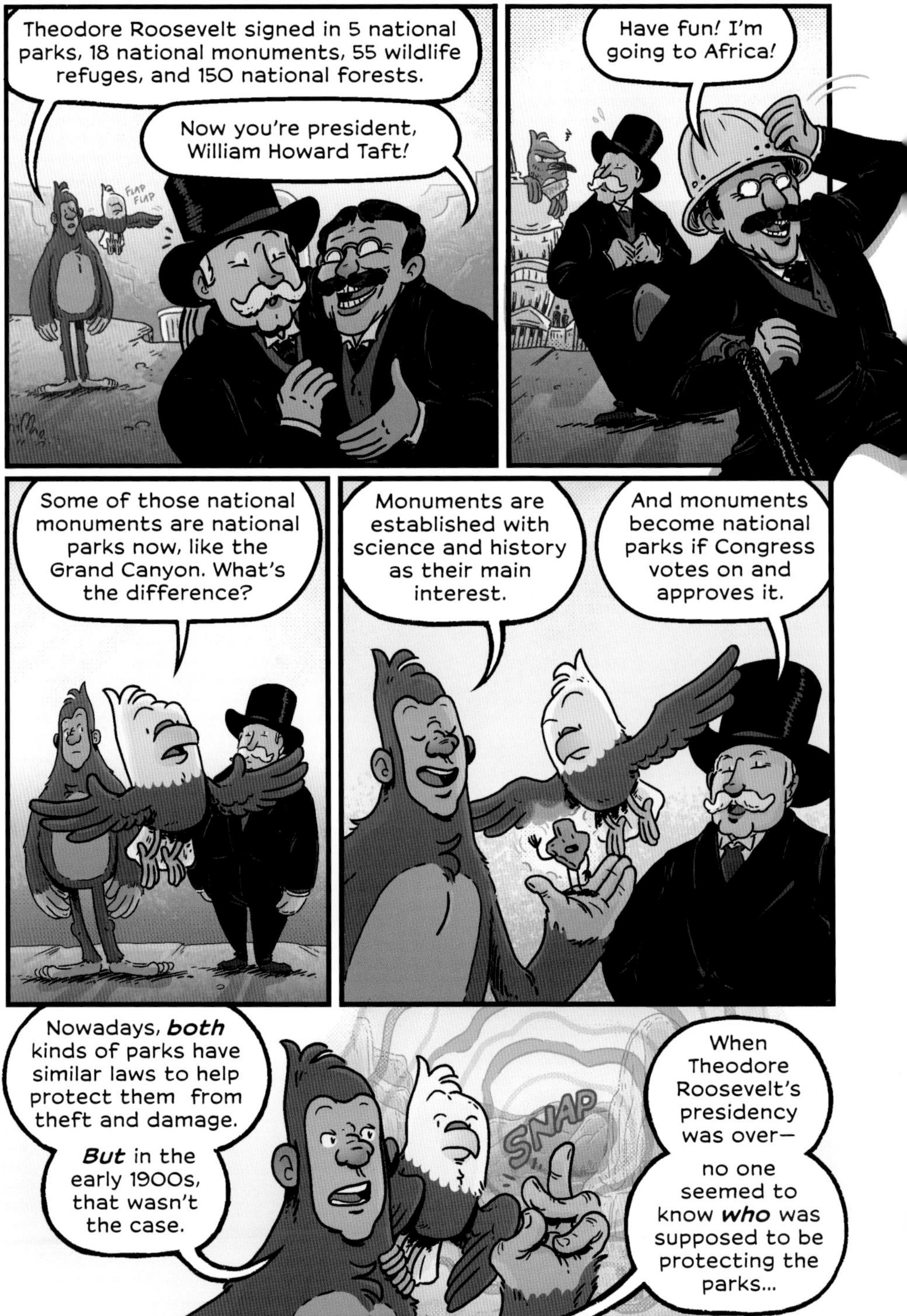
Theodore Roosevelt signed in 5 national parks, 18 national monuments, 55 wildlife refuges, and 150 national forests.
Now you're president, William Howard Taft!
FLAP FLAP
Have fun! I'm going to Africa!
Some of those national monuments are national parks now, like the Grand Canyon. What's the difference?
Monuments are established with science and history as their main interest.
And monuments become national parks if Congress votes on and approves it.
Nowadays, ***both*** kinds of parks have similar laws to help protect them from theft and damage.
But in the early 1900s, that wasn't the case.
SNAP
When Theodore Roosevelt's presidency was over—
no one seemed to know ***who*** was supposed to be protecting the parks...

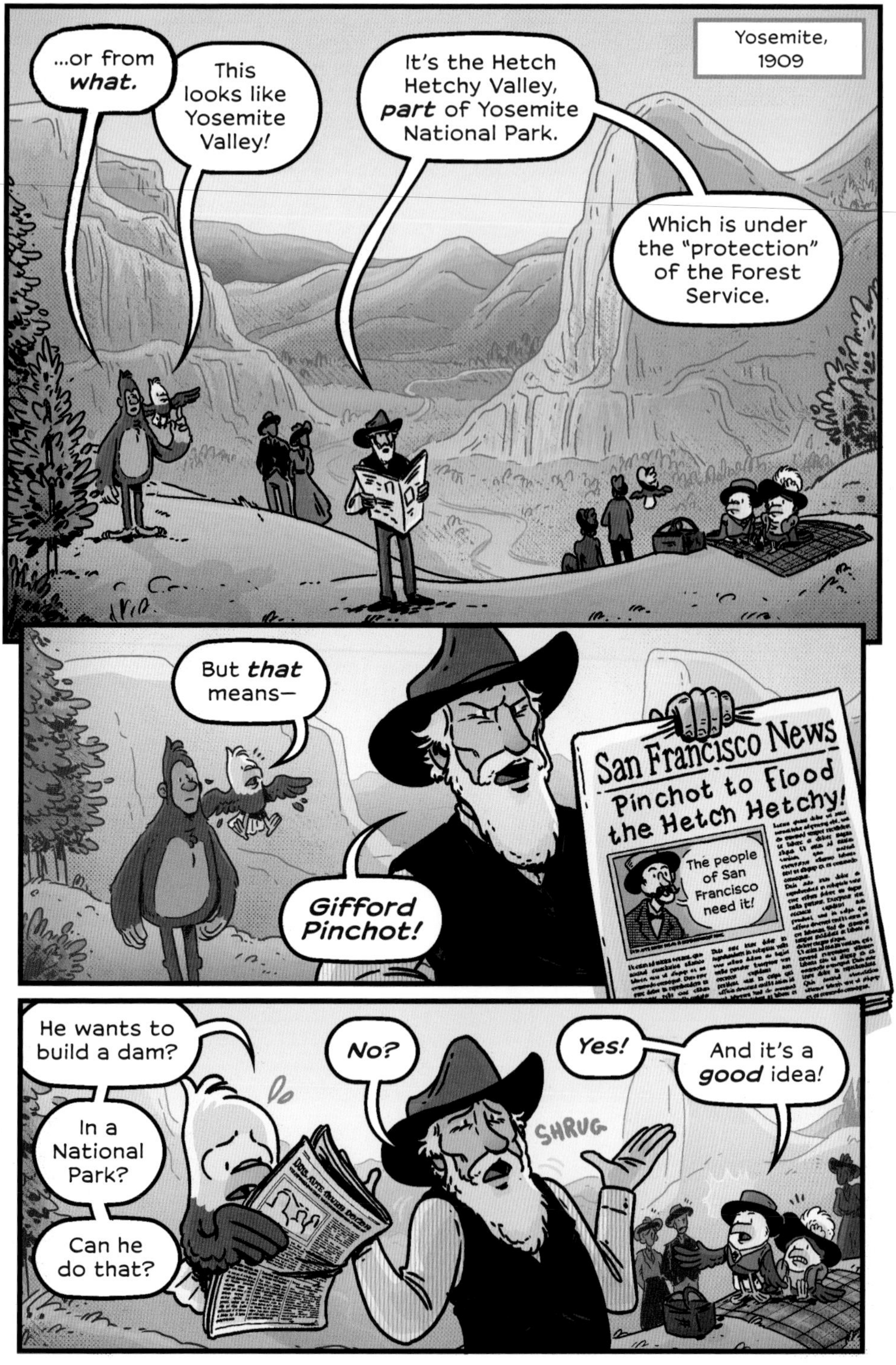
Yosemite, 1909
...or from *what.*
This looks like Yosemite Valley!
It's the Hetch Hetchy Valley, *part* of Yosemite National Park.
Which is under the "protection" of the Forest Service.
But *that* means—
Gifford Pinchot!
San Francisco News
Pinchot to Flood the Hetch Hetchy!
The people of San Francisco need it!
He wants to build a dam?
In a National Park?
Can he do that?
No?
SHRUG
Yes!
And it's a *good* idea!

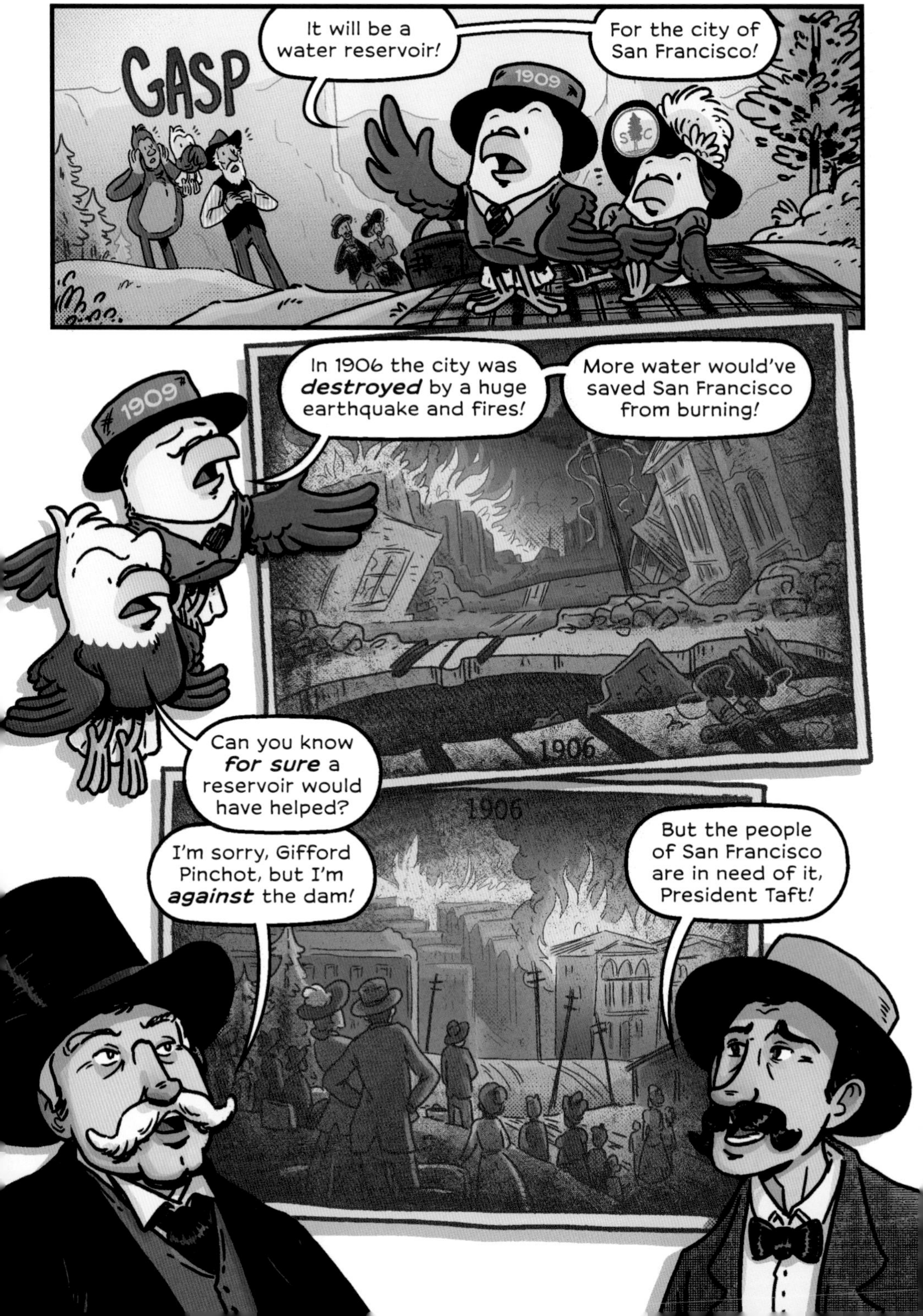
GASP
It will be a water reservoir!
For the city of San Francisco!
1909
S C
1909
In 1906 the city was *destroyed* by a huge earthquake and fires!
More water would've saved San Francisco from burning!
1906
Can you know *for sure* a reservoir would have helped?
1906
I'm sorry, Gifford Pinchot, but I'm *against* the dam!
But the people of San Francisco are in need of it, President Taft!

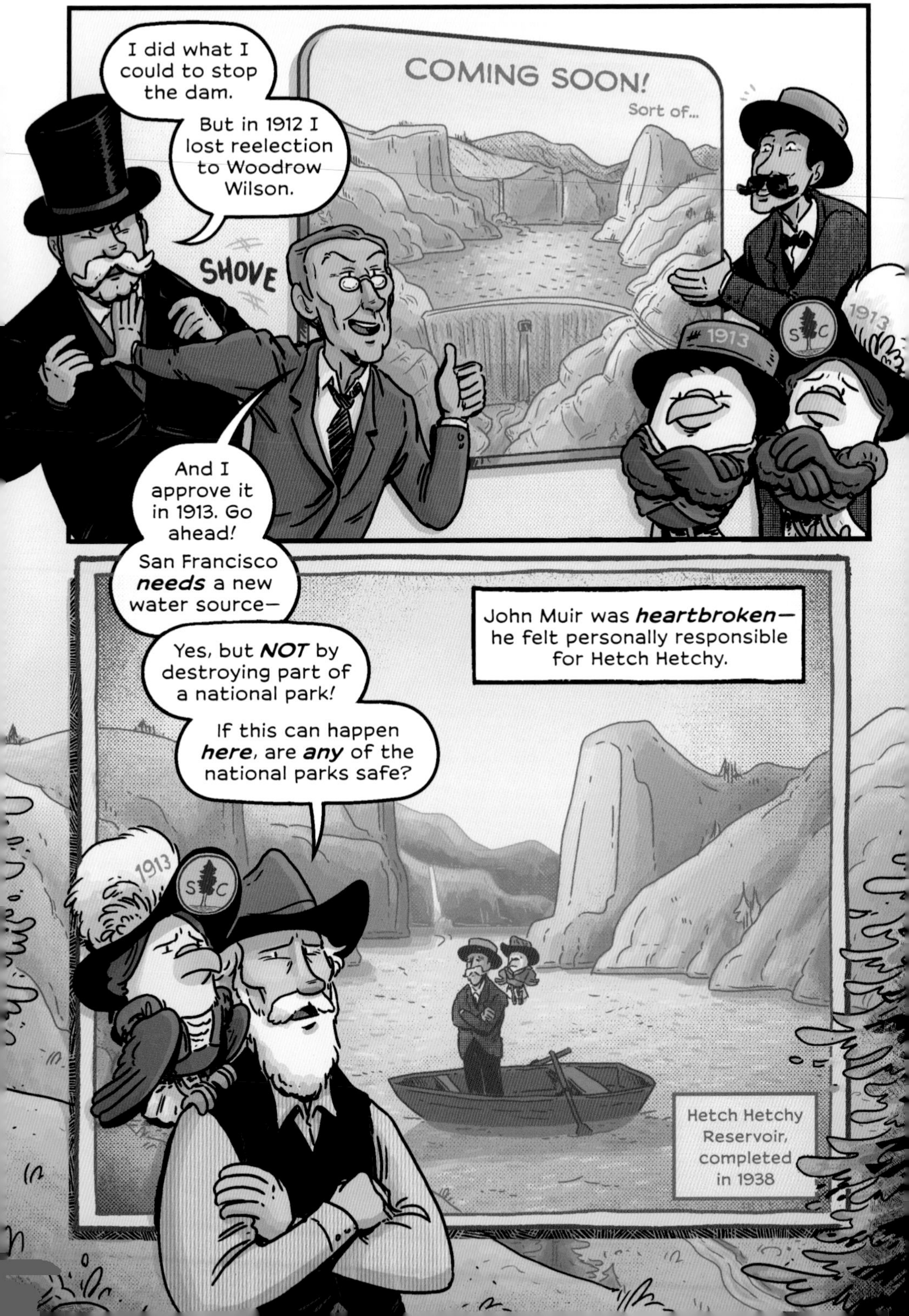
I did what I could to stop the dam.
But in 1912 I lost reelection to Woodrow Wilson.
COMING SOON!
Sort of...
SHOVE
And I approve it in 1913. Go ahead!
San Francisco *needs* a new water source—
1913
1913
1913
John Muir was ***heartbroken***—he felt personally responsible for Hetch Hetchy.
Yes, but ***NOT*** by destroying part of a national park!
If this can happen ***here***, are ***any*** of the national parks safe?
1913
Hetch Hetchy Reservoir, completed in 1938

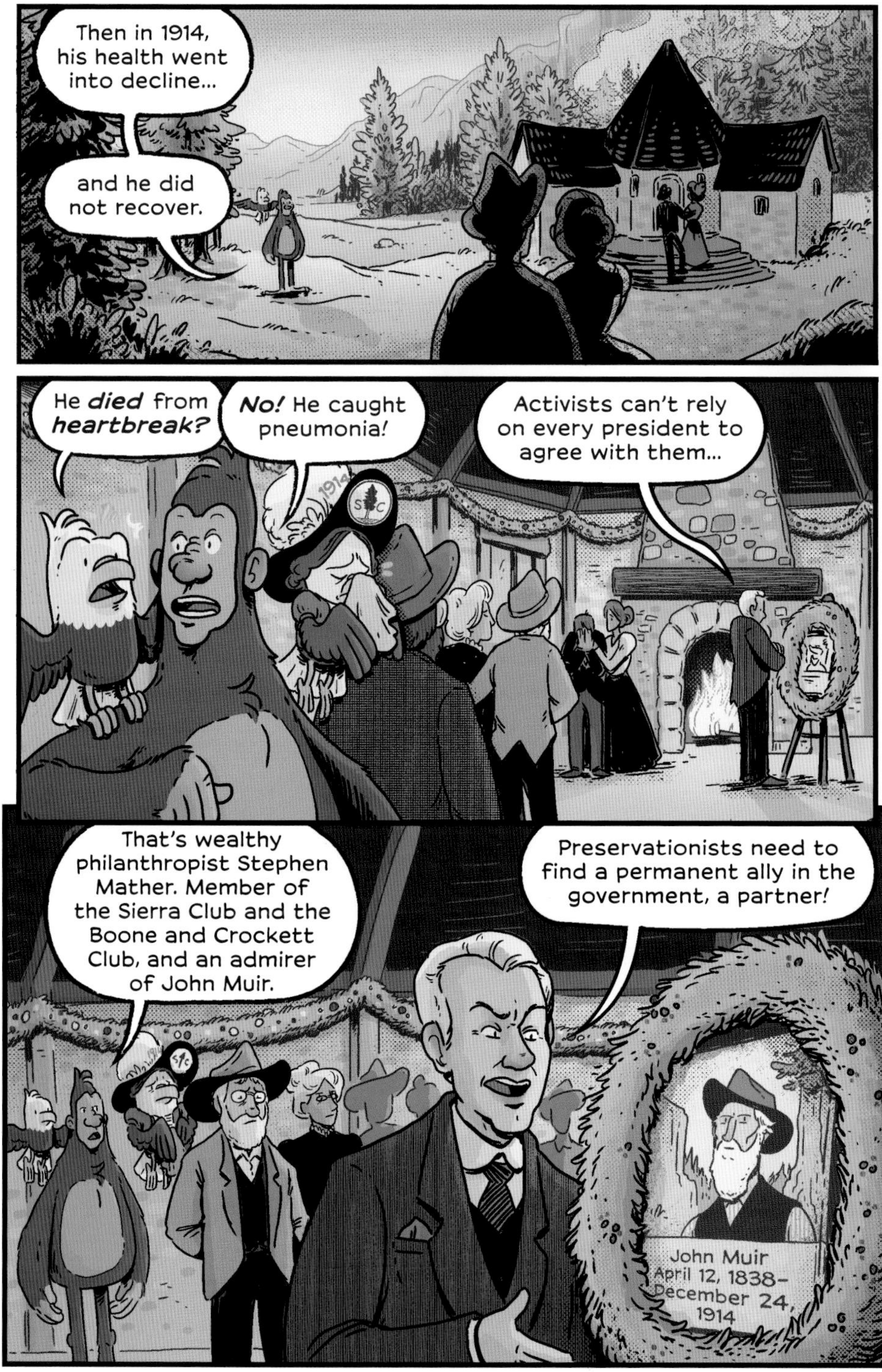
Then in 1914, his health went into decline...
and he did not recover.
He *died* from ***heartbreak?***
No! He caught pneumonia!
Activists can't rely on every president to agree with them...
That's wealthy philanthropist Stephen Mather. Member of the Sierra Club and the Boone and Crockett Club, and an admirer of John Muir.
Preservationists need to find a permanent ally in the government, a partner!
John Muir April 12, 1838– December 24, 1914

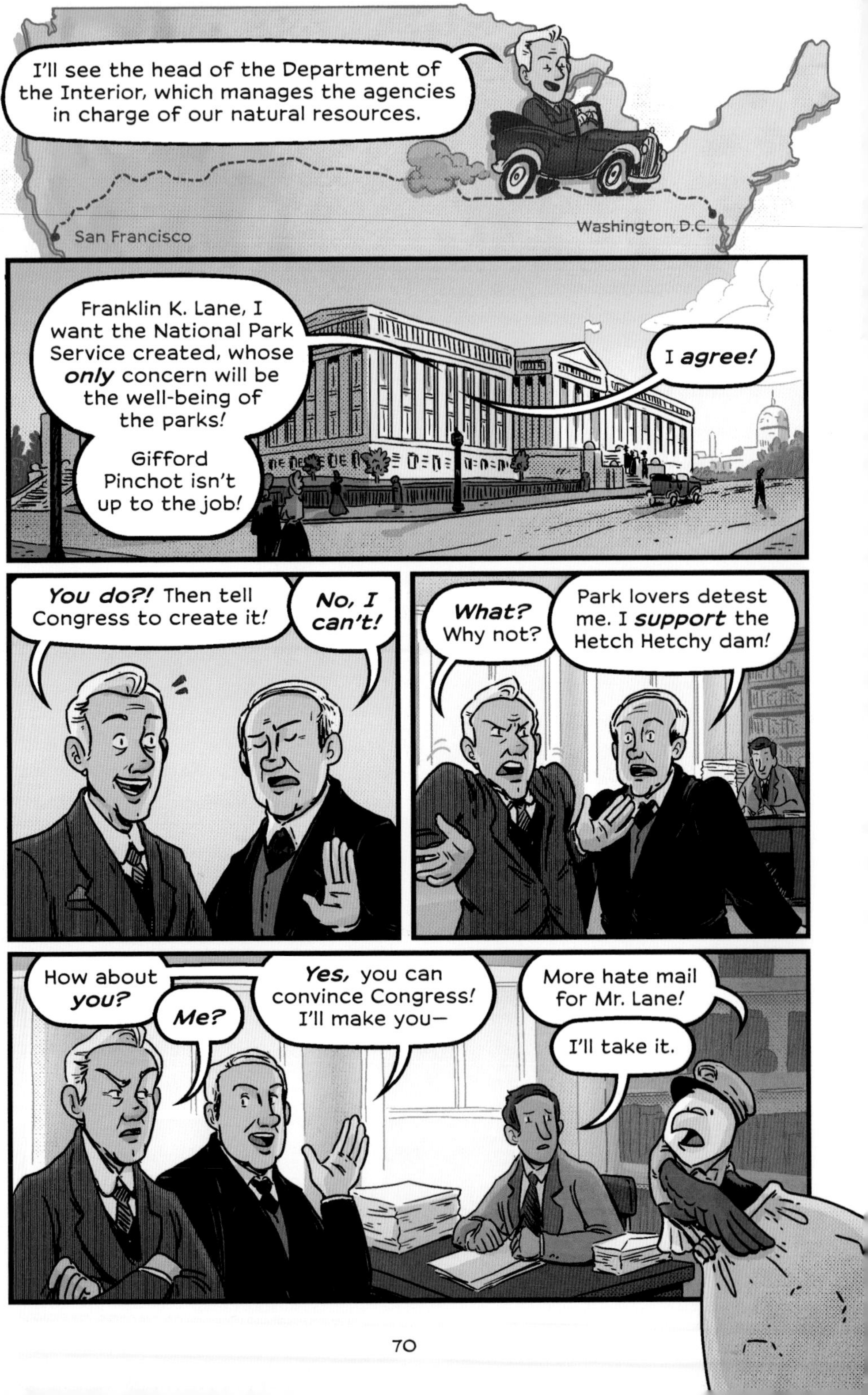
I'll see the head of the Department of the Interior, which manages the agencies in charge of our natural resources.
San Francisco
Washington, D.C.
Franklin K. Lane, I want the National Park Service created, whose *only* concern will be the well-being of the parks!
Gifford Pinchot isn't up to the job!
I *agree!*
You do?! Then tell Congress to create it!
No, I can't!
What? Why not?
Park lovers detest me. I *support* the Hetch Hetchy dam!
How about *you?*
Me?
Yes, you can convince Congress! I'll make you—
More hate mail for Mr. Lane!
I'll take it.

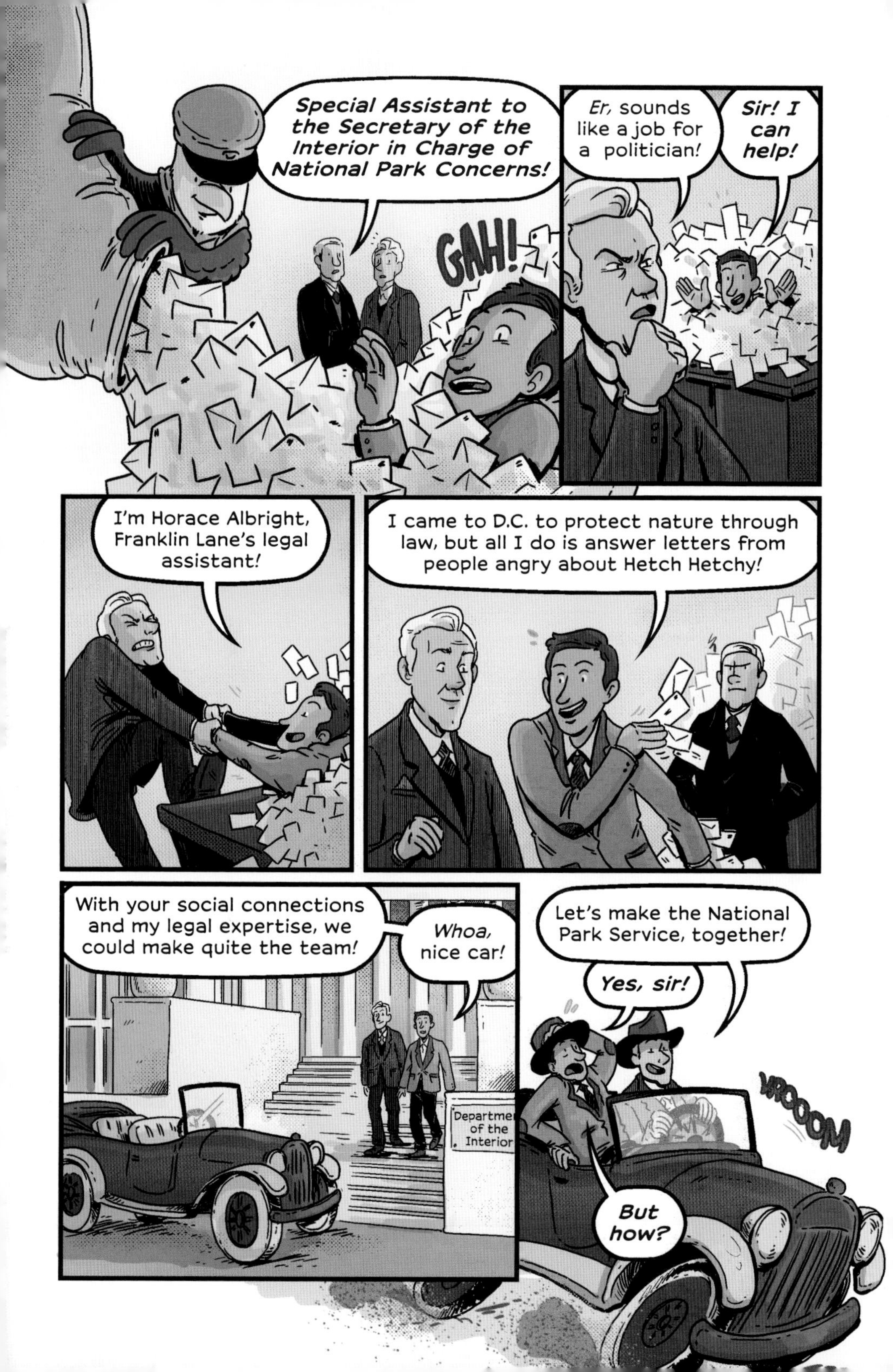
Special Assistant to the Secretary of the Interior in Charge of National Park Concerns!
GAH!
Er, sounds like a job for a politician!
Sir! I can help!
I'm Horace Albright, Franklin Lane's legal assistant!
I came to D.C. to protect nature through law, but all I do is answer letters from people angry about Hetch Hetchy!
With your social connections and my legal expertise, we could make quite the team!
Whoa, nice car!
Department of the Interior
Let's make the National Park Service, together!
Yes, sir!
VROOOM
But how?

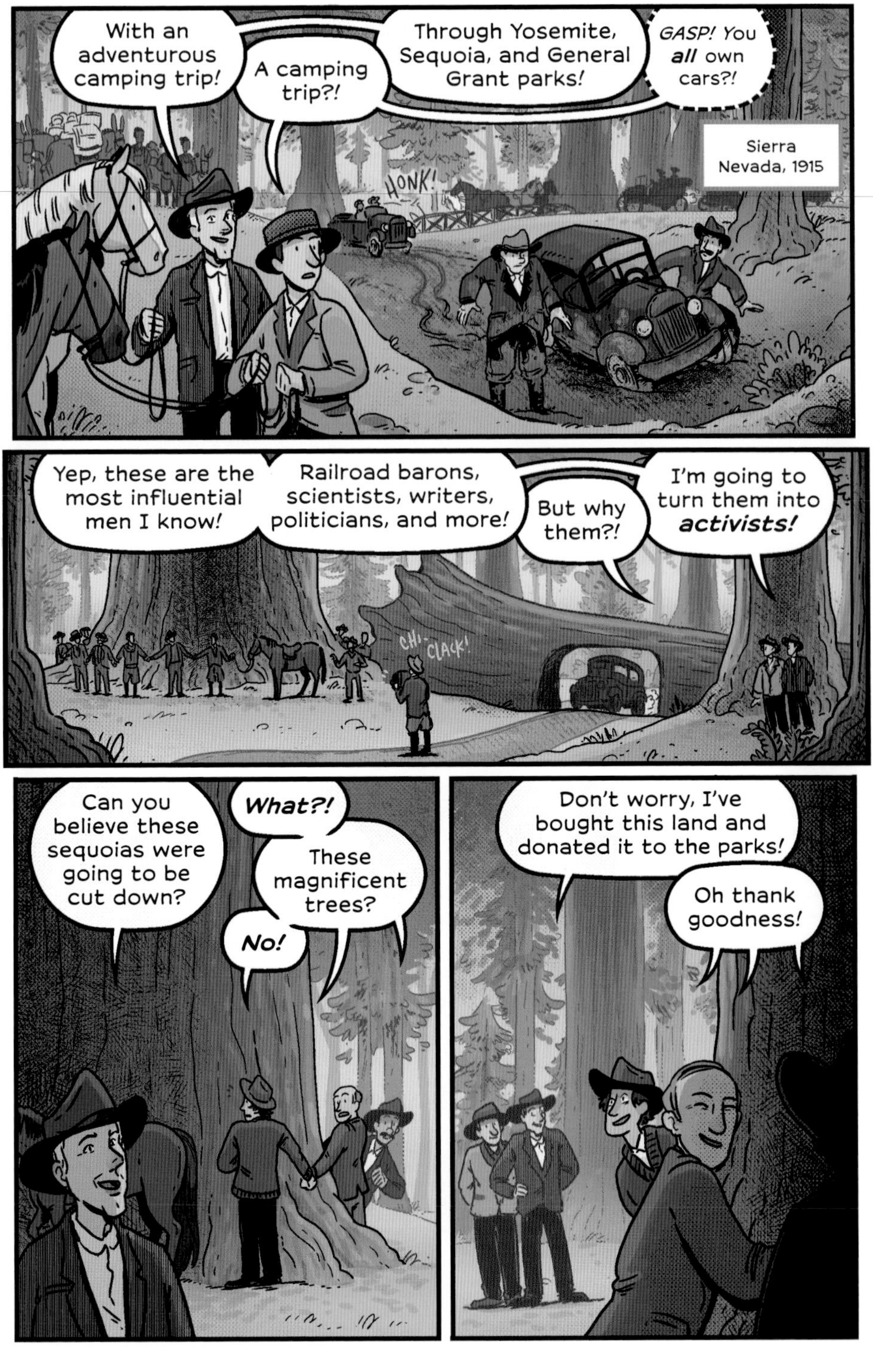
Sierra Nevada, 1915
With an adventurous camping trip!
A camping trip?!
Through Yosemite, Sequoia, and General Grant parks!
GASP! You *all* own cars?!
HONK!
Yep, these are the most influential men I know!
Railroad barons, scientists, writers, politicians, and more!
But why them?!
I'm going to turn them into ***activists!***
CHI-CLACK!
Can you believe these sequoias were going to be cut down?
What?!
These magnificent trees?
No!
Don't worry, I've bought this land and donated it to the parks!
Oh thank goodness!

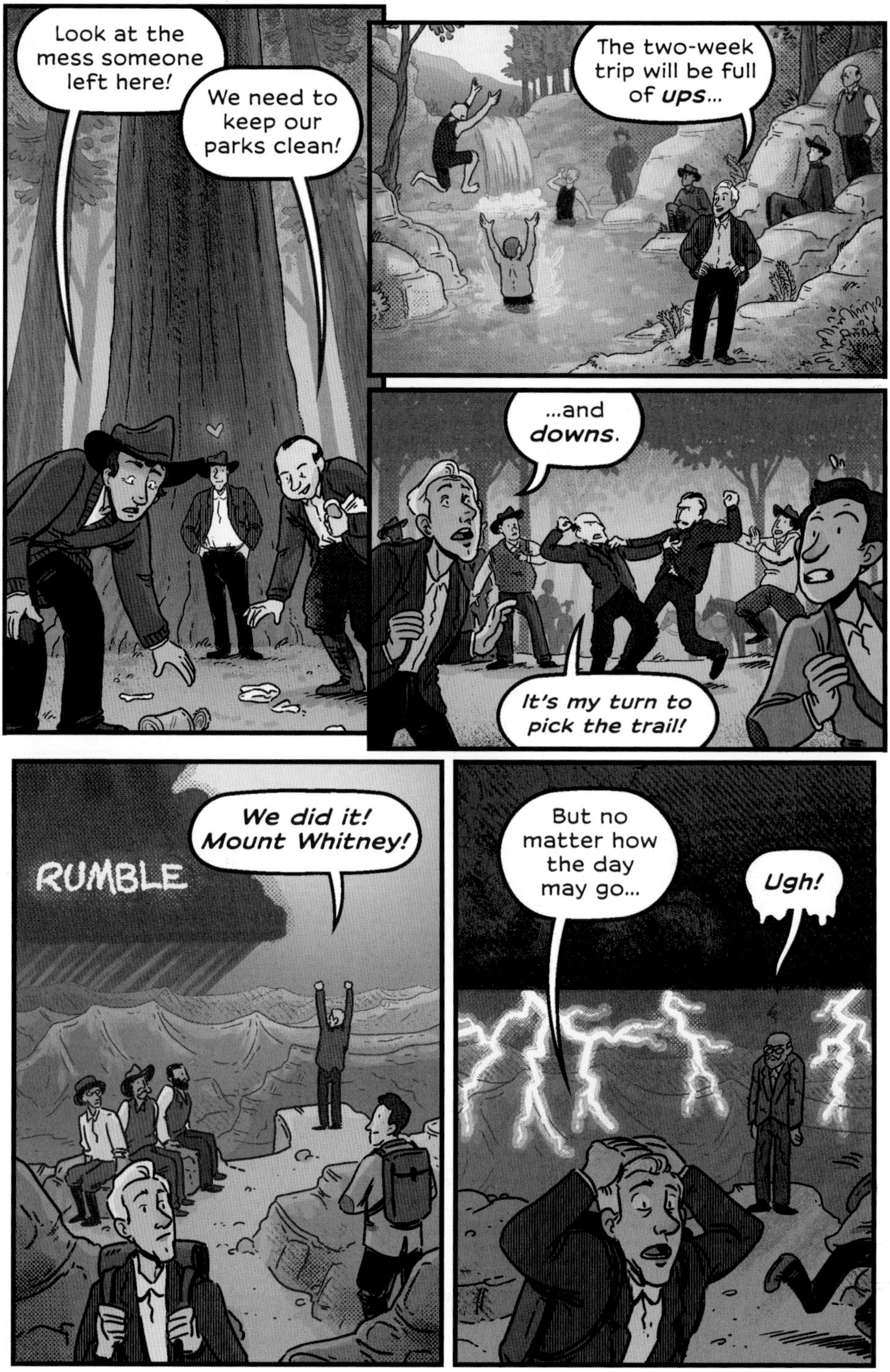

Look at the mess someone left here!
We need to keep our parks clean!
The two-week trip will be full of *ups*...
...and *downs*.
It's my turn to pick the trail!
We did it! Mount Whitney!
RUMBLE
But no matter how the day may go...
Ugh!

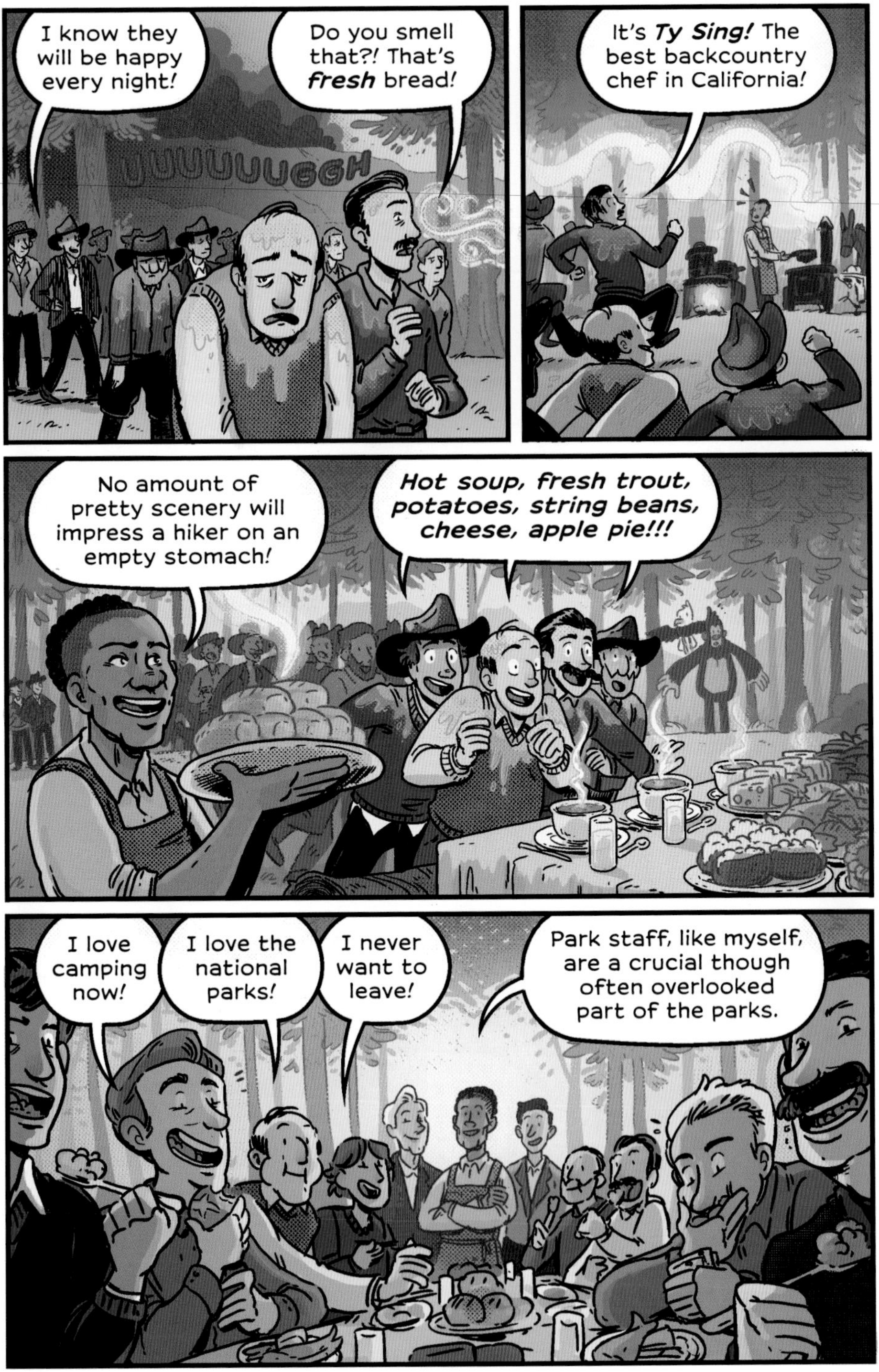

I know they will be happy every night!
Do you smell that?! That's ***fresh*** bread!
UUUUUUGGH
It's ***Ty Sing!*** The best backcountry chef in California!
No amount of pretty scenery will impress a hiker on an empty stomach!
Hot soup, fresh trout, potatoes, string beans, cheese, apple pie!!!
I love camping now!
I love the national parks!
I never want to leave!
Park staff, like myself, are a crucial though often overlooked part of the parks.

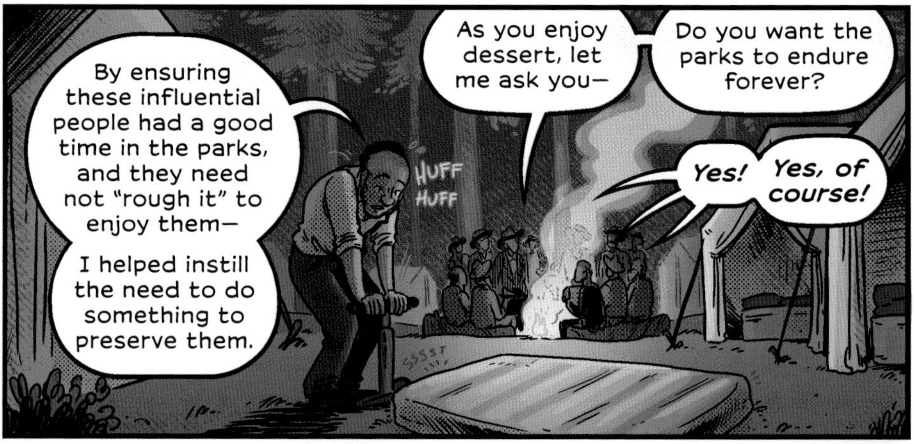
By ensuring these influential people had a good time in the parks, and they need not "rough it" to enjoy them—
I helped instill the need to do something to preserve them.
HUFF HUFF
SSSST
As you enjoy dessert, let me ask you—
Do you want the parks to endure forever?
Yes!
Yes, of course!

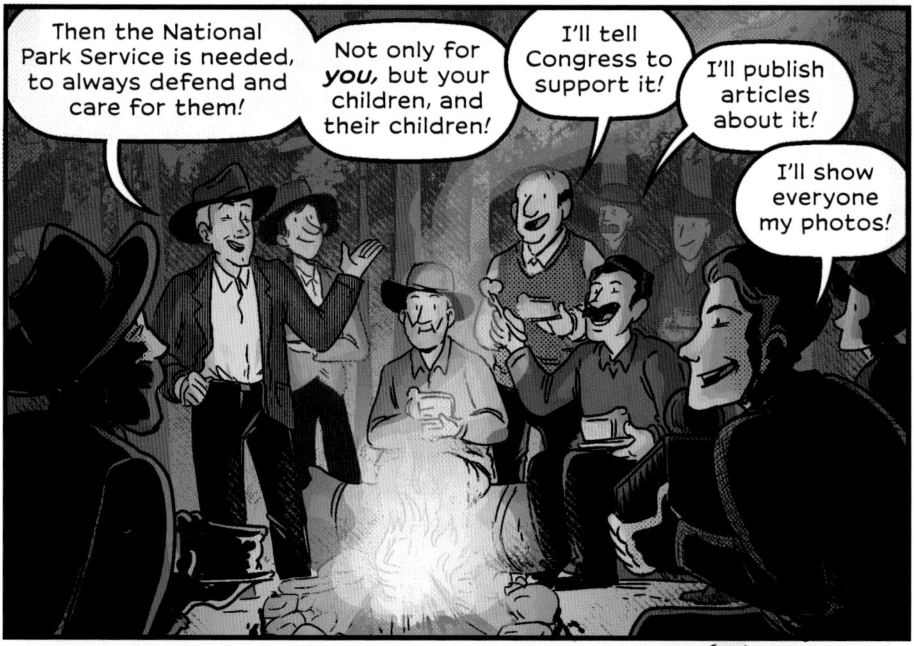
Then the National Park Service is needed, to always defend and care for them!
Not only for ***you,*** but your children, and their children!
I'll tell Congress to support it!
I'll publish articles about it!
I'll show everyone my photos!

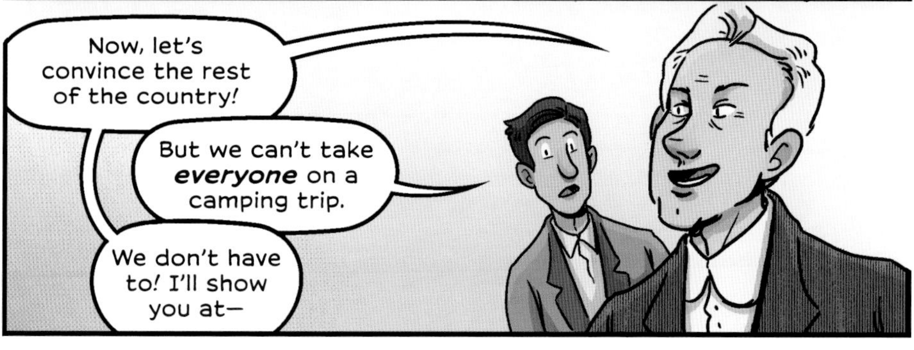
Now, let's convince the rest of the country!
But we can't take ***everyone*** on a camping trip.
We don't have to! I'll show you at—

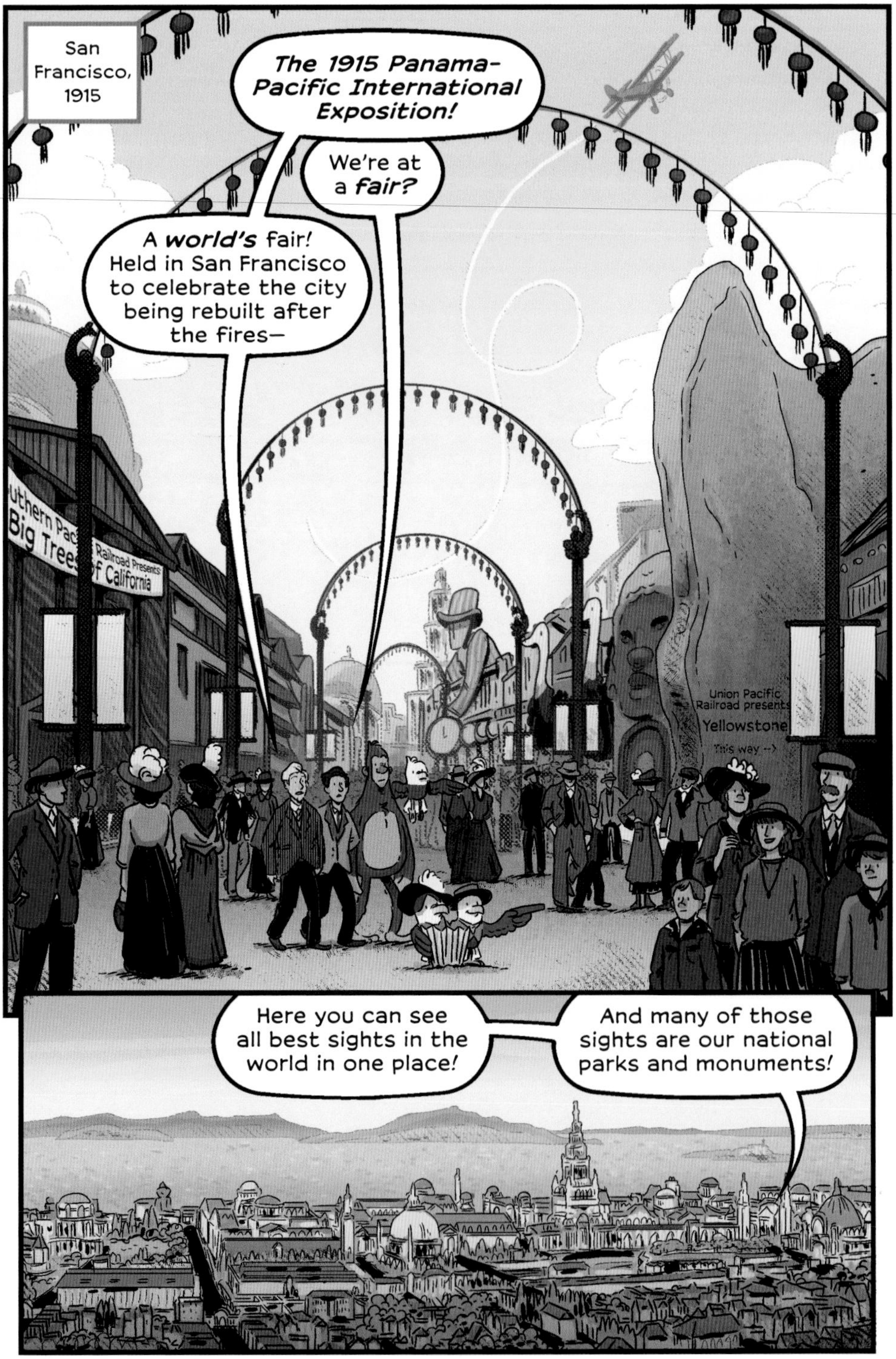
San Francisco, 1915
The 1915 Panama-Pacific International Exposition!
We're at a ***fair?***
A ***world's*** fair! Held in San Francisco to celebrate the city being rebuilt after the fires—
Southern Pacific Railroad Presents Big Trees of California
Union Pacific Railroad presents Yellowstone
This way -->
Here you can see all best sights in the world in one place!
And many of those sights are our national parks and monuments!

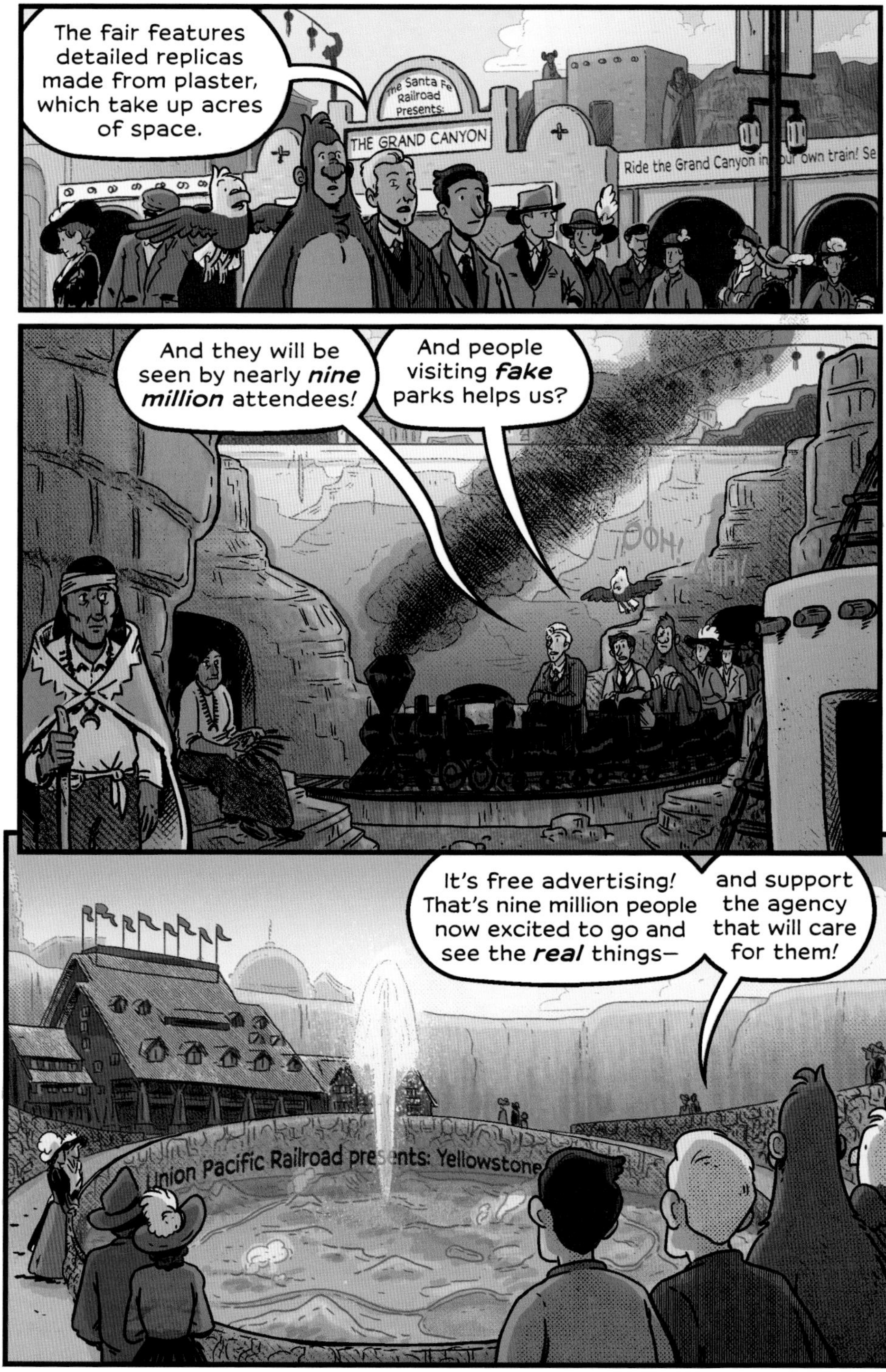
The fair features detailed replicas made from plaster, which take up acres of space.
The Santa Fe Railroad Presents:
THE GRAND CANYON
Ride the Grand Canyon in your own train! Se
And they will be seen by nearly ***nine million*** attendees!
And people visiting ***fake*** parks helps us?
OOH! AHH!
It's free advertising! That's nine million people now excited to go and see the ***real*** things—
and support the agency that will care for them!
Union Pacific Railroad presents: Yellowstone

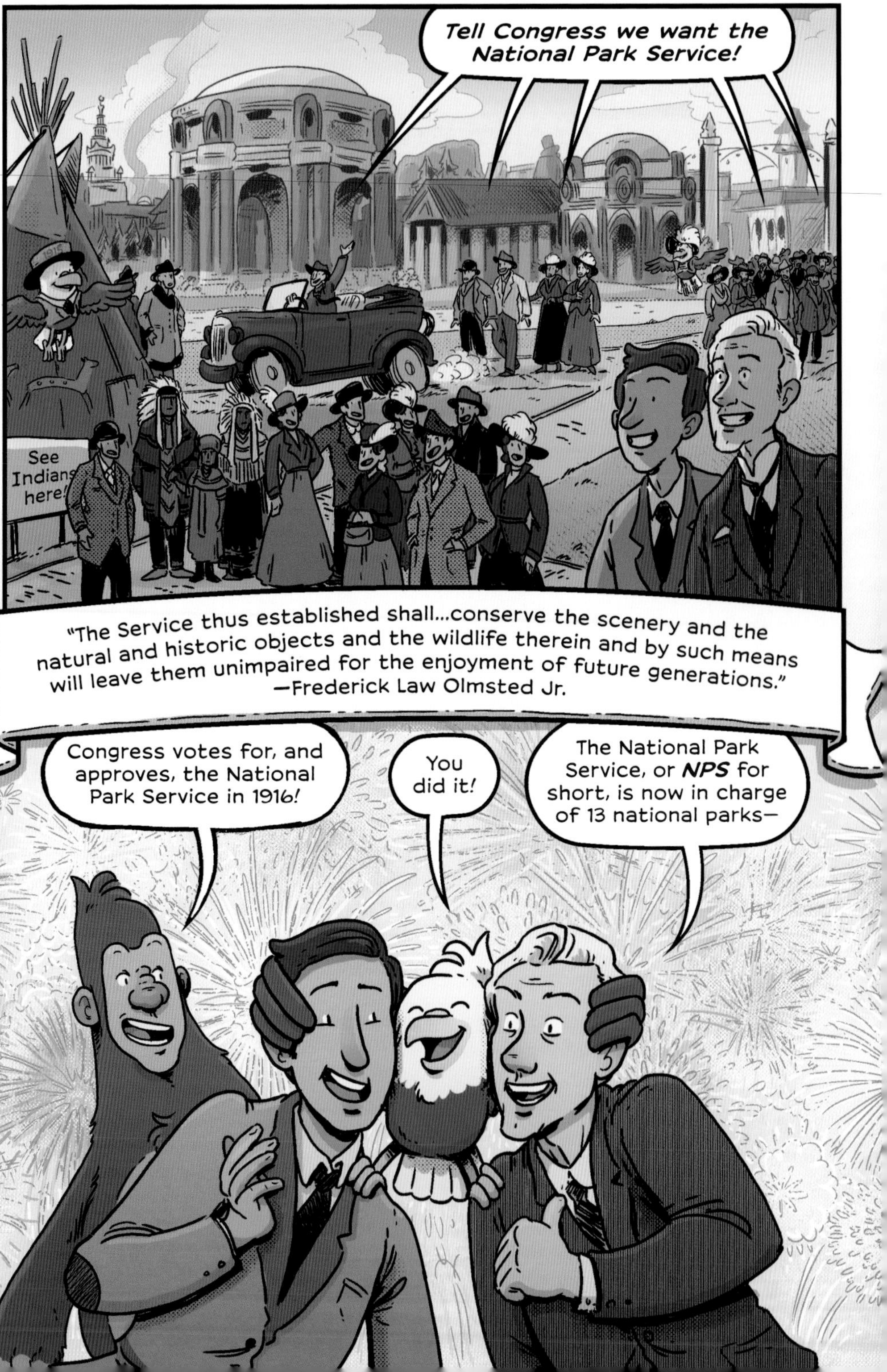
Tell Congress we want the National Park Service!
See Indians here!
1915
"The Service thus established shall...conserve the scenery and the natural and historic objects and the wildlife therein and by such means will leave them unimpaired for the enjoyment of future generations."
—Frederick Law Olmsted Jr.
Congress votes for, and approves, the National Park Service in 1916!
You did it!
The National Park Service, or ***NPS*** for short, is now in charge of 13 national parks—

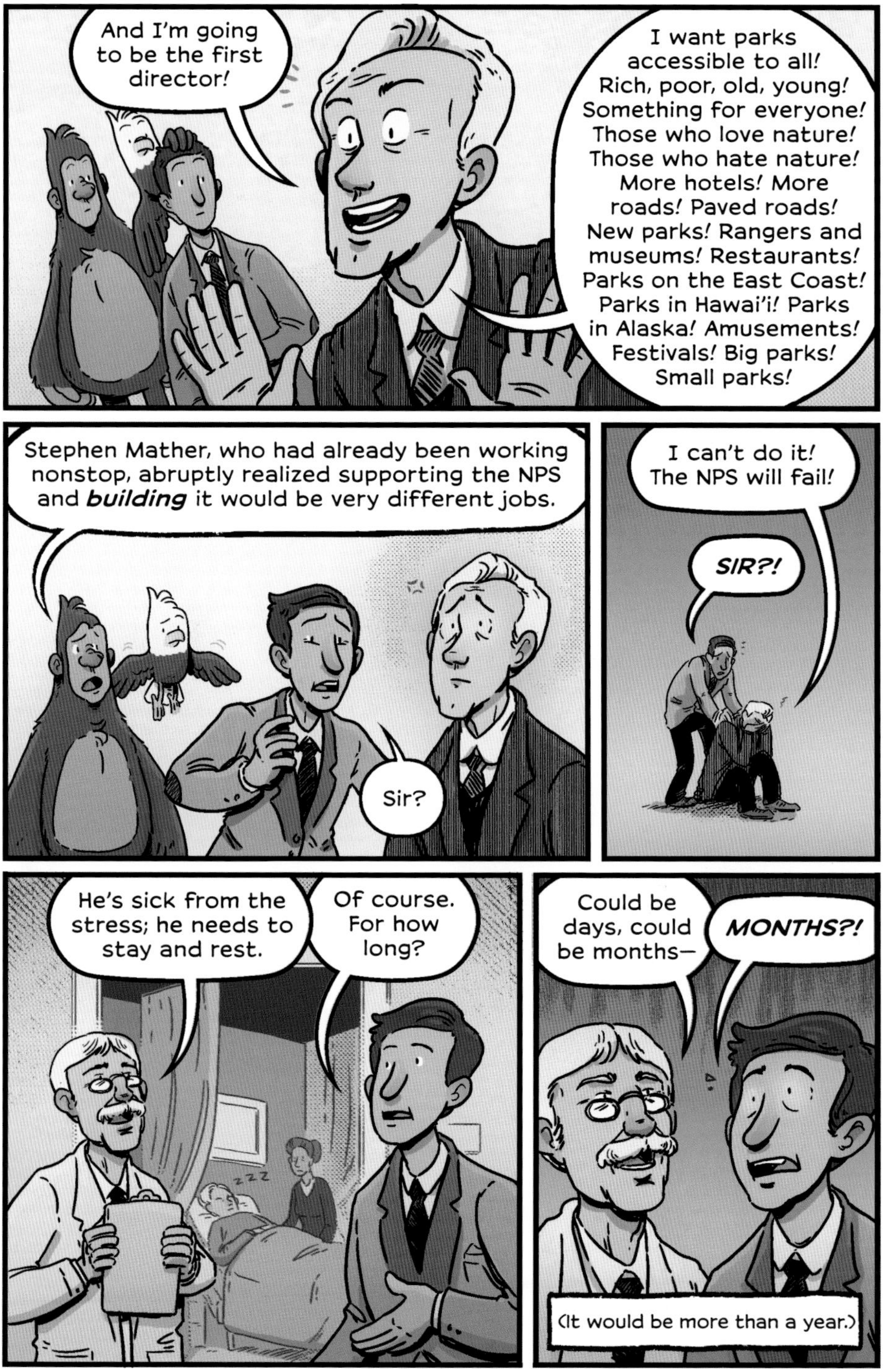
And I'm going to be the first director!
I want parks accessible to all! Rich, poor, old, young! Something for everyone! Those who love nature! Those who hate nature! More hotels! More roads! Paved roads! New parks! Rangers and museums! Restaurants! Parks on the East Coast! Parks in Hawai'i! Parks in Alaska! Amusements! Festivals! Big parks! Small parks!
Stephen Mather, who had already been working nonstop, abruptly realized supporting the NPS and ***building*** it would be very different jobs.
Sir?
I can't do it! The NPS will fail!
SIR?!
He's sick from the stress; he needs to stay and rest.
Of course. For how long?
Could be days, could be months—
MONTHS?!
(It would be more than a year.)

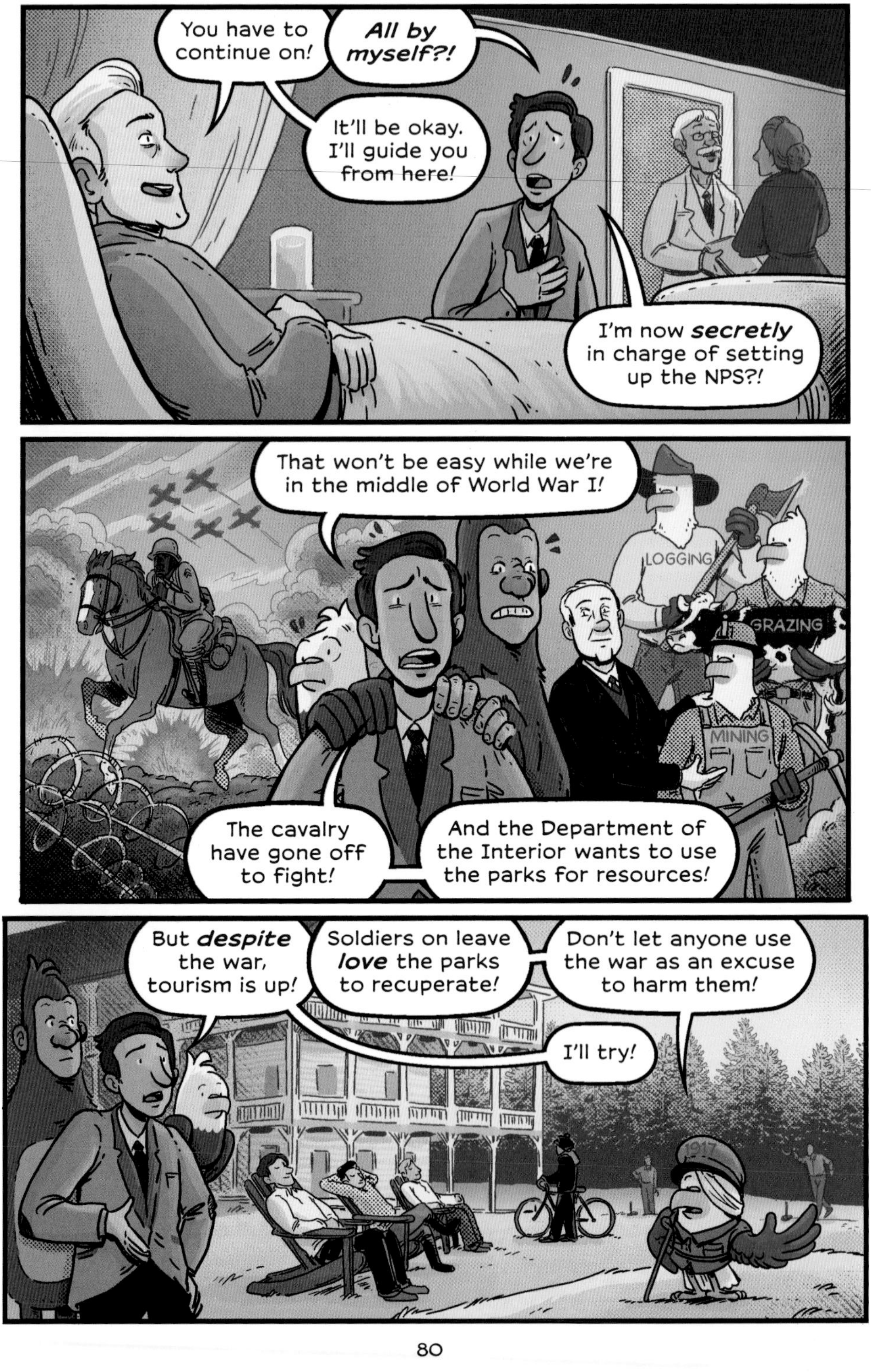

You have to continue on!
All by myself?!
It'll be okay. I'll guide you from here!
I'm now *secretly* in charge of setting up the NPS?!
That won't be easy while we're in the middle of World War I!
LOGGING
GRAZING
MINING
The cavalry have gone off to fight!
And the Department of the Interior wants to use the parks for resources!
But *despite* the war, tourism is up!
Soldiers on leave *love* the parks to recuperate!
Don't let anyone use the war as an excuse to harm them!
I'll try!
1917

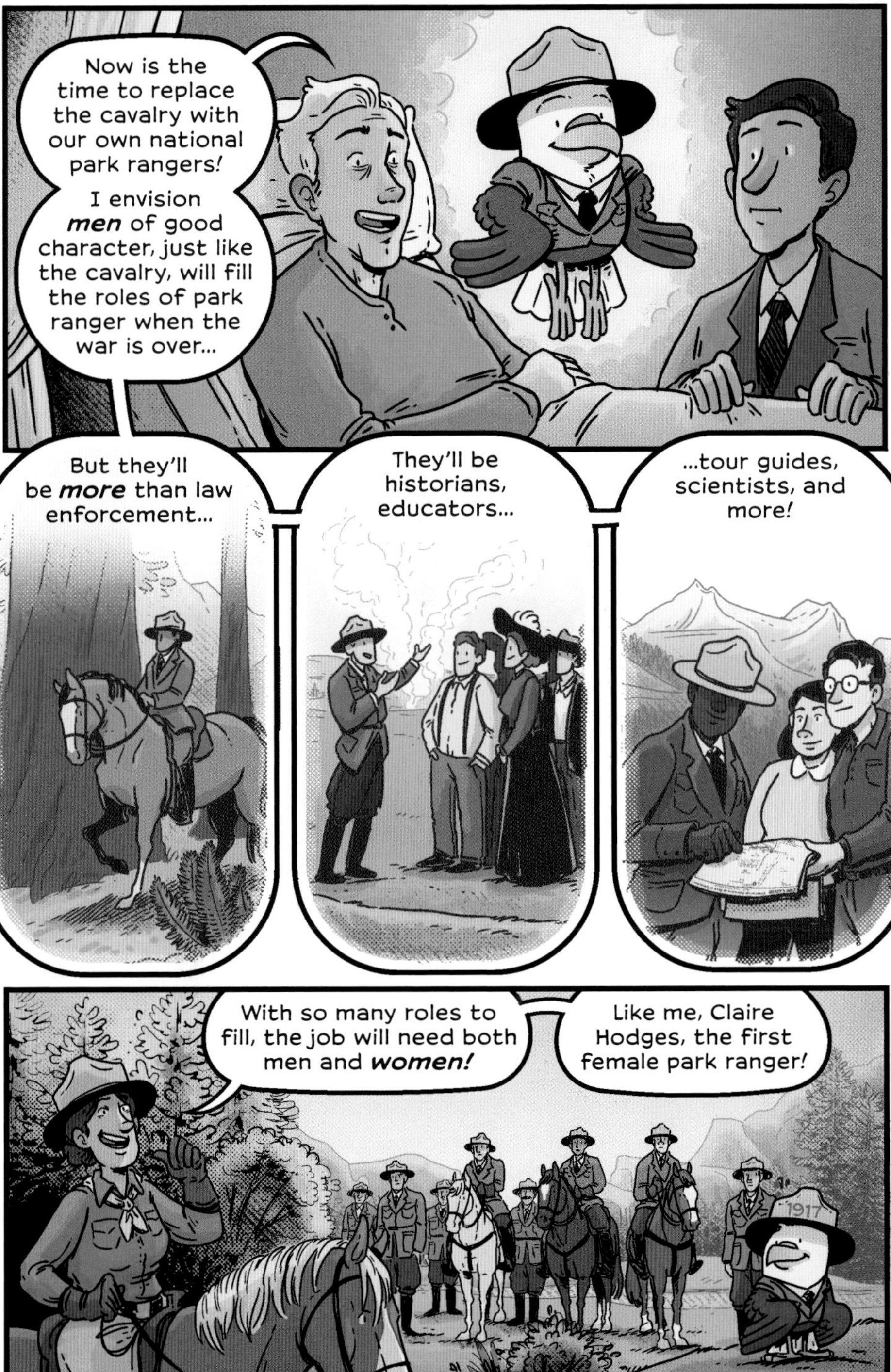
Now is the time to replace the cavalry with our own national park rangers!
I envision ***men*** of good character, just like the cavalry, will fill the roles of park ranger when the war is over...
But they'll be ***more*** than law enforcement...
They'll be historians, educators...
...tour guides, scientists, and more!
With so many roles to fill, the job will need both men and ***women!***
Like me, Claire Hodges, the first female park ranger!
1917

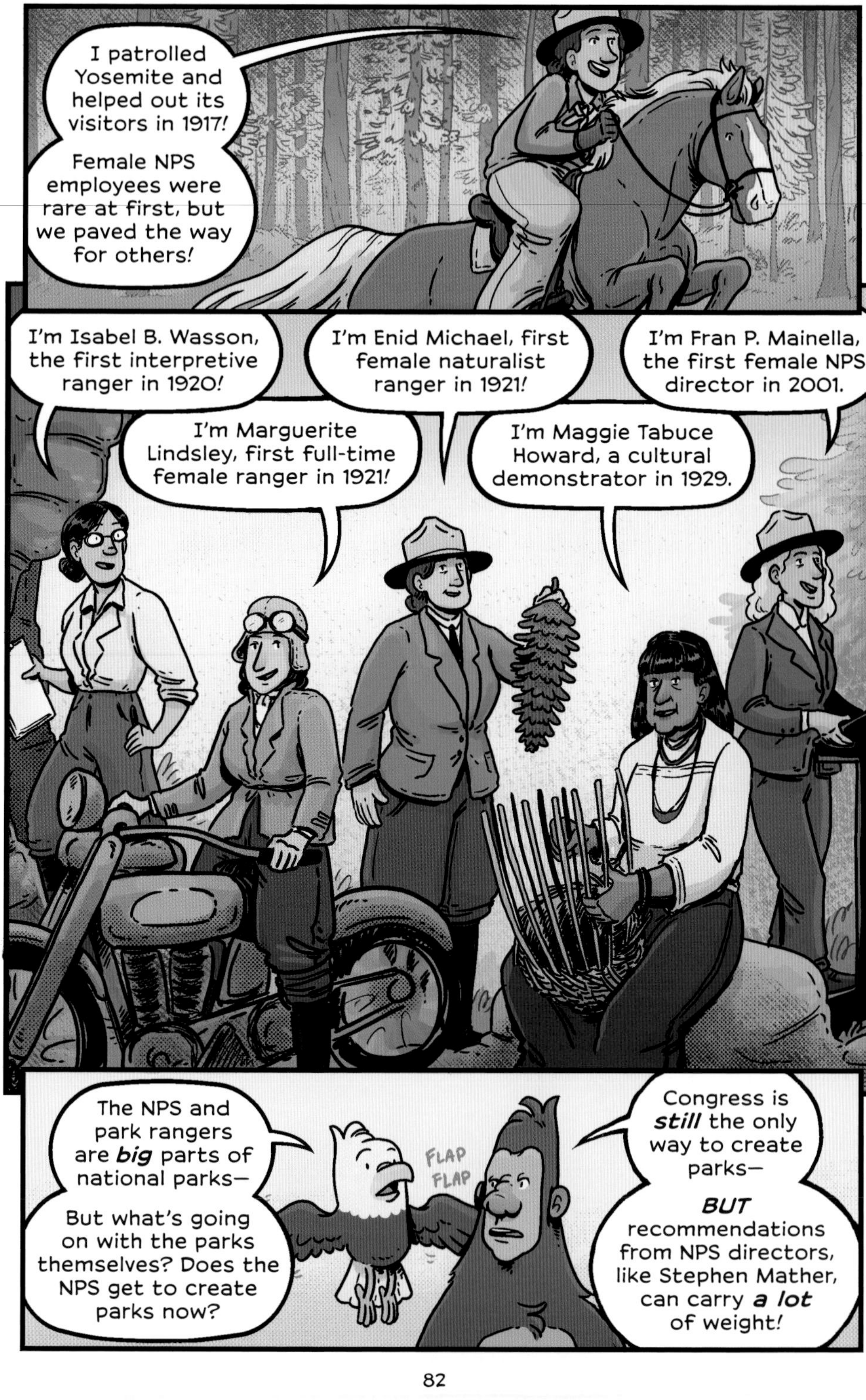
I patrolled Yosemite and helped out its visitors in 1917!
Female NPS employees were rare at first, but we paved the way for others!
I'm Isabel B. Wasson, the first interpretive ranger in 1920!
I'm Marguerite Lindsley, first full-time female ranger in 1921!
I'm Enid Michael, first female naturalist ranger in 1921!
I'm Maggie Tabuce Howard, a cultural demonstrator in 1929.
I'm Fran P. Mainella, the first female NPS director in 2001.
The NPS and park rangers are ***big*** parts of national parks—
But what's going on with the parks themselves? Does the NPS get to create parks now?
FLAP FLAP
Congress is ***still*** the only way to create parks—
BUT recommendations from NPS directors, like Stephen Mather, can carry ***a lot*** of weight!

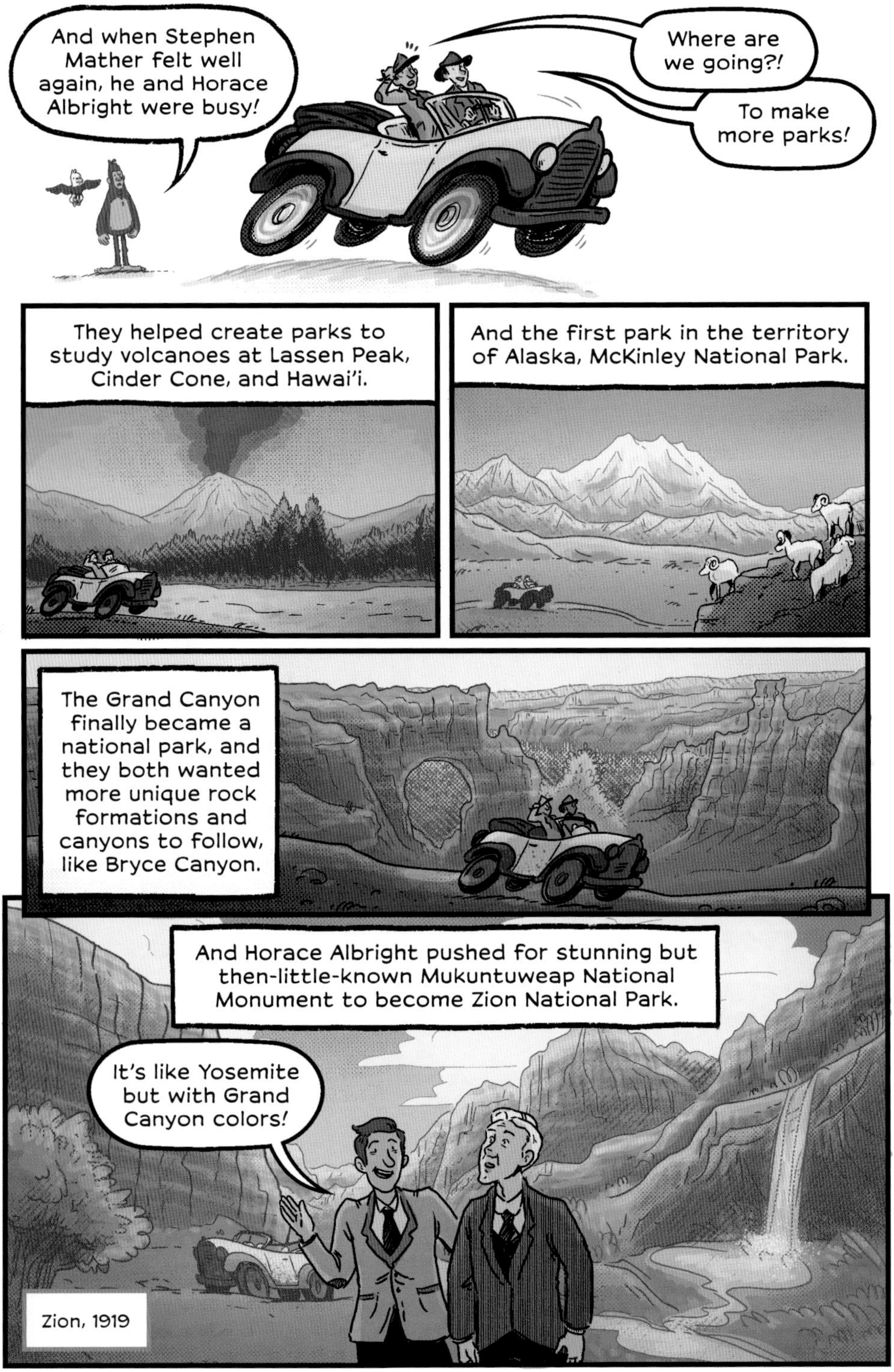
And when Stephen Mather felt well again, he and Horace Albright were busy!
Where are we going?!
To make more parks!
They helped create parks to study volcanoes at Lassen Peak, Cinder Cone, and Hawai'i.
And the first park in the territory of Alaska, McKinley National Park.
The Grand Canyon finally became a national park, and they both wanted more unique rock formations and canyons to follow, like Bryce Canyon.
And Horace Albright pushed for stunning but then-little-known Mukuntuweap National Monument to become Zion National Park.
It's like Yosemite but with Grand Canyon colors!
Zion, 1919

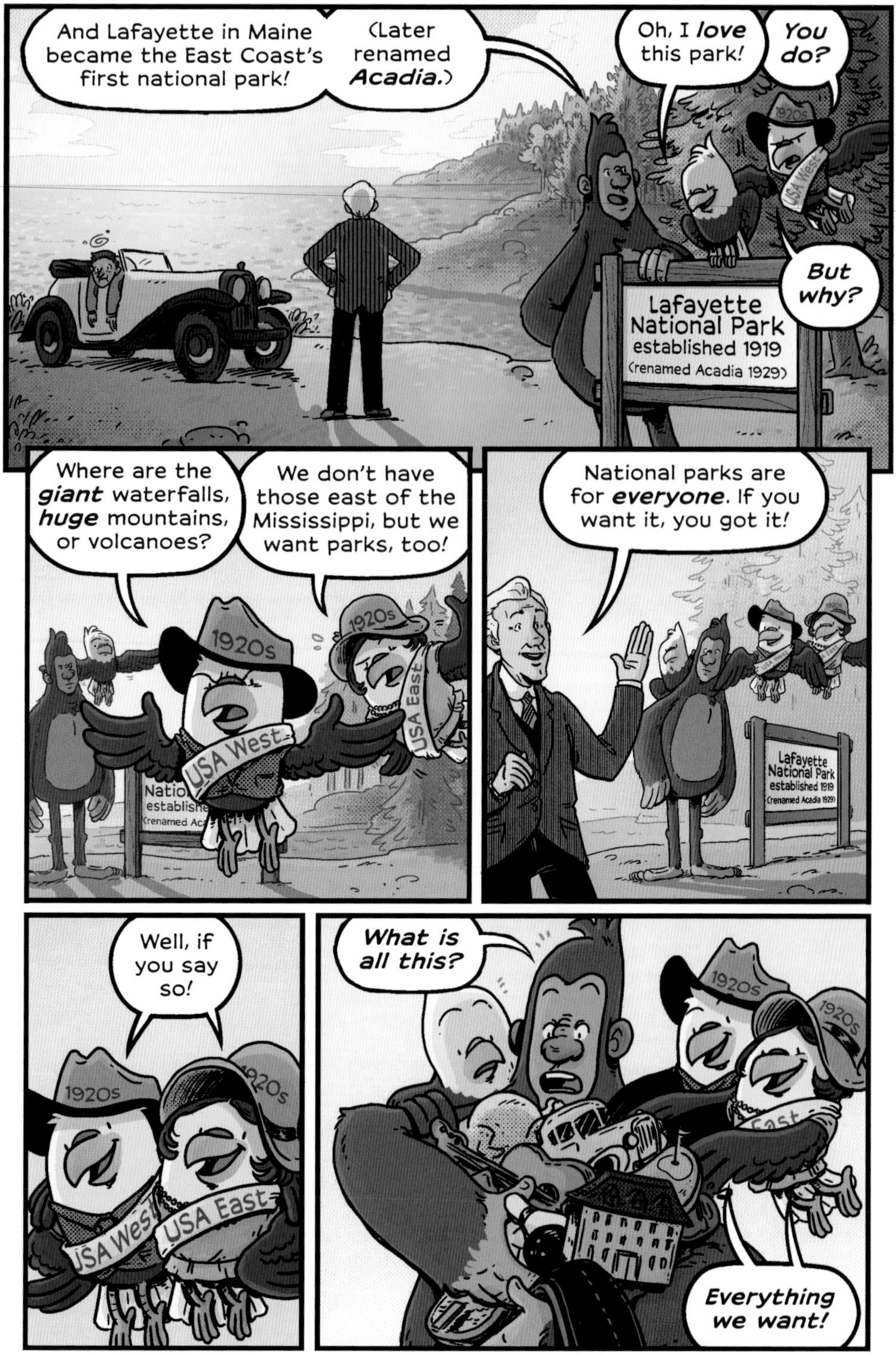
And Lafayette in Maine became the East Coast's first national park!
(Later renamed *Acadia.*)
Oh, I *love* this park!
You do?
But why?
Lafayette National Park established 1919 (renamed Acadia 1929)
1920s
USA West
Where are the ***giant*** waterfalls, ***huge*** mountains, or volcanoes?
We don't have those east of the Mississippi, but we want parks, too!
1920s
USA West
USA East
National parks are for ***everyone***. If you want it, you got it!
Lafayette National Park established 1919 (renamed Acadia 1929)
Well, if you say so!
1920s
USA West
USA East
What is all this?
Everything we want!

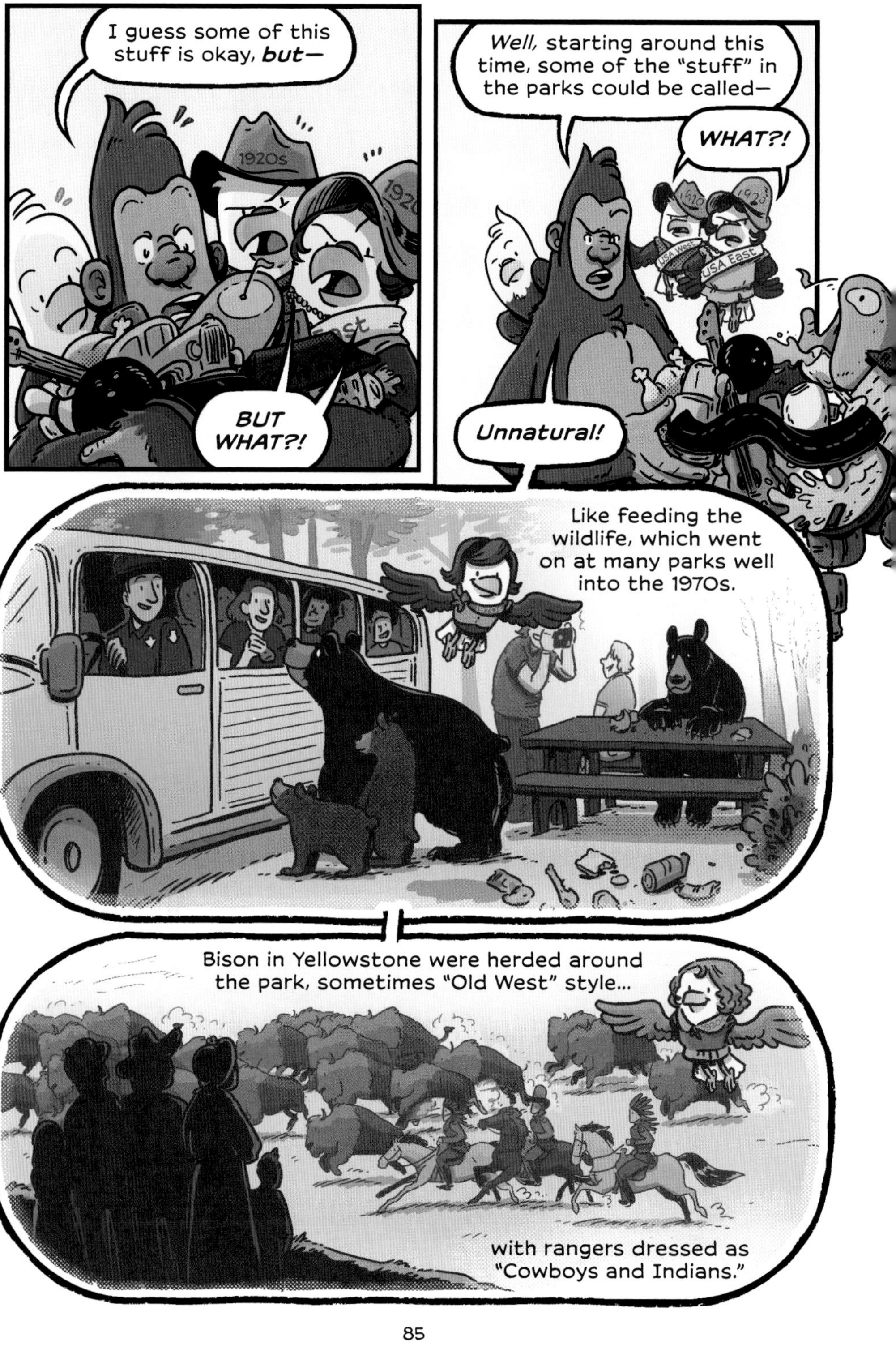
I guess some of this stuff is okay, ***but***—
BUT WHAT?!
Well, starting around this time, some of the "stuff" in the parks could be called—
WHAT?!
Unnatural!
1920s
USA West
USA East
Like feeding the wildlife, which went on at many parks well into the 1970s.
Bison in Yellowstone were herded around the park, sometimes "Old West" style...
with rangers dressed as "Cowboys and Indians."

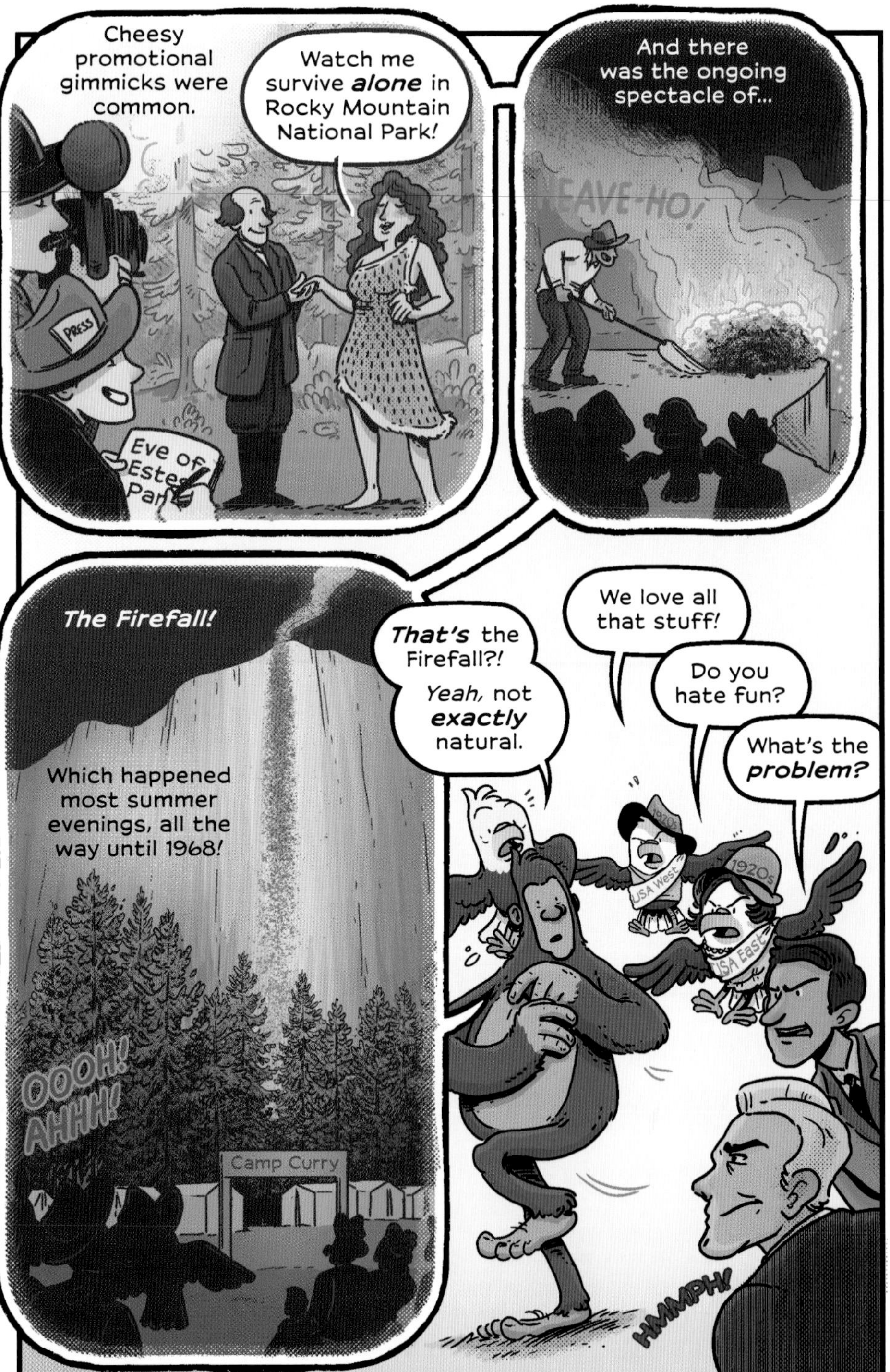
Cheesy promotional gimmicks were common.
Watch me survive *alone* in Rocky Mountain National Park!
PRESS
And there was the ongoing spectacle of...
The Firefall!
Which happened most summer evenings, all the way until 1968!
OOOH! AHHH!
Camp Curry
That's the Firefall?!
Yeah, not ***exactly*** natural.
We love all that stuff!
Do you hate fun?
What's the ***problem?***
USA West
1920s
USA East
HMMPH!

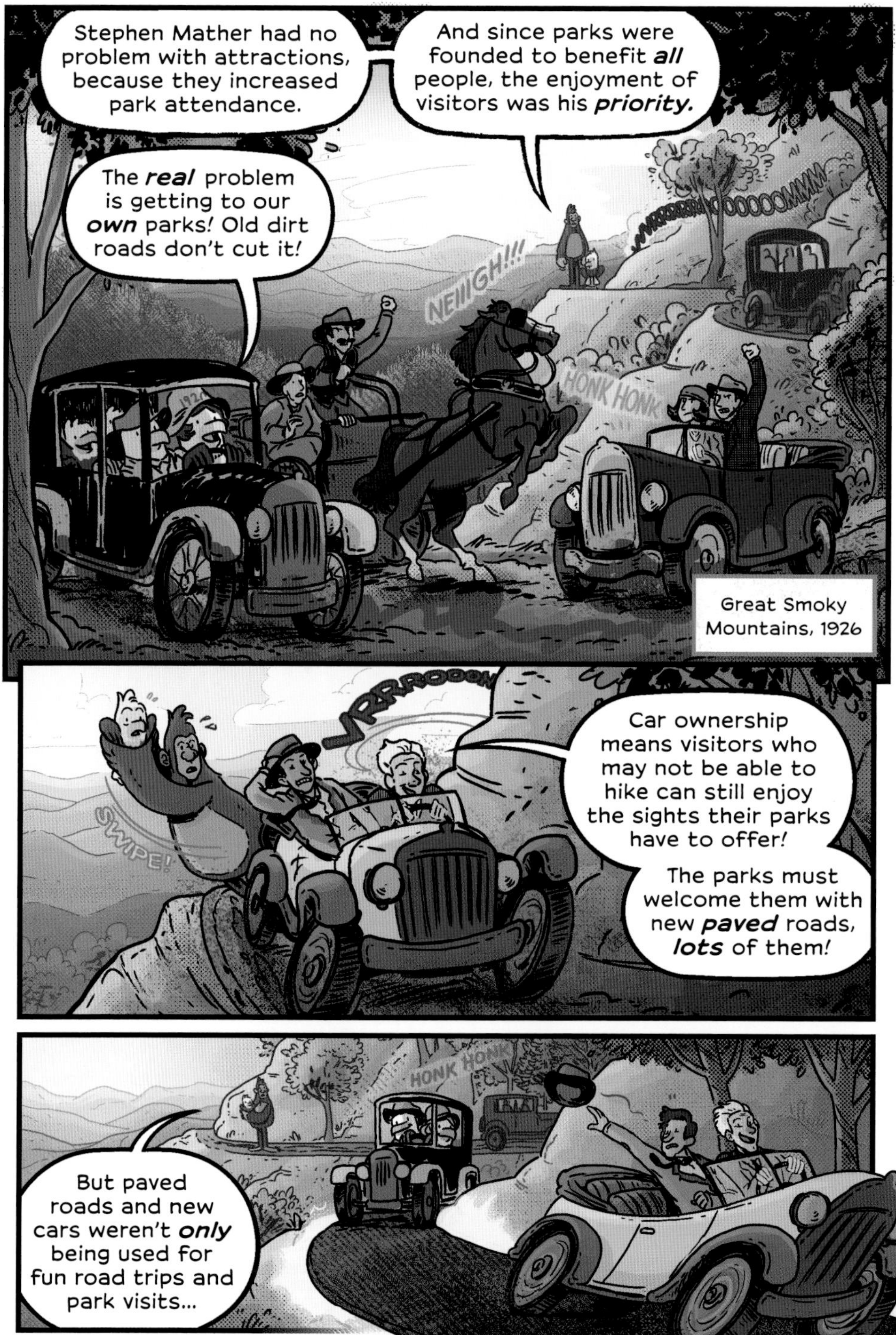
Stephen Mather had no problem with attractions, because they increased park attendance.
And since parks were founded to benefit ***all*** people, the enjoyment of visitors was his ***priority.***
The ***real*** problem is getting to our ***own*** parks! Old dirt roads don't cut it!
NEIIIGH!!!
HONK HONK
Great Smoky Mountains, 1926
VRRROOOM
Car ownership means visitors who may not be able to hike can still enjoy the sights their parks have to offer!
The parks must welcome them with new ***paved*** roads, ***lots*** of them!
SWIPE!
HONK HONK
But paved roads and new cars weren't ***only*** being used for fun road trips and park visits...

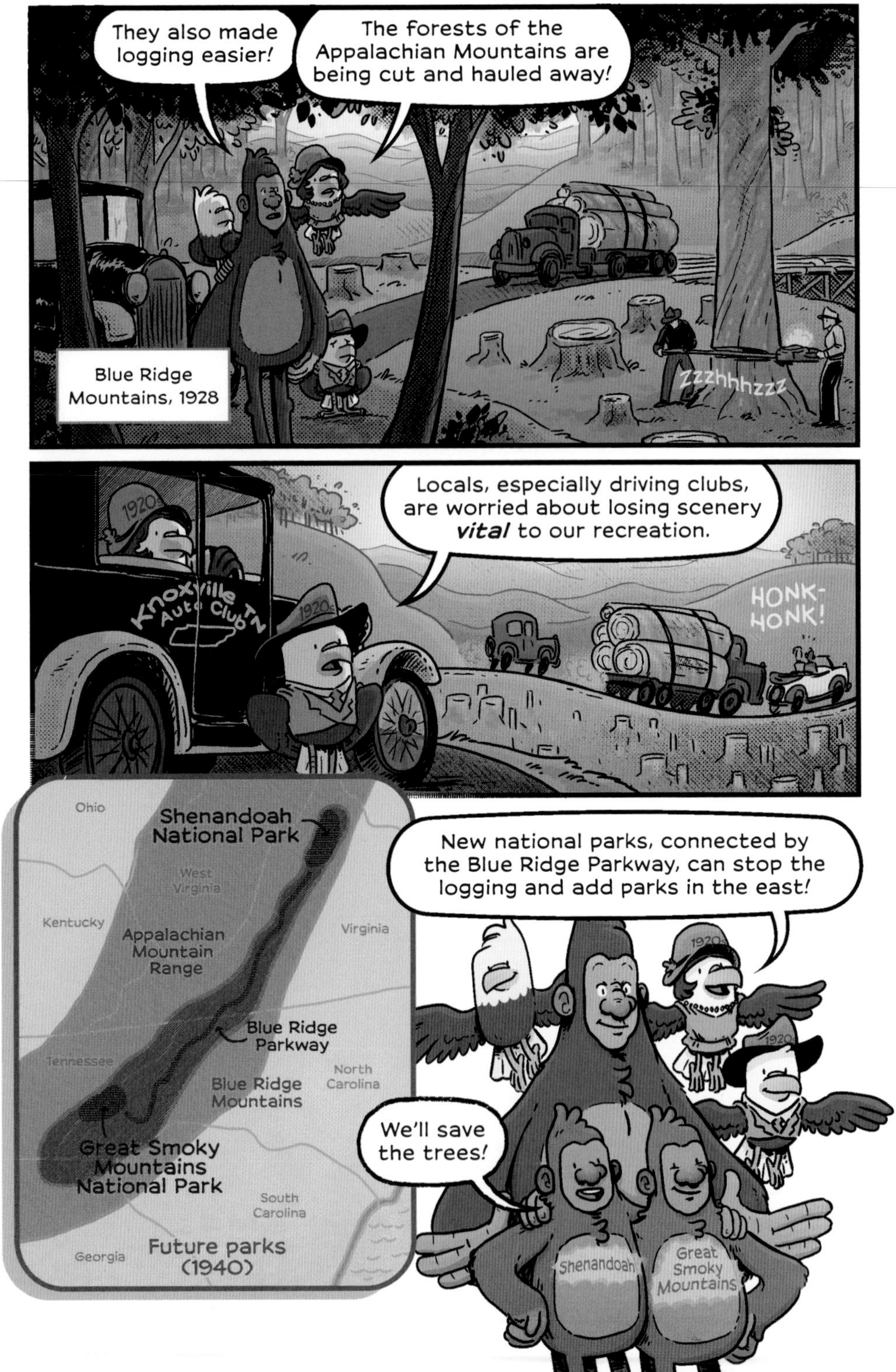
Blue Ridge Mountains, 1928
They also made logging easier!
The forests of the Appalachian Mountains are being cut and hauled away!
Zzzhhhzzz
Locals, especially driving clubs, are worried about losing scenery ***vital*** to our recreation.
Knoxville TN Auto Club
1920s
HONK-HONK!
Ohio
Shenandoah National Park
West Virginia
Kentucky
Appalachian Mountain Range
Virginia
Blue Ridge Parkway
Tennessee
North Carolina
Blue Ridge Mountains
Great Smoky Mountains National Park
South Carolina
Georgia
Future parks (1940)
New national parks, connected by the Blue Ridge Parkway, can stop the logging and add parks in the east!
We'll save the trees!
Shenandoah
Great Smoky Mountains

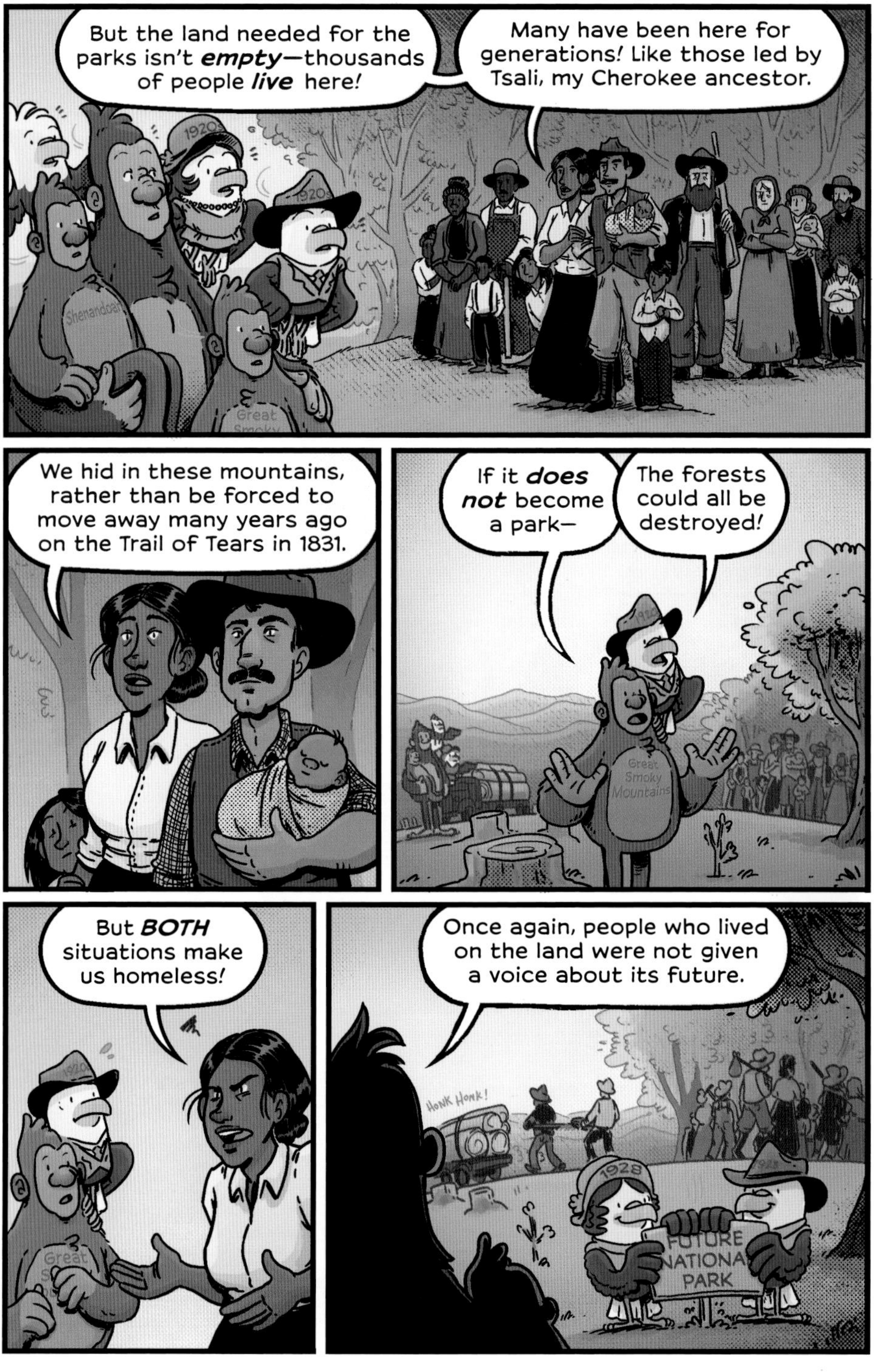

But the land needed for the parks isn't ***empty***—thousands of people ***live*** here!
Many have been here for generations! Like those led by Tsali, my Cherokee ancestor.
1920s
Shenandoah
Great Smoky
We hid in these mountains, rather than be forced to move away many years ago on the Trail of Tears in 1831.
If it ***does not*** become a park—
The forests could all be destroyed!
Great Smoky Mountains
But ***BOTH*** situations make us homeless!
Great
Once again, people who lived on the land were not given a voice about its future.
HONK HONK!
1928
FUTURE NATIONA PARK

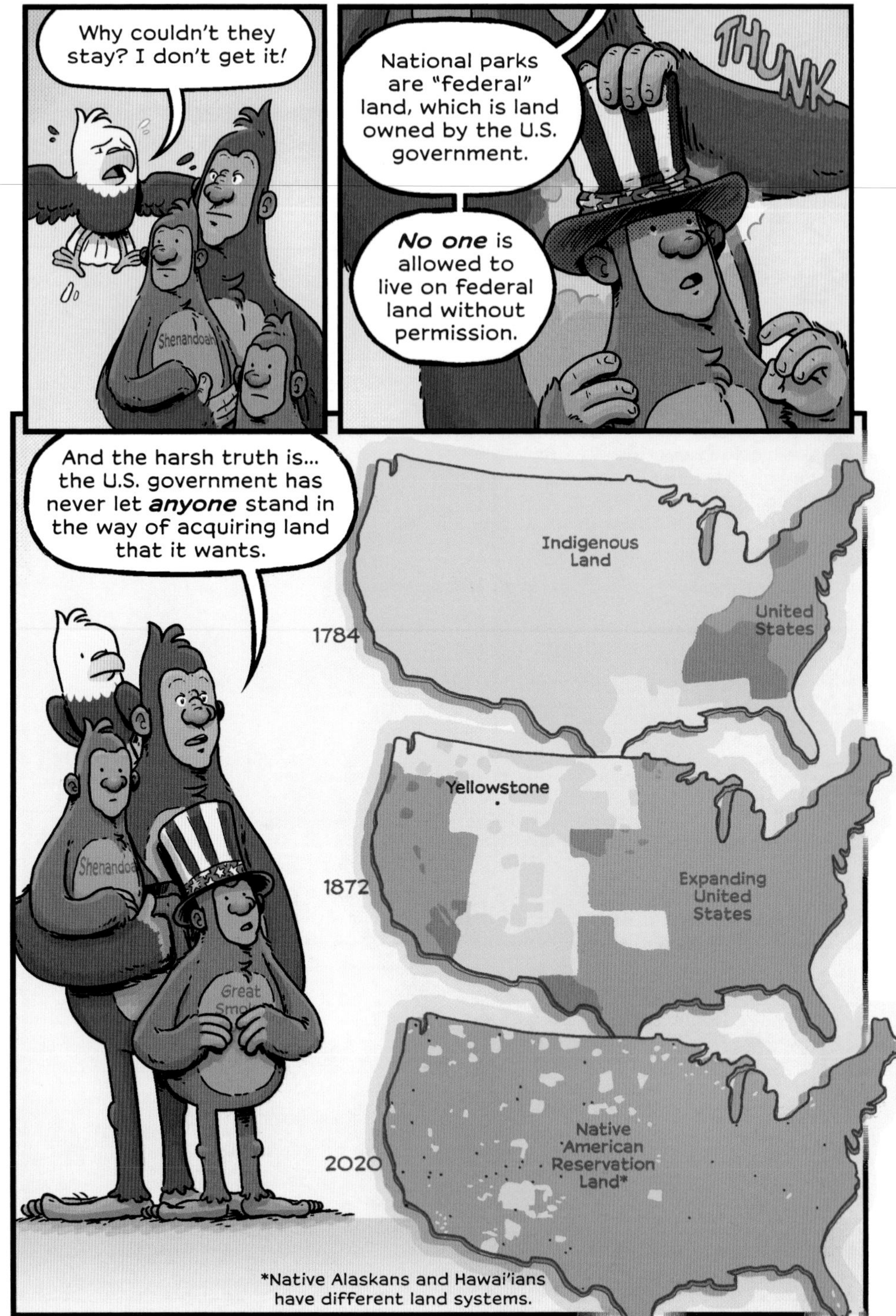
Why couldn't they stay? I don't get it!
National parks are "federal" land, which is land owned by the U.S. government.
THUNK
No one is allowed to live on federal land without permission.
And the harsh truth is... the U.S. government has never let ***anyone*** stand in the way of acquiring land that it wants.
Shenandoah
Shenandoah
Great Smo
1784
Indigenous Land
United States
1872
Yellowstone
Expanding United States
2020
Native American Reservation Land*
*Native Alaskans and Hawai'ians have different land systems.

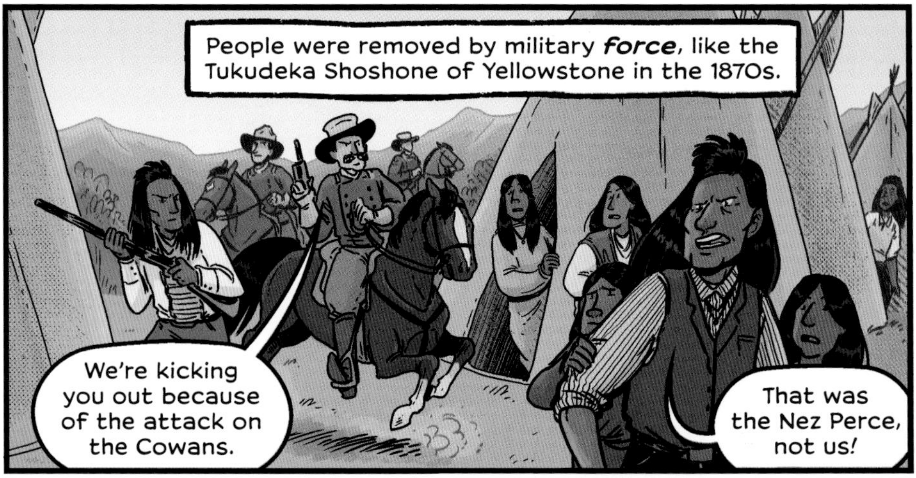
People were removed by military *force*, like the Tukudeka Shoshone of Yellowstone in the 1870s.
We're kicking you out because of the attack on the Cowans.
That was the Nez Perce, not us!

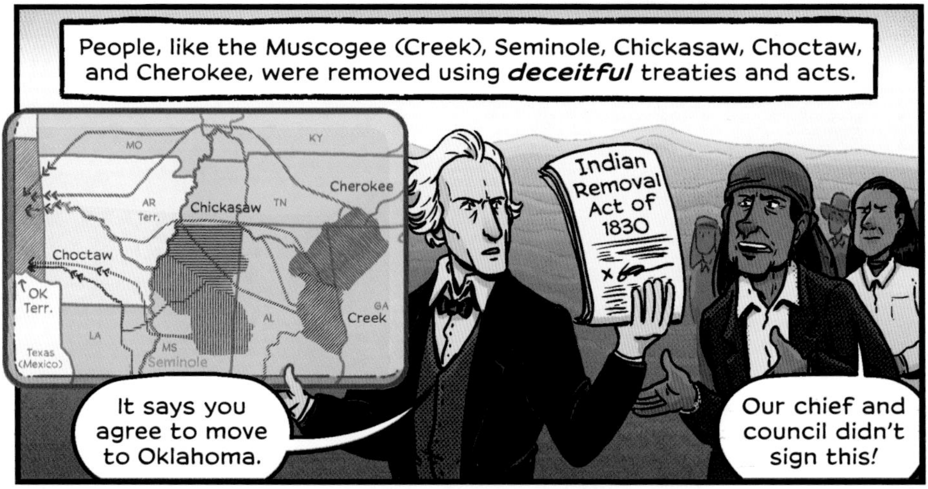
People, like the Muscogee (Creek), Seminole, Chickasaw, Choctaw, and Cherokee, were removed using *deceitful* treaties and acts.
MO
KY
Cherokee
AR Terr.
Chickasaw
TN
Choctaw
OK Terr.
GA
Creek
AL
LA
MS
Seminole
Texas (Mexico)
Indian Removal Act of 1830
It says you agree to move to Oklahoma.
Our chief and council didn't sign this!

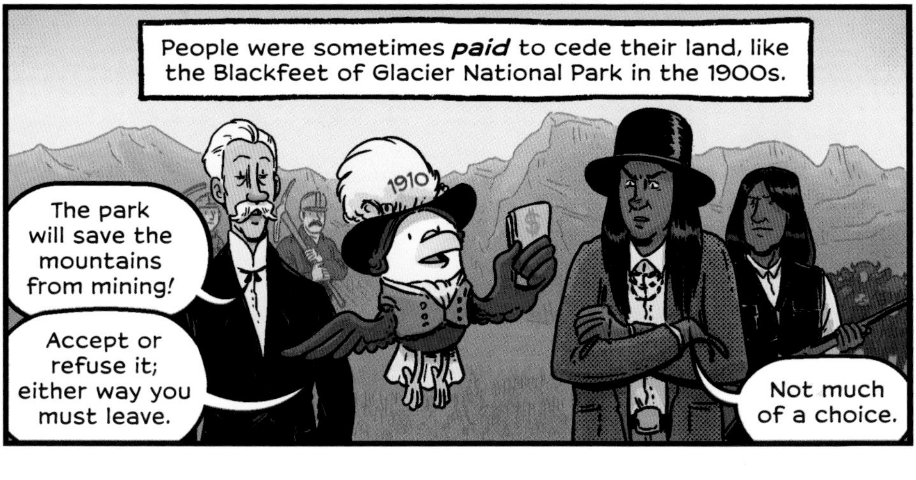
People were sometimes *paid* to cede their land, like the Blackfeet of Glacier National Park in the 1900s.
1910
The park will save the mountains from mining!
Accept or refuse it; either way you must leave.
Not much of a choice.

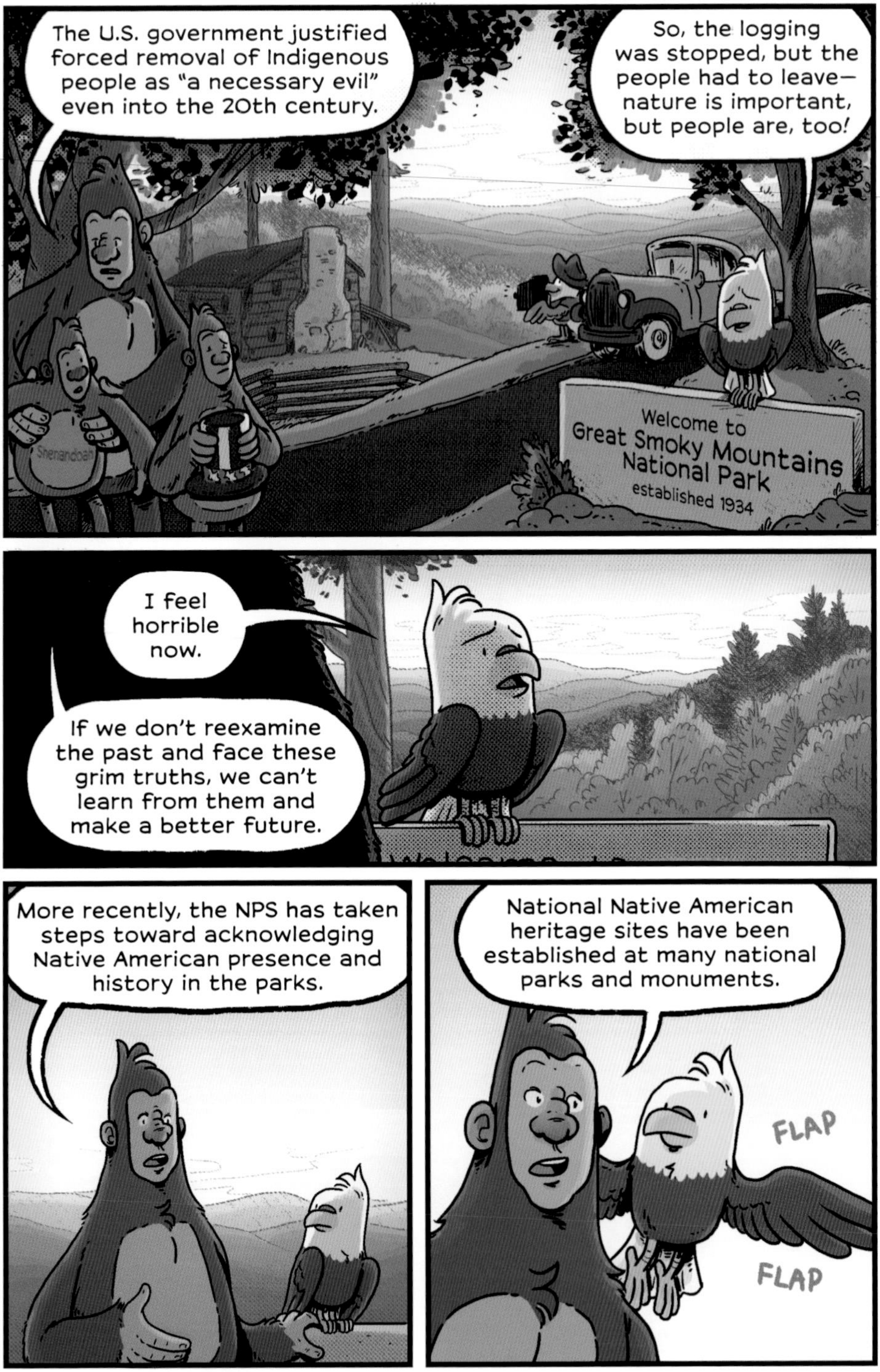
The U.S. government justified forced removal of Indigenous people as "a necessary evil" even into the 20th century.
So, the logging was stopped, but the people had to leave—nature is important, but people are, too!
Shenandoah
Welcome to Great Smoky Mountains National Park established 1934
I feel horrible now.
If we don't reexamine the past and face these grim truths, we can't learn from them and make a better future.
More recently, the NPS has taken steps toward acknowledging Native American presence and history in the parks.
National Native American heritage sites have been established at many national parks and monuments.
FLAP
FLAP

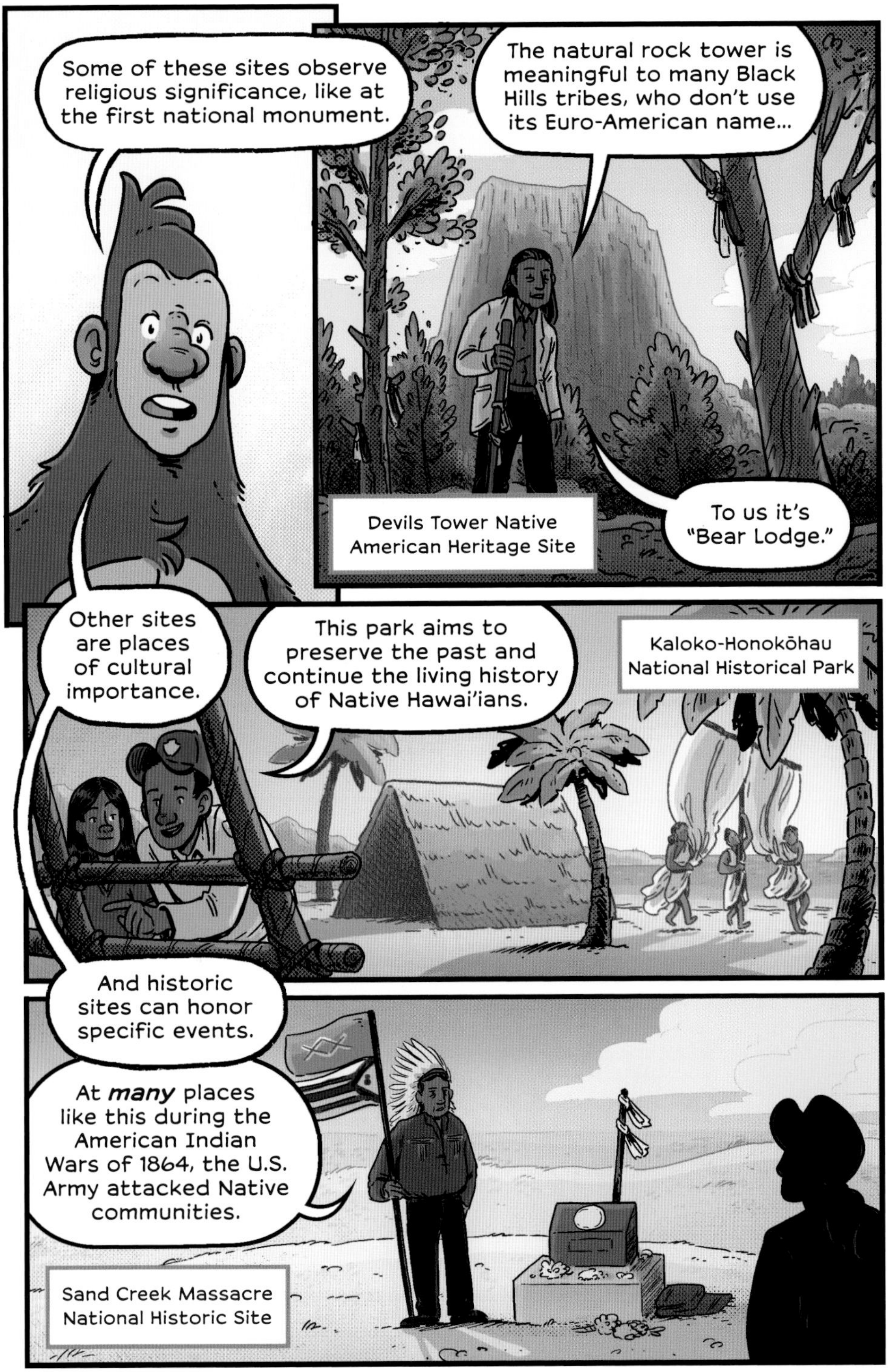

Some of these sites observe religious significance, like at the first national monument.
The natural rock tower is meaningful to many Black Hills tribes, who don't use its Euro-American name...
To us it's "Bear Lodge."
Devils Tower Native American Heritage Site
Other sites are places of cultural importance.
Kaloko-Honokōhau National Historical Park
This park aims to preserve the past and continue the living history of Native Hawai'ians.
And historic sites can honor specific events.
At *many* places like this during the American Indian Wars of 1864, the U.S. Army attacked Native communities.
Sand Creek Massacre National Historic Site

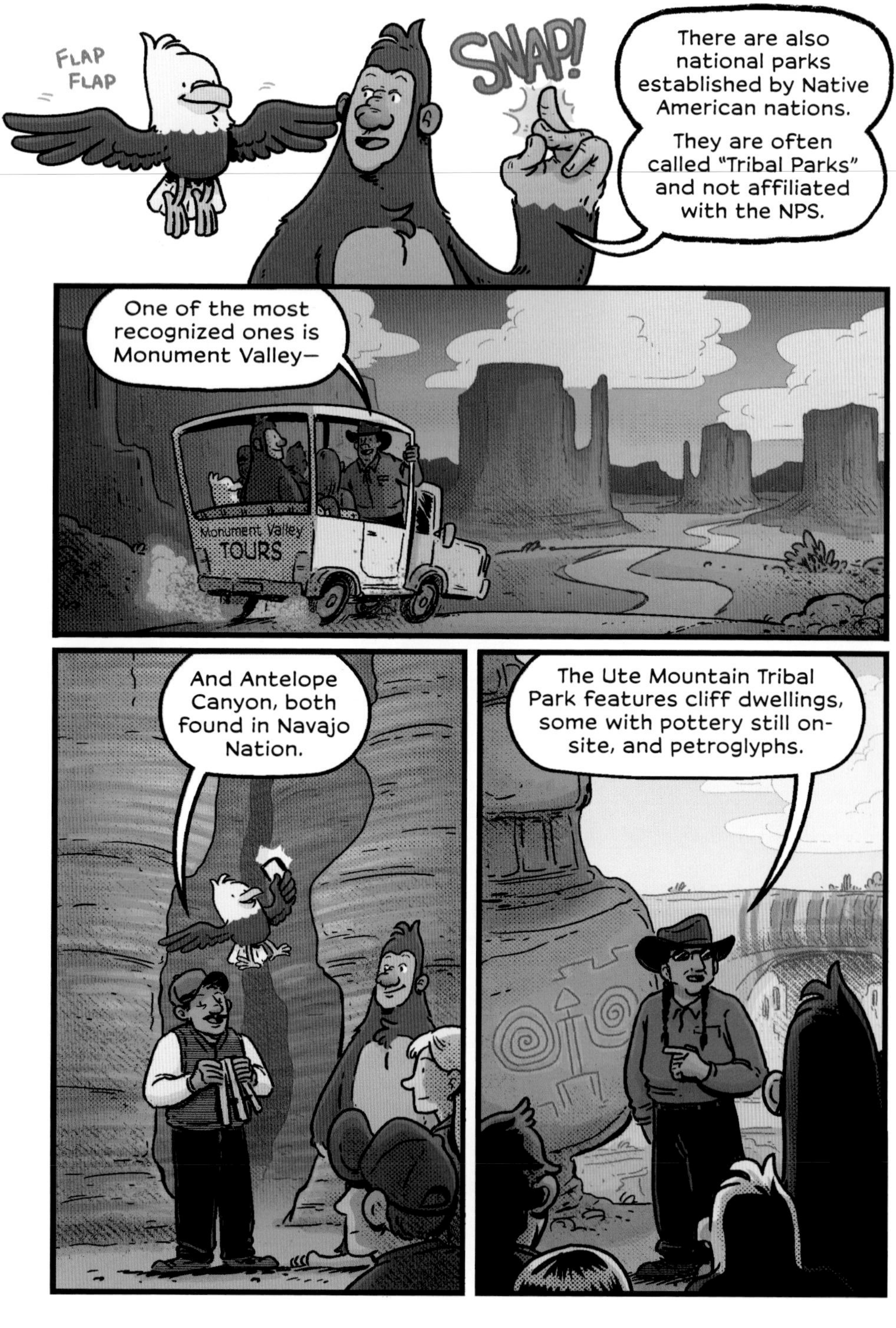
FLAP FLAP
SNAP!
There are also national parks established by Native American nations.
They are often called "Tribal Parks" and not affiliated with the NPS.
One of the most recognized ones is Monument Valley—
Monument Valley TOURS
And Antelope Canyon, both found in Navajo Nation.
The Ute Mountain Tribal Park features cliff dwellings, some with pottery still on-site, and petroglyphs.

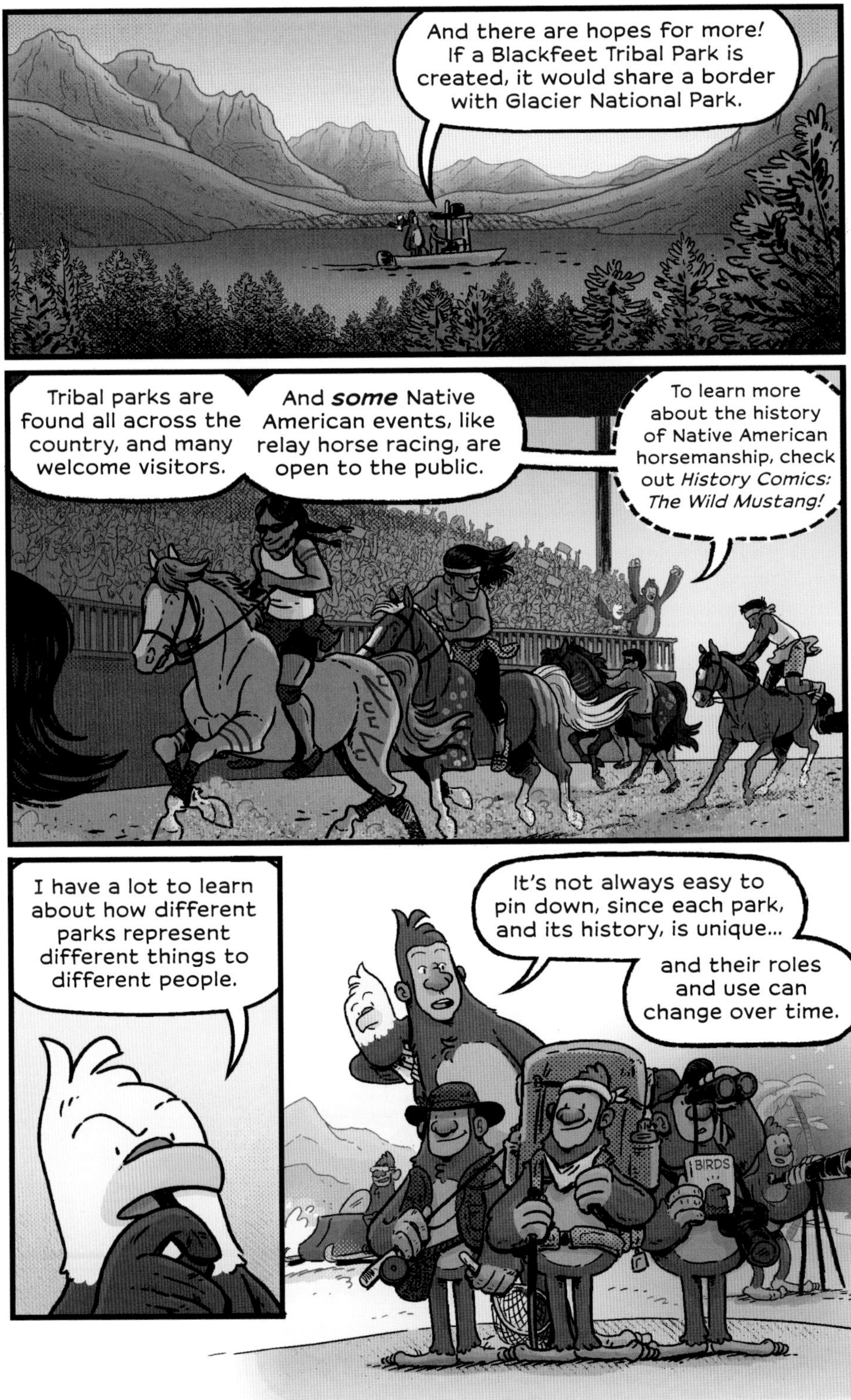
And there are hopes for more! If a Blackfeet Tribal Park is created, it would share a border with Glacier National Park.
Tribal parks are found all across the country, and many welcome visitors.
And *some* Native American events, like relay horse racing, are open to the public.
To learn more about the history of Native American horsemanship, check out *History Comics: The Wild Mustang!*
I have a lot to learn about how different parks represent different things to different people.
It's not always easy to pin down, since each park, and its history, is unique...
and their roles and use can change over time.
BIRDS

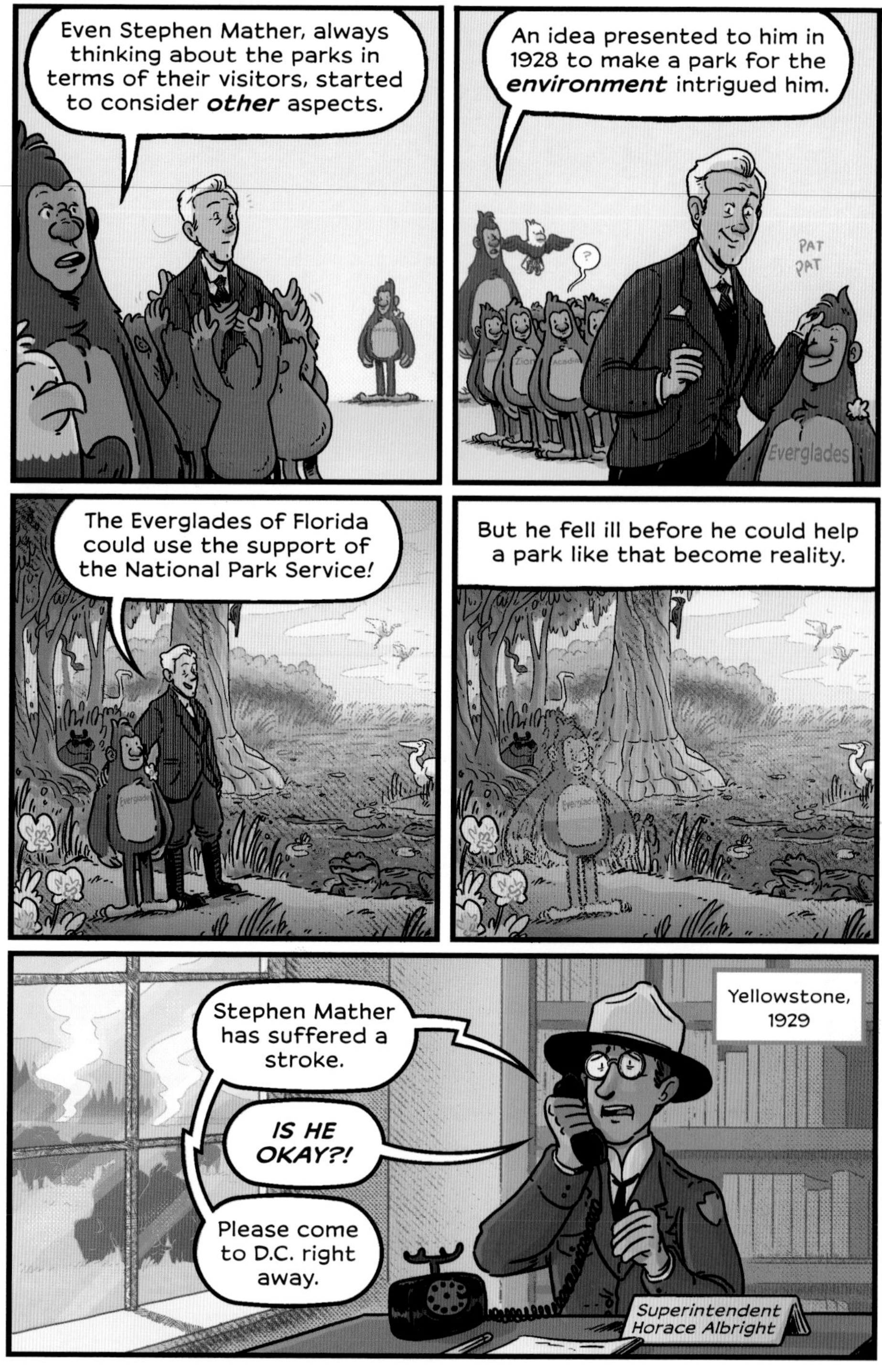
Even Stephen Mather, always thinking about the parks in terms of their visitors, started to consider *other* aspects.
An idea presented to him in 1928 to make a park for the ***environment*** intrigued him.
?
PAT PAT
Zion
Acadia
Everglades
The Everglades of Florida could use the support of the National Park Service!
Everglades
But he fell ill before he could help a park like that become reality.
Everglades
Yellowstone, 1929
Stephen Mather has suffered a stroke.
IS HE OKAY?!
Please come to D.C. right away.
Superintendent Horace Albright

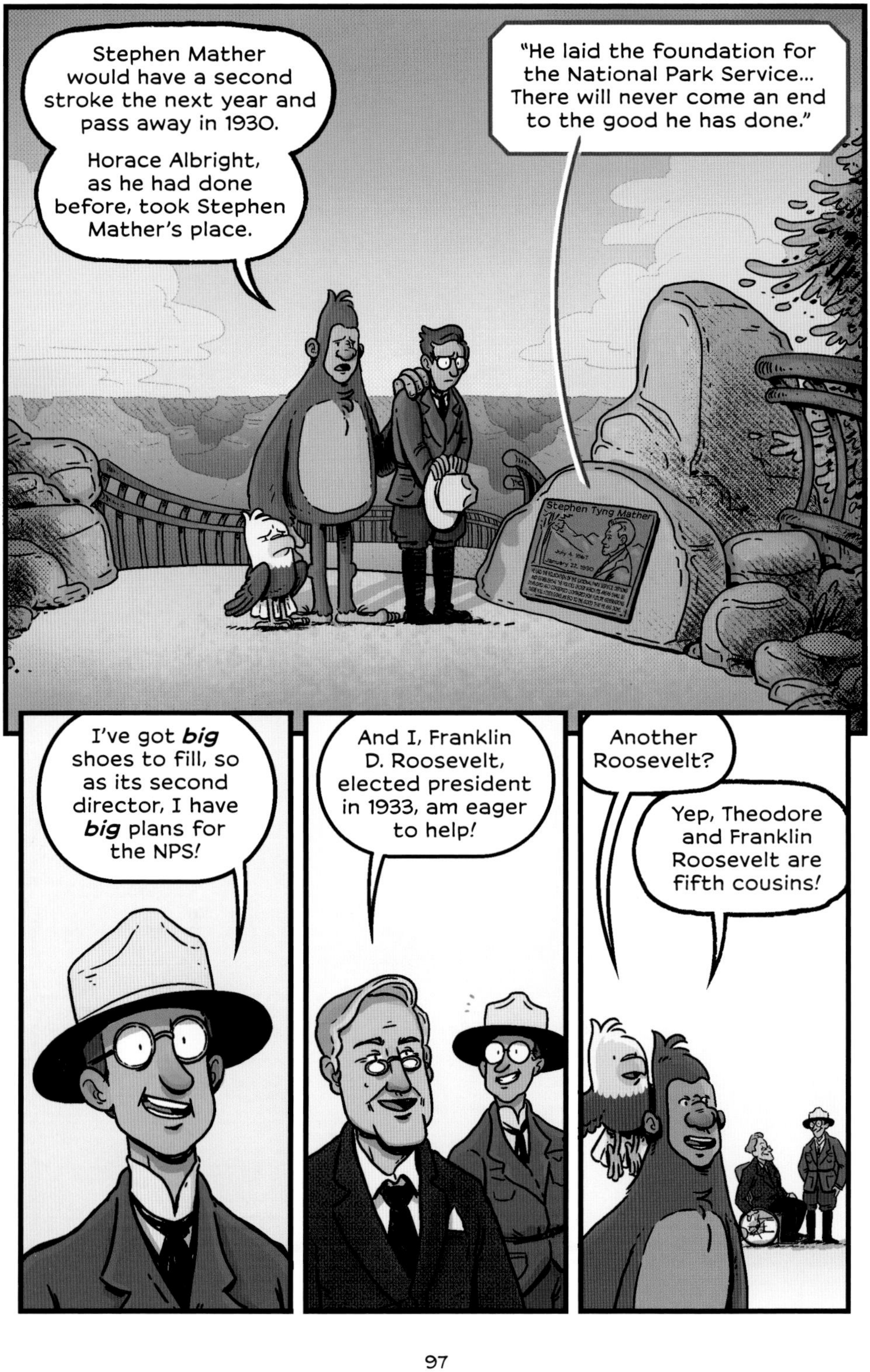
Stephen Mather would have a second stroke the next year and pass away in 1930.
Horace Albright, as he had done before, took Stephen Mather's place.
"He laid the foundation for the National Park Service... There will never come an end to the good he has done."
Stephen Tyng Mather
July 4, 1867
January 22, 1930
I've got **big** shoes to fill, so as its second director, I have **big** plans for the NPS!
And I, Franklin D. Roosevelt, elected president in 1933, am eager to help!
Another Roosevelt?
Yep, Theodore and Franklin Roosevelt are fifth cousins!

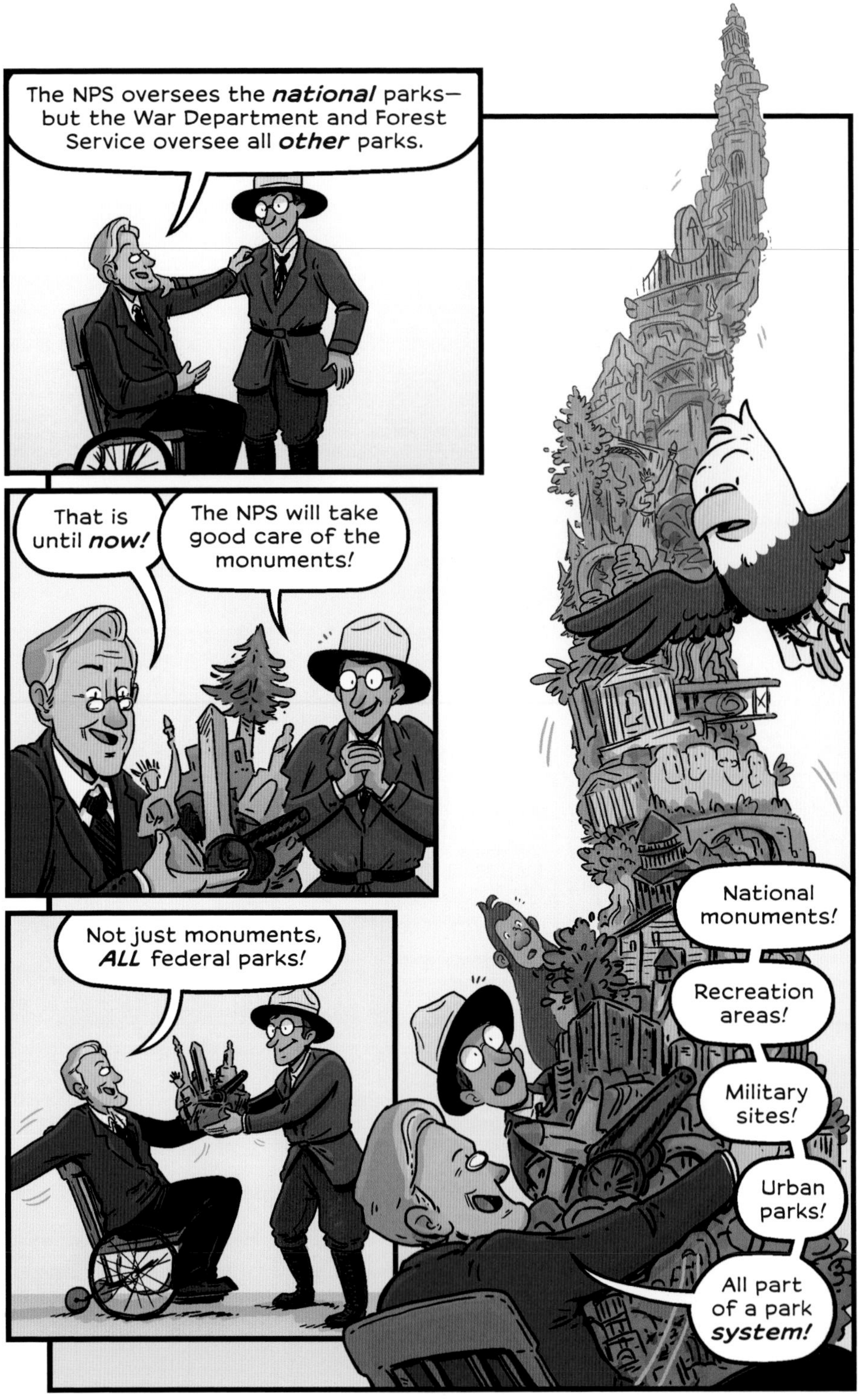

The NPS oversees the ***national*** parks—but the War Department and Forest Service oversee all ***other*** parks.
That is until ***now!***
The NPS will take good care of the monuments!
Not just monuments, ***ALL*** federal parks!
National monuments!
Recreation areas!
Military sites!
Urban parks!
All part of a park ***system!***

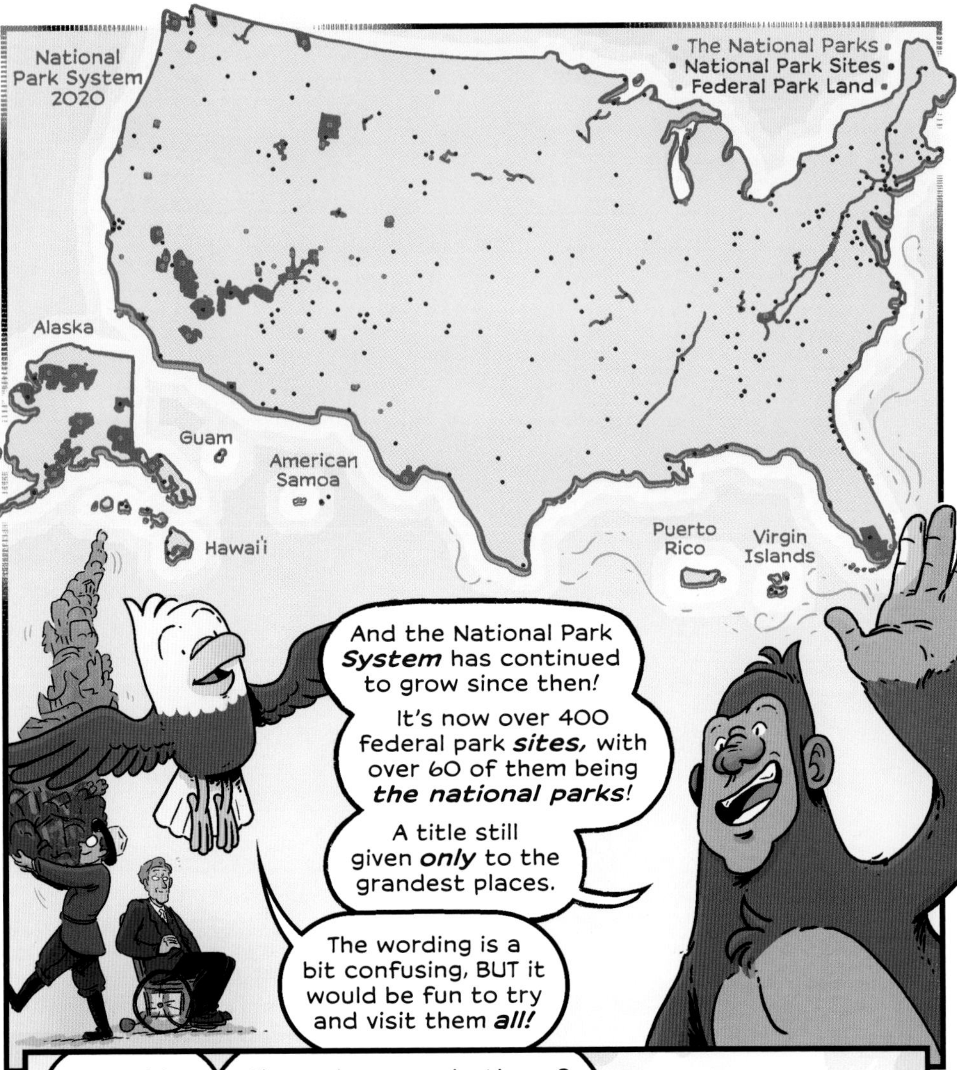
National Park System 2020
The National Parks
National Park Sites
Federal Park Land
Alaska
Guam
American Samoa
Hawai'i
Puerto Rico
Virgin Islands
And the National Park ***System*** has continued to grow since then!
It's now over 400 federal park ***sites,*** with over 60 of them being ***the national parks!***
A title still given ***only*** to the grandest places.
The wording is a bit confusing, BUT it would be fun to try and visit them ***all!***

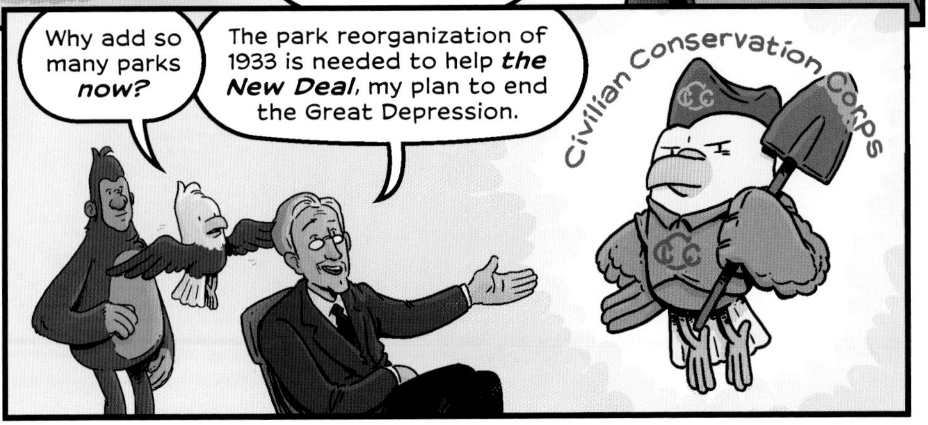
Why add so many parks *now?*
The park reorganization of 1933 is needed to help ***the New Deal***, my plan to end the Great Depression.
Civilian Conservation Corps

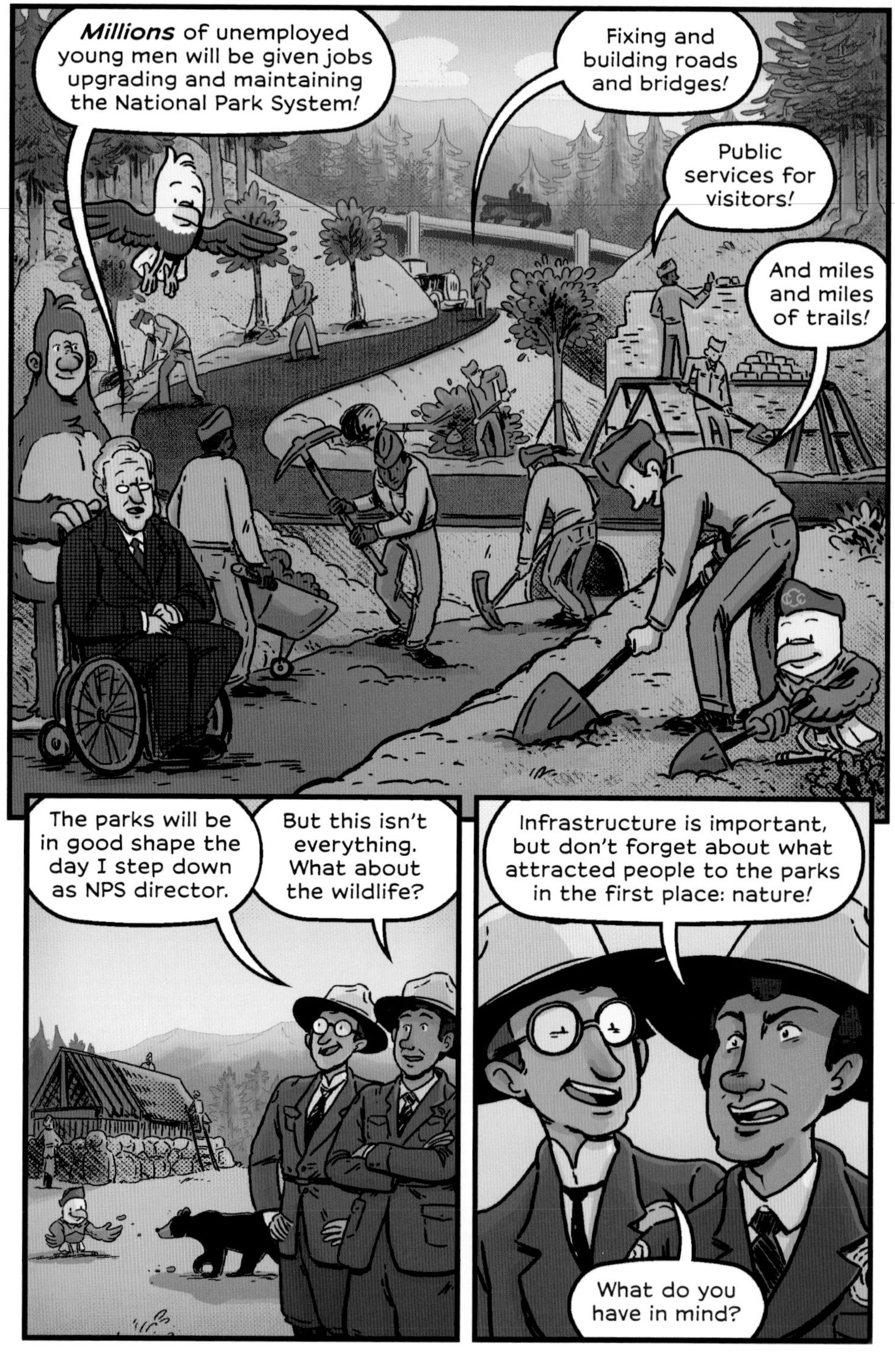
Millions of unemployed young men will be given jobs upgrading and maintaining the National Park System!
Fixing and building roads and bridges!
Public services for visitors!
And miles and miles of trails!
The parks will be in good shape the day I step down as NPS director.
But this isn't everything. What about the wildlife?
Infrastructure is important, but don't forget about what attracted people to the parks in the first place: nature!
What do you have in mind?

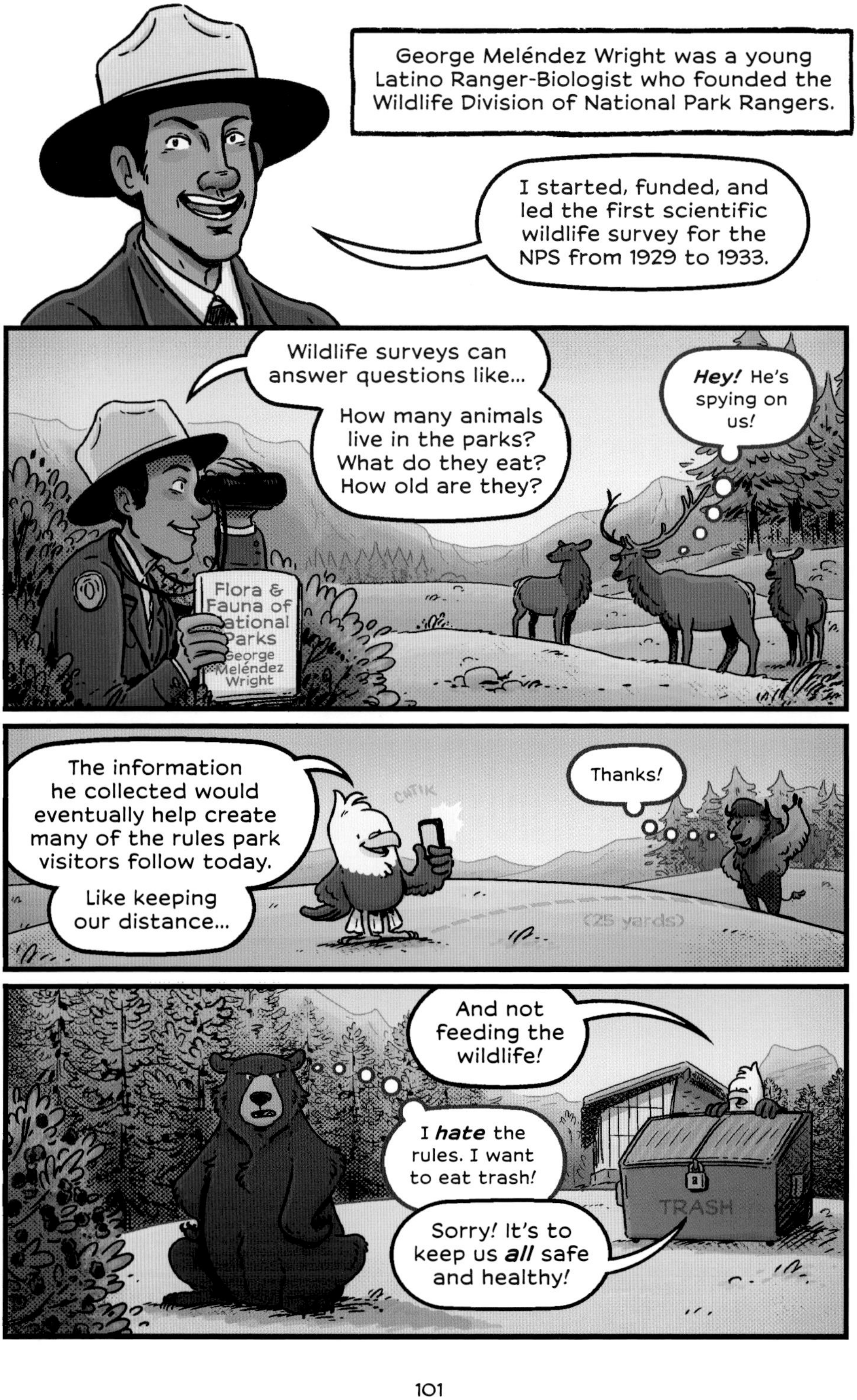
George Meléndez Wright was a young Latino Ranger-Biologist who founded the Wildlife Division of National Park Rangers.
I started, funded, and led the first scientific wildlife survey for the NPS from 1929 to 1933.
Wildlife surveys can answer questions like...
How many animals live in the parks? What do they eat? How old are they?
Flora & Fauna of National Parks George Meléndez Wright
Hey! He's spying on us!
The information he collected would eventually help create many of the rules park visitors follow today.
Like keeping our distance...
CHTIK
Thanks!
(25 yards)
And not feeding the wildlife!
I ***hate*** the rules. I want to eat trash!
TRASH
Sorry! It's to keep us ***all*** safe and healthy!

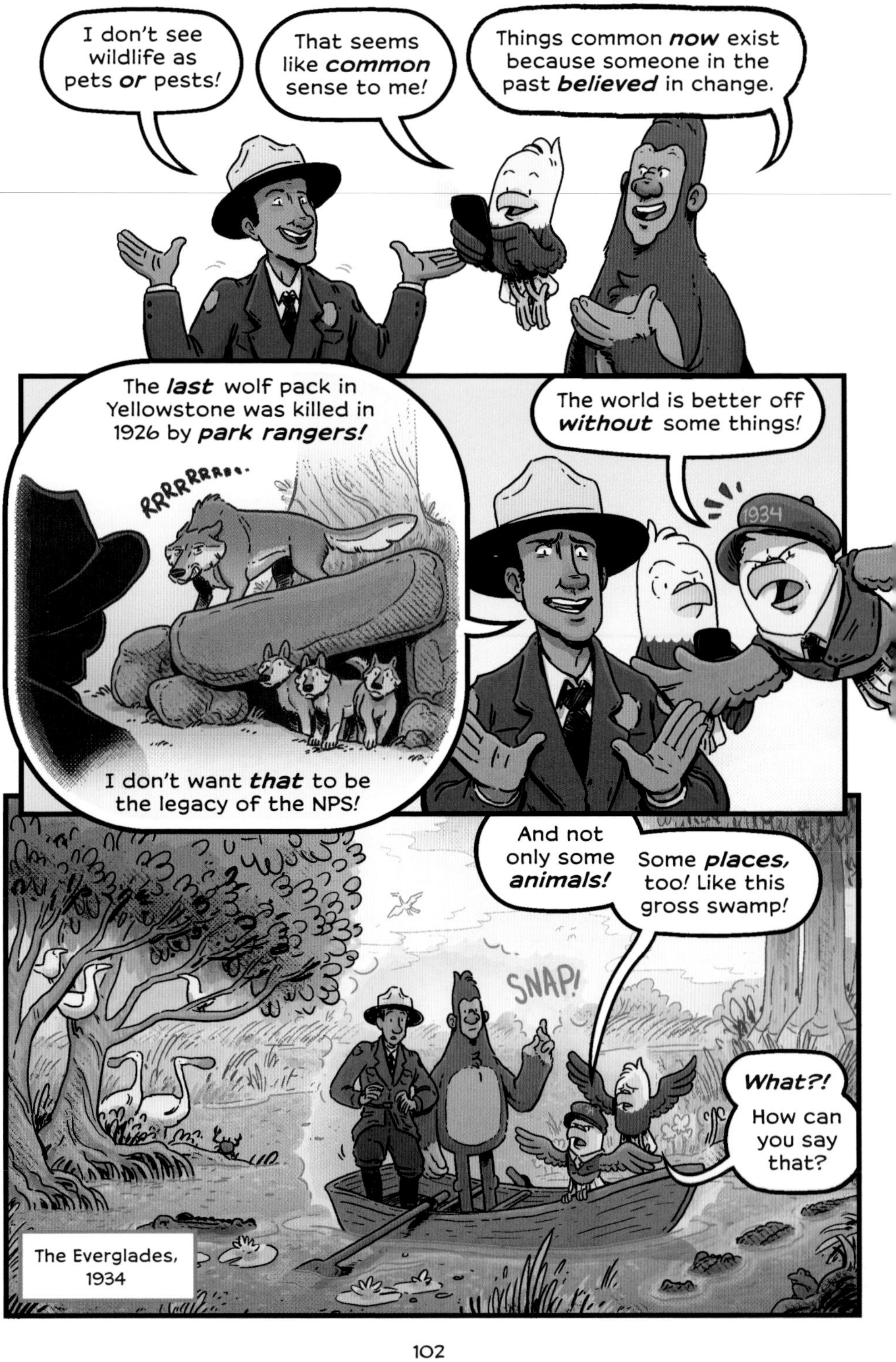

I don't see wildlife as pets *or* pests!
That seems like ***common*** sense to me!
Things common ***now*** exist because someone in the past ***believed*** in change.
The ***last*** wolf pack in Yellowstone was killed in 1926 by ***park rangers!***
RRRRRRR...
I don't want ***that*** to be the legacy of the NPS!
The world is better off ***without*** some things!
1934
And not only some ***animals!***
Some ***places,*** too! Like this gross swamp!
SNAP!
What?!
How can you say that?
The Everglades, 1934

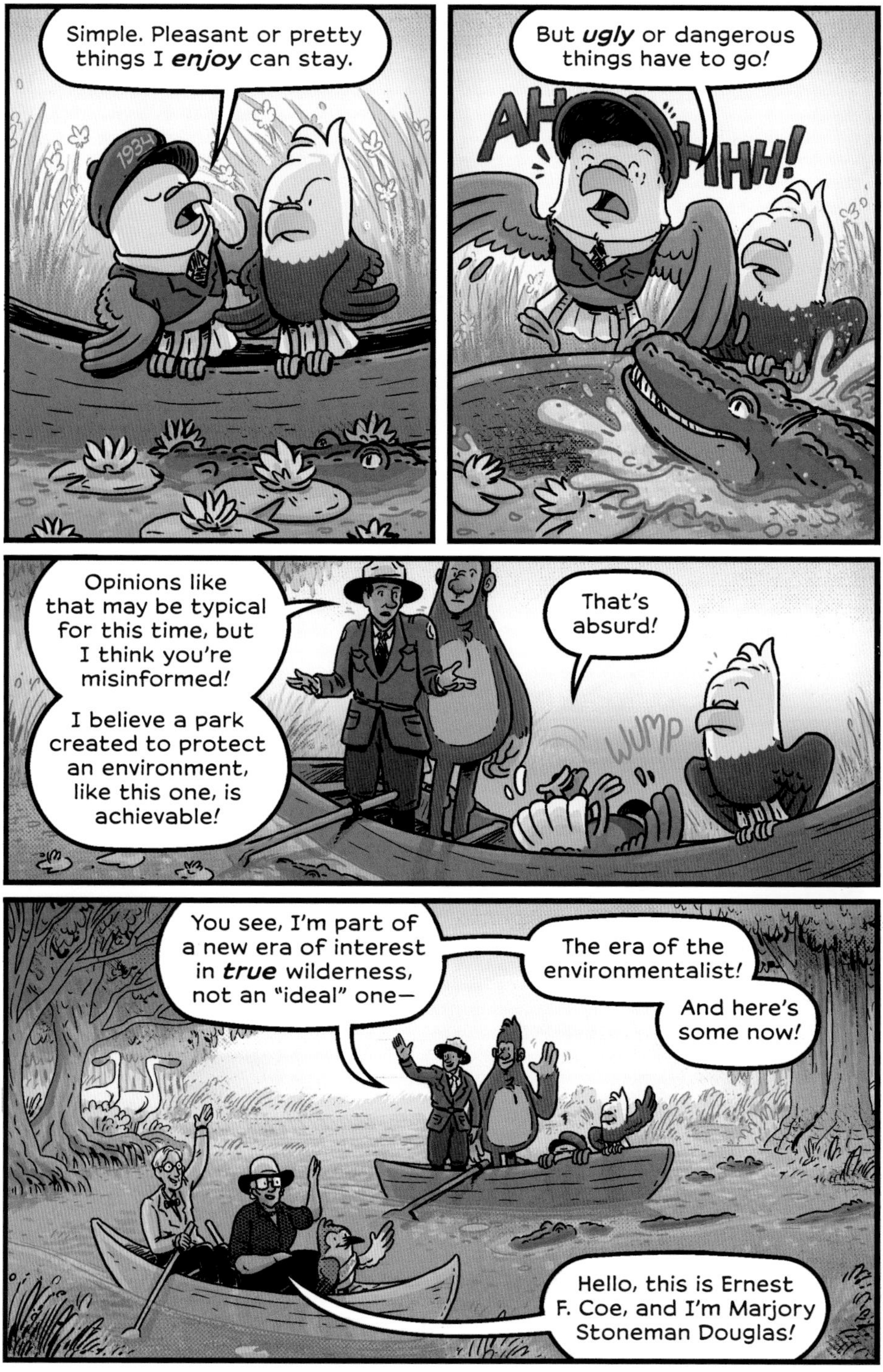

Simple. Pleasant or pretty things I ***enjoy*** can stay.
But ***ugly*** or dangerous things have to go!
AHHHHH!
Opinions like that may be typical for this time, but I think you're misinformed!
I believe a park created to protect an environment, like this one, is achievable!
That's absurd!
WUMP
You see, I'm part of a new era of interest in ***true*** wilderness, not an "ideal" one—
The era of the environmentalist!
And here's some now!
Hello, this is Ernest F. Coe, and I'm Marjory Stoneman Douglas!

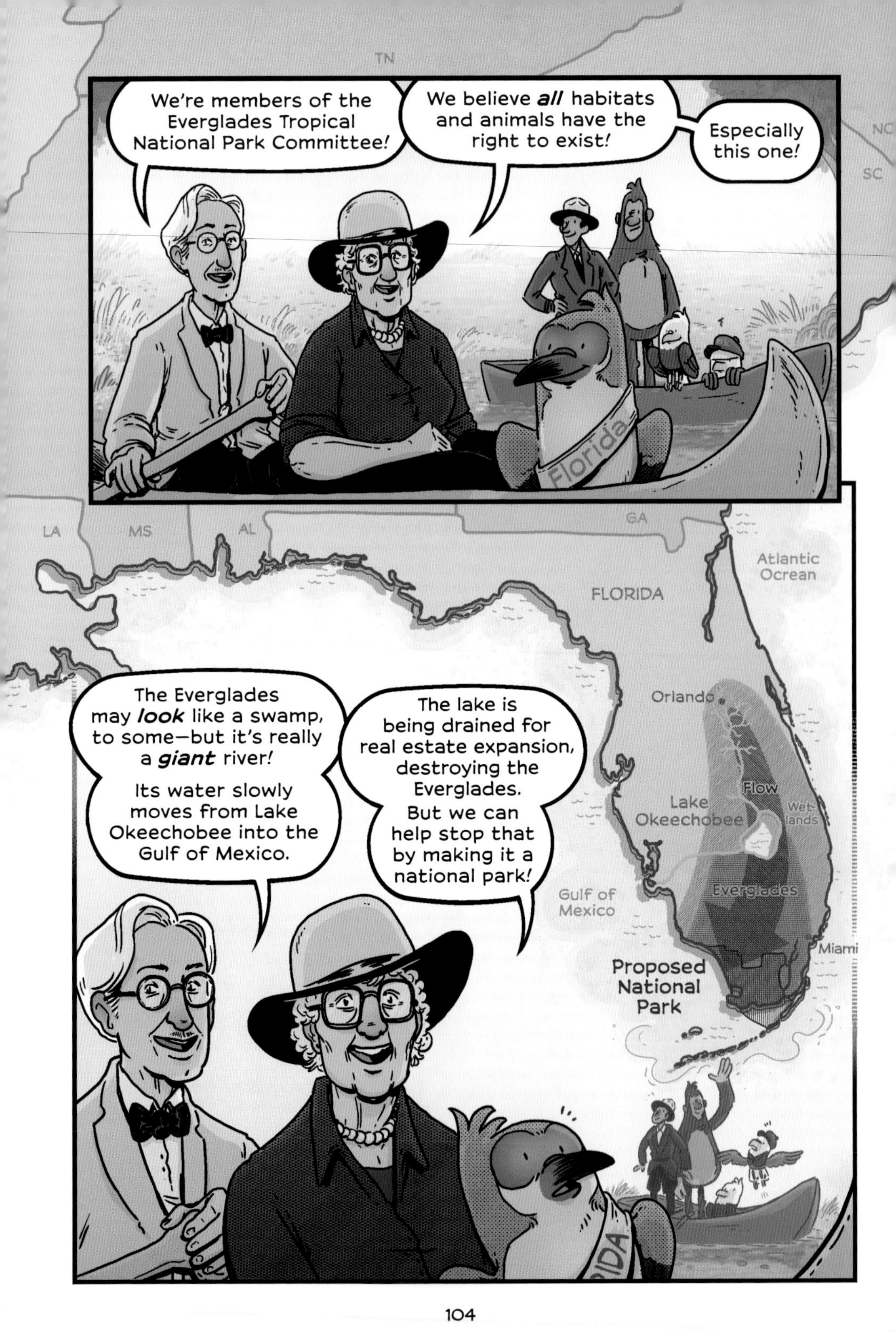
TN
NC
SC
We're members of the Everglades Tropical National Park Committee!
We believe *all* habitats and animals have the right to exist!
Especially this one!
Florida
LA
MS
AL
GA
Atlantic Ocrean
FLORIDA
The Everglades may *look* like a swamp, to some—but it's really a *giant* river!
Its water slowly moves from Lake Okeechobee into the Gulf of Mexico.
The lake is being drained for real estate expansion, destroying the Everglades.
But we can help stop that by making it a national park!
Orlando
Flow
Lake Okeechobee
Wet-lands
Everglades
Gulf of Mexico
Miami
Proposed National Park
IDA

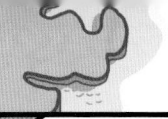

Marjory Stoneman Douglas, we need *millions* of acres donated to the NPS to create this park! It won't be *easy!*

No, it won't, but as a lifelong activist, I know it's *possible!* And I hope my book *The Everglades: River of Grass* will help people understand this *unique* wilderness.

THE Everglades
RIVER OF GRASS
MARJORY STONEMAN DOUGLAS
Illustrated by ROBERT FINK
RIVERS OF AMERICA

"Vast glittering openness, wider than the enormous visible round of the horizon... The miracle of the light pours over the green and brown expanse of saw grass and water, shining and slow-moving below, the grass and water that is the meaning and the central fact of the Everglades."

Wait, this place is part of what makes me, *me?*

Yes! And I need your help to save it!

Together, it will take us *years* to convince the public an environment without fuzzy animals or scenic drives is *worth* conserving.

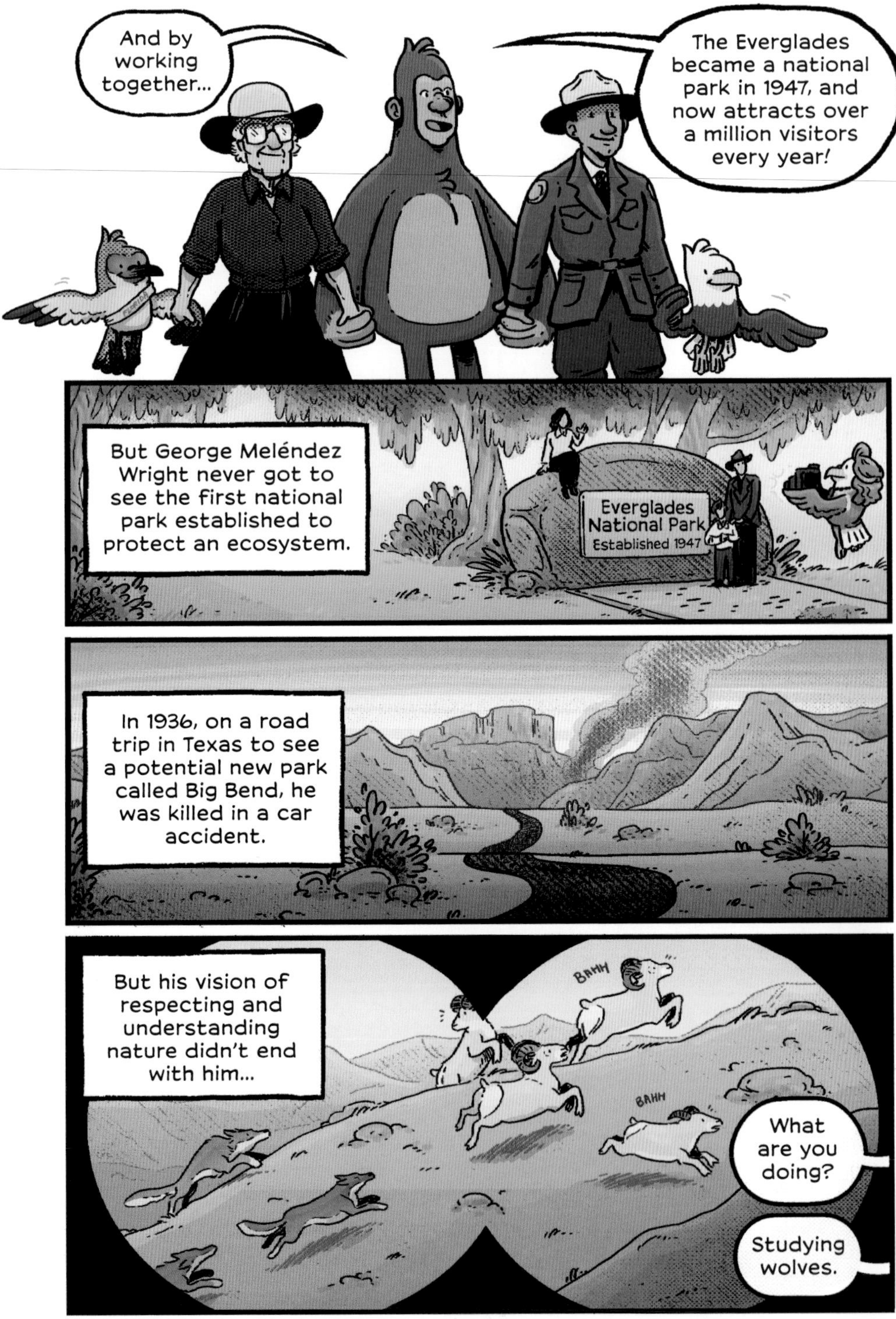
And by working together...
The Everglades became a national park in 1947, and now attracts over a million visitors every year!
But George Meléndez Wright never got to see the first national park established to protect an ecosystem.
Everglades National Park Established 1947
In 1936, on a road trip in Texas to see a potential new park called Big Bend, he was killed in a car accident.
But his vision of respecting and understanding nature didn't end with him...
BAHH
BAHH
What are you doing?
Studying wolves.

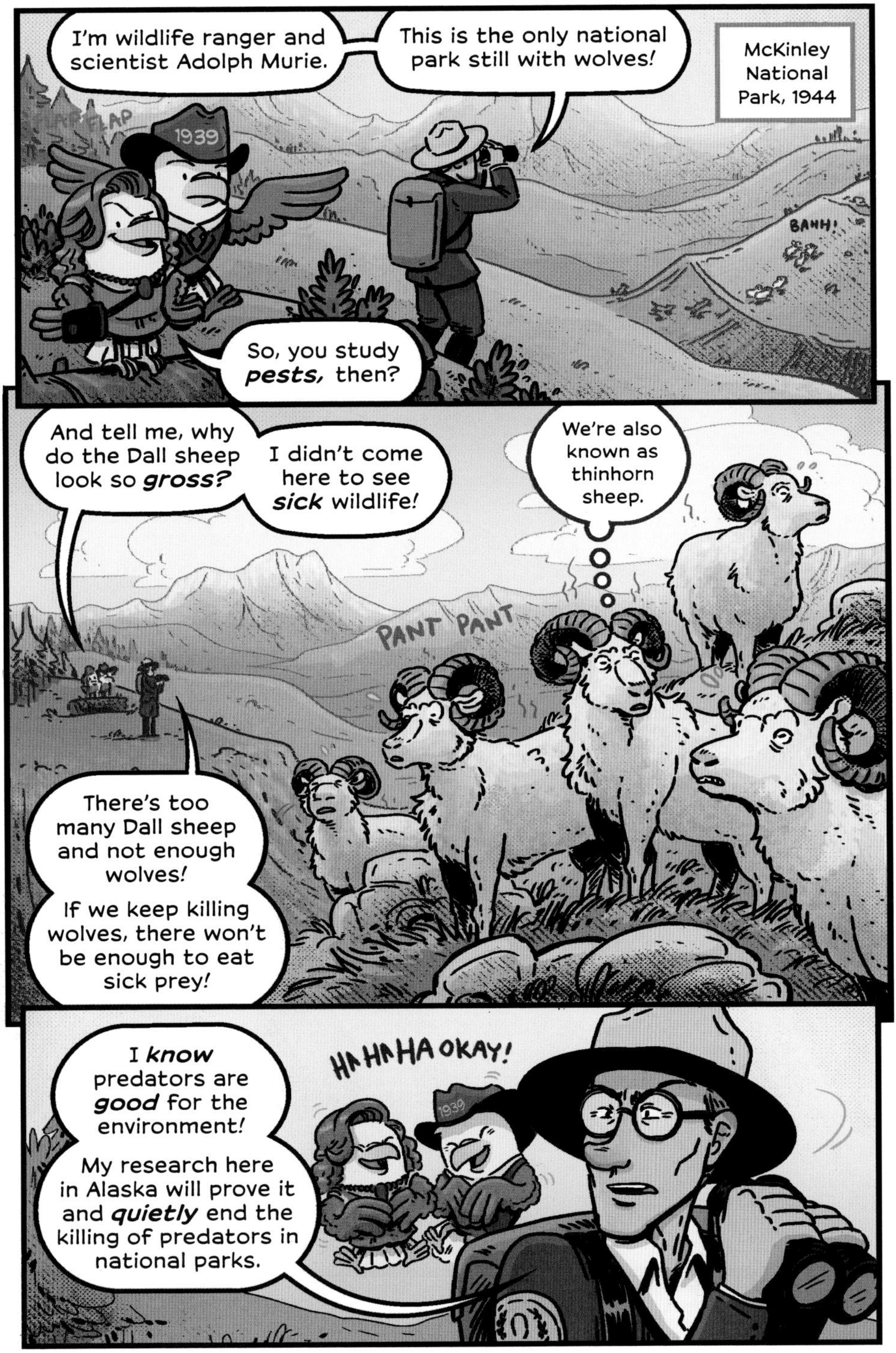
McKinley National Park, 1944
I'm wildlife ranger and scientist Adolph Murie.
This is the only national park still with wolves!
FLAP
1939
BAHH!
So, you study *pests,* then?
And tell me, why do the Dall sheep look so *gross?*
I didn't come here to see *sick* wildlife!
We're also known as thinhorn sheep.
PANT PANT
There's too many Dall sheep and not enough wolves!
If we keep killing wolves, there won't be enough to eat sick prey!
I *know* predators are *good* for the environment!
My research here in Alaska will prove it and *quietly* end the killing of predators in national parks.
HAHAHA OKAY!

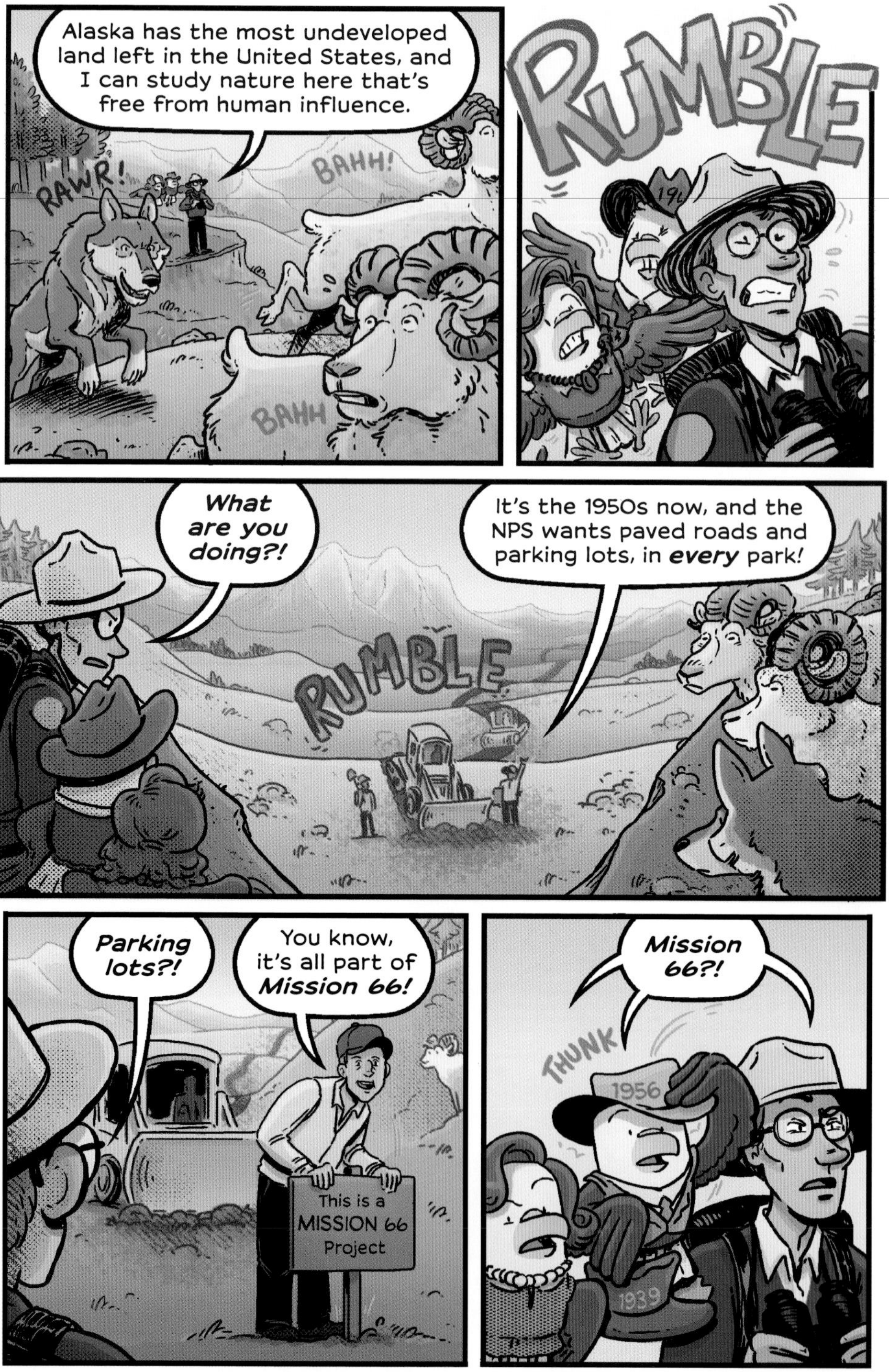
Alaska has the most undeveloped land left in the United States, and I can study nature here that's free from human influence.
RAWR!
BAHH!
BAHH
RUMBLE
What are you doing?!
It's the 1950s now, and the NPS wants paved roads and parking lots, in *every* park!
RUMBLE
Parking lots?!
You know, it's all part of *Mission 66!*
This is a MISSION 66 Project
Mission 66?!
THUNK
1956
1939

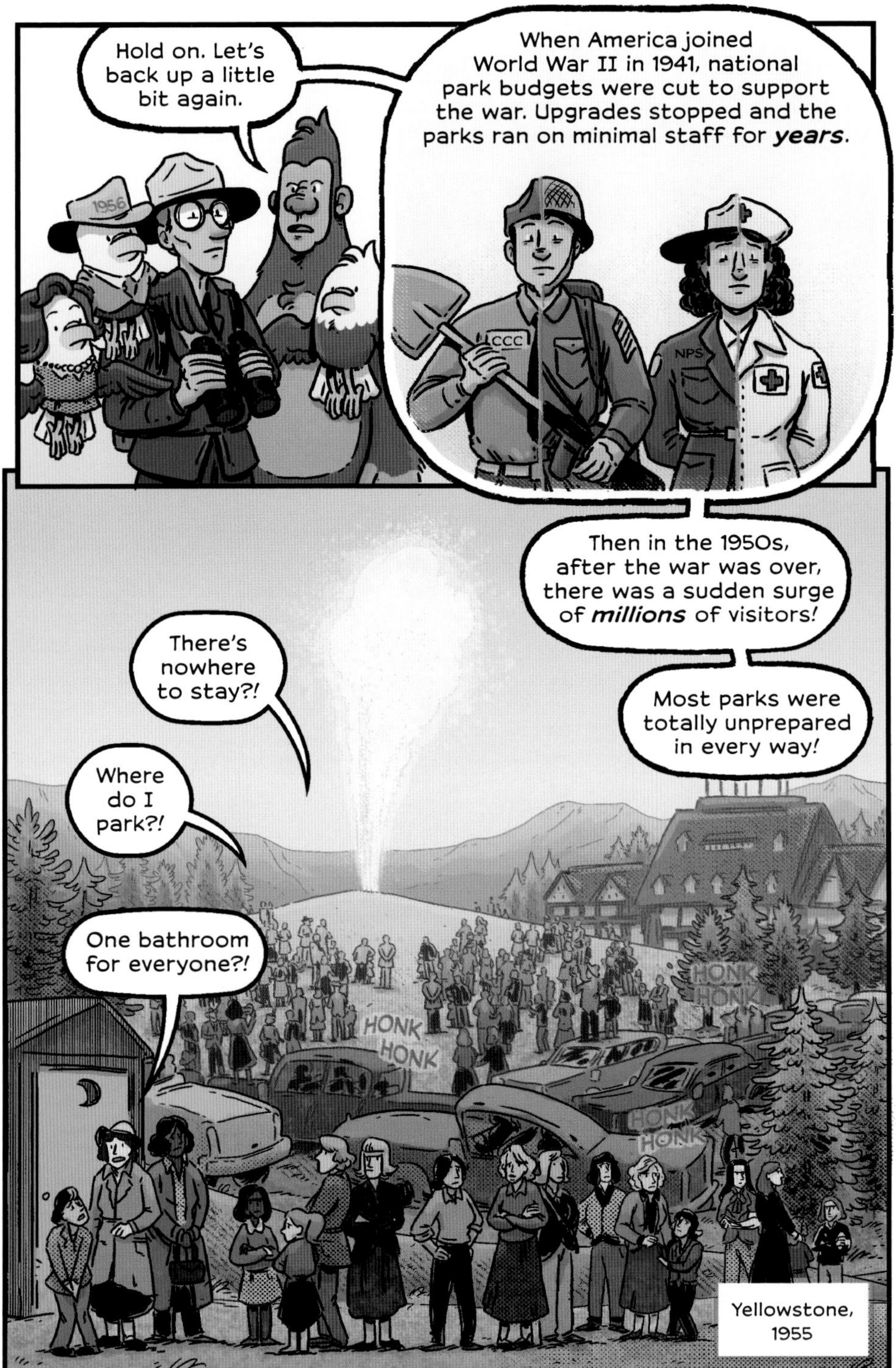
Hold on. Let's back up a little bit again.
When America joined World War II in 1941, national park budgets were cut to support the war. Upgrades stopped and the parks ran on minimal staff for *years*.
1956
CCC
NPS
Then in the 1950s, after the war was over, there was a sudden surge of *millions* of visitors!
Most parks were totally unprepared in every way!
There's nowhere to stay?!
Where do I park?!
One bathroom for everyone?!
HONK HONK
HONK HONK
HONK HONK
Yellowstone, 1955

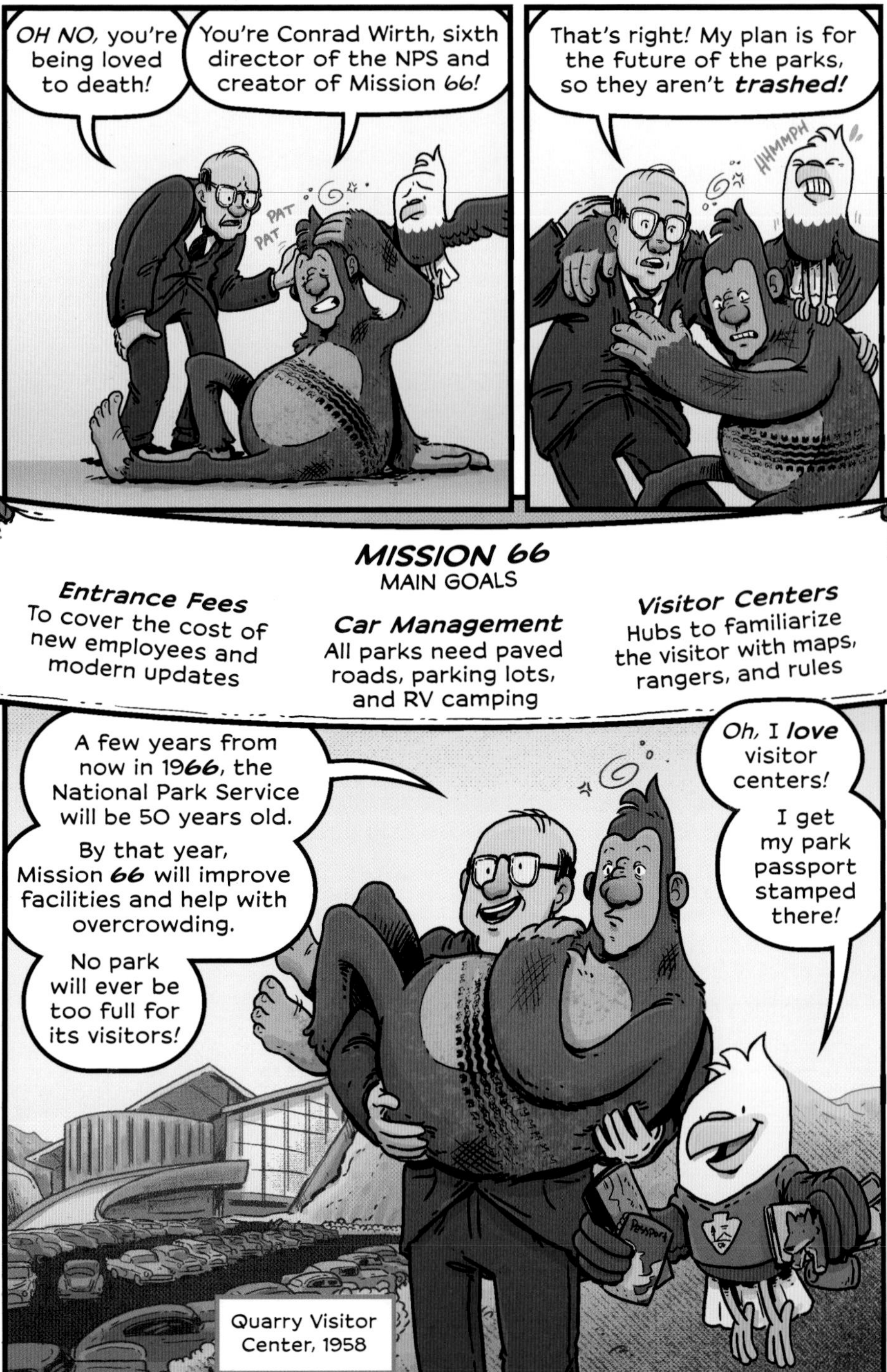
OH NO, you're being loved to death!
You're Conrad Wirth, sixth director of the NPS and creator of Mission *66*!
PAT PAT
That's right! My plan is for the future of the parks, so they aren't ***trashed!***
HHMMPH
MISSION 66
MAIN GOALS
Entrance Fees
To cover the cost of new employees and modern updates
Car Management
All parks need paved roads, parking lots, and RV camping
Visitor Centers
Hubs to familiarize the visitor with maps, rangers, and rules
A few years from now in 19**66**, the National Park Service will be 50 years old.
By that year, Mission **66** will improve facilities and help with overcrowding.
No park will ever be too full for its visitors!
Oh, I ***love*** visitor centers!
I get my park passport stamped there!
Passport
Quarry Visitor Center, 1958

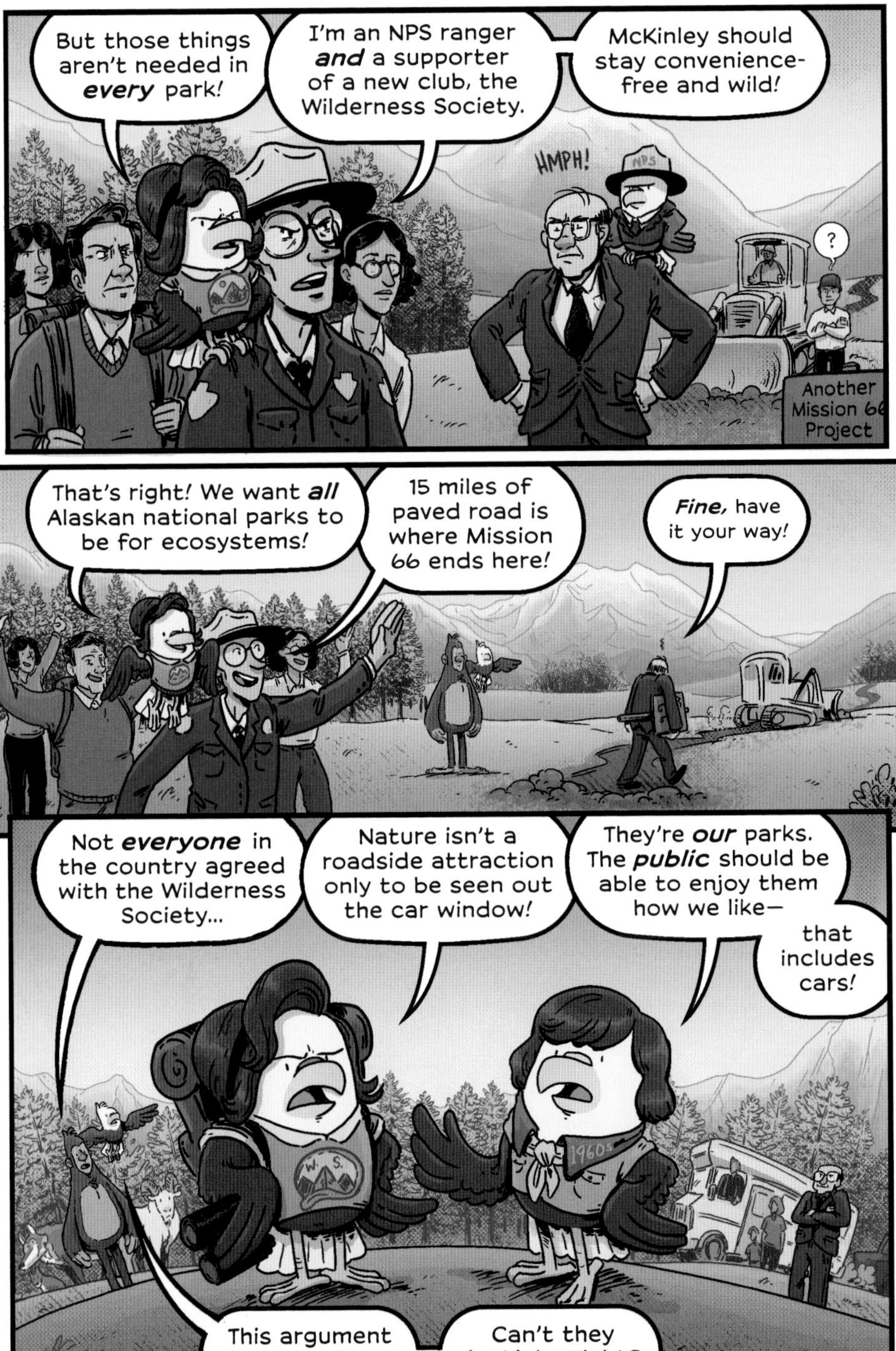

But those things aren't needed in ***every*** park!
I'm an NPS ranger ***and*** a supporter of a new club, the Wilderness Society.
McKinley should stay convenience-free and wild!
HMPH!
NPS
?
Another Mission 66 Project
That's right! We want ***all*** Alaskan national parks to be for ecosystems!
15 miles of paved road is where Mission 66 ends here!
Fine, have it your way!
Not ***everyone*** in the country agreed with the Wilderness Society...
Nature isn't a roadside attraction only to be seen out the car window!
They're ***our*** parks. The ***public*** should be able to enjoy them how we like—
that includes cars!
W. S.
1960s
This argument feels familiar—
Can't they ***both*** be right?

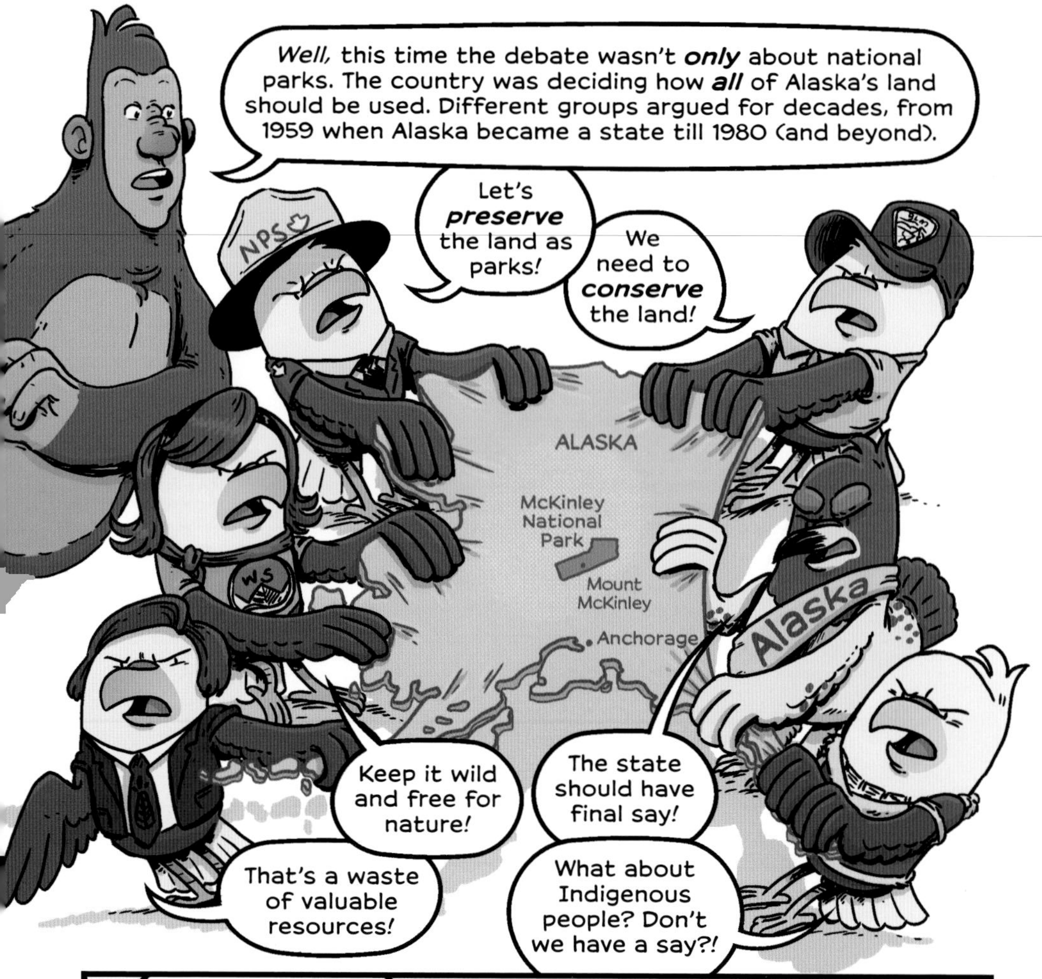
Well, this time the debate wasn't ***only*** about national parks. The country was deciding how ***all*** of Alaska's land should be used. Different groups argued for decades, from 1959 when Alaska became a state till 1980 (and beyond).
Let's ***preserve*** the land as parks!
We need to ***conserve*** the land!
ALASKA
McKinley National Park
Mount McKinley
Anchorage
Keep it wild and free for nature!
The state should have final say!
That's a waste of valuable resources!
What about Indigenous people? Don't we have a say?!

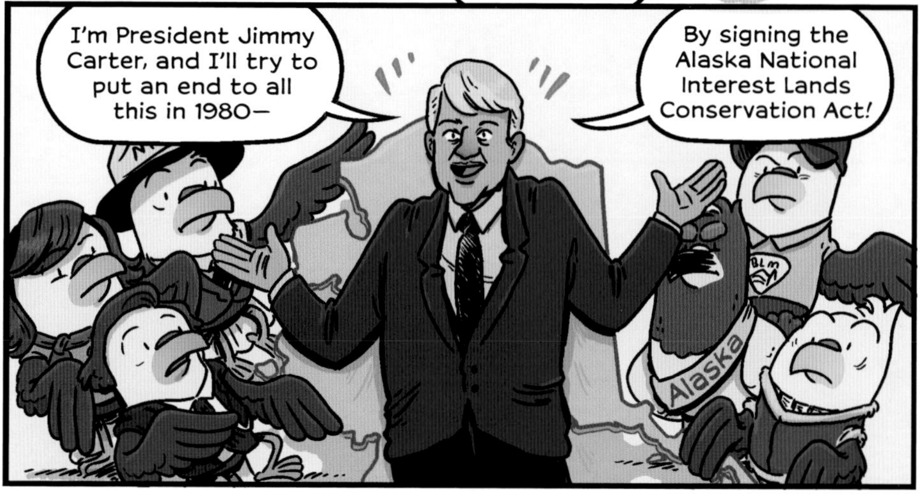
I'm President Jimmy Carter, and I'll try to put an end to all this in 1980—
By signing the Alaska National Interest Lands Conservation Act!

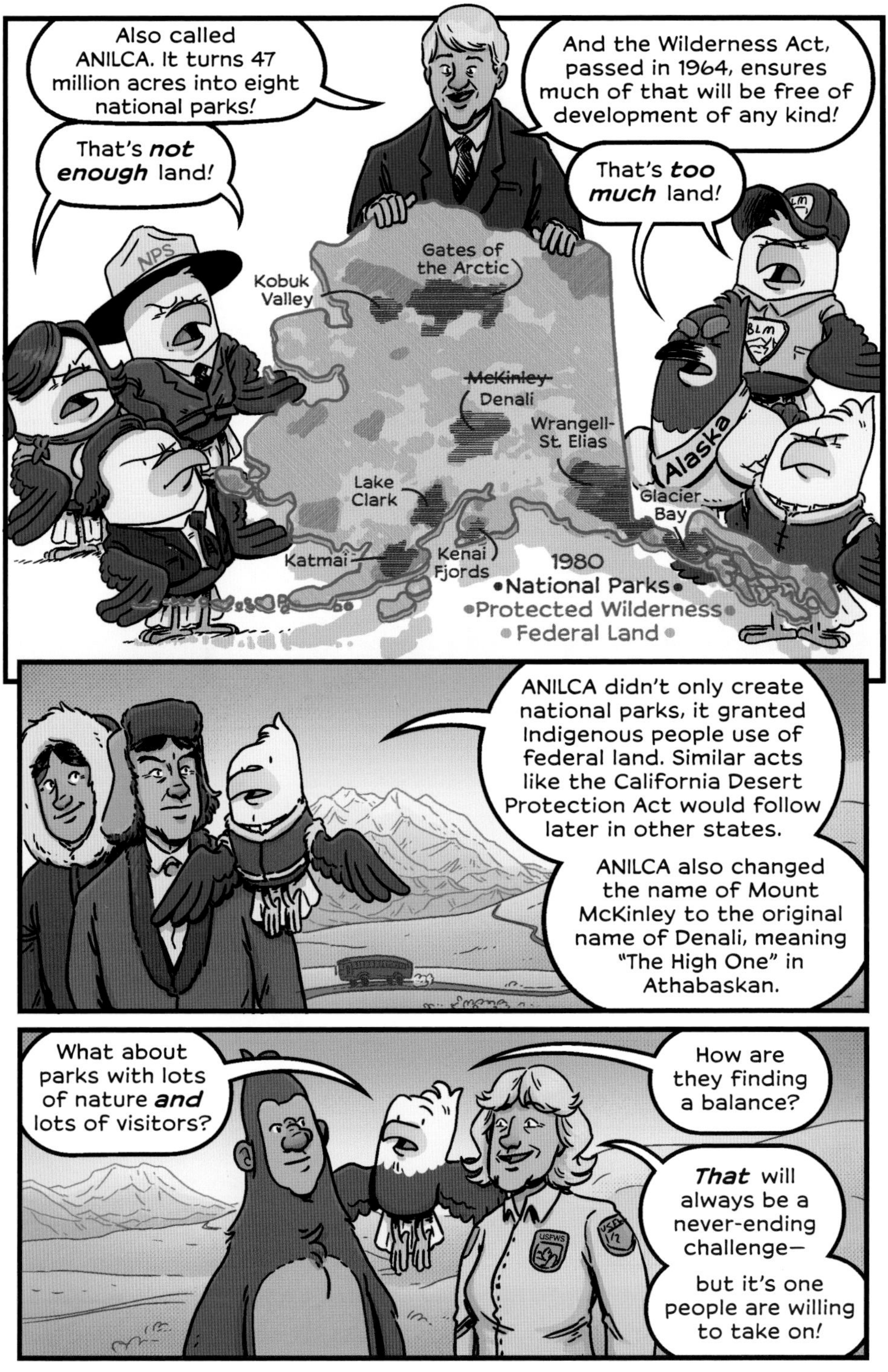
Also called ANILCA. It turns 47 million acres into eight national parks!
That's ***not enough*** land!
And the Wilderness Act, passed in 1964, ensures much of that will be free of development of any kind!
That's ***too much*** land!
NPS
Gates of the Arctic
Kobuk Valley
~~McKinley~~
Denali
Wrangell-St. Elias
Lake Clark
Glacier Bay
Katmai
Kenai Fjords
1980
National Parks
Protected Wilderness
Federal Land
BLM
Alaska
ANILCA didn't only create national parks, it granted Indigenous people use of federal land. Similar acts like the California Desert Protection Act would follow later in other states.
ANILCA also changed the name of Mount McKinley to the original name of Denali, meaning "The High One" in Athabaskan.
What about parks with lots of nature ***and*** lots of visitors?
How are they finding a balance?
That will always be a never-ending challenge—
but it's one people are willing to take on!
USFWS

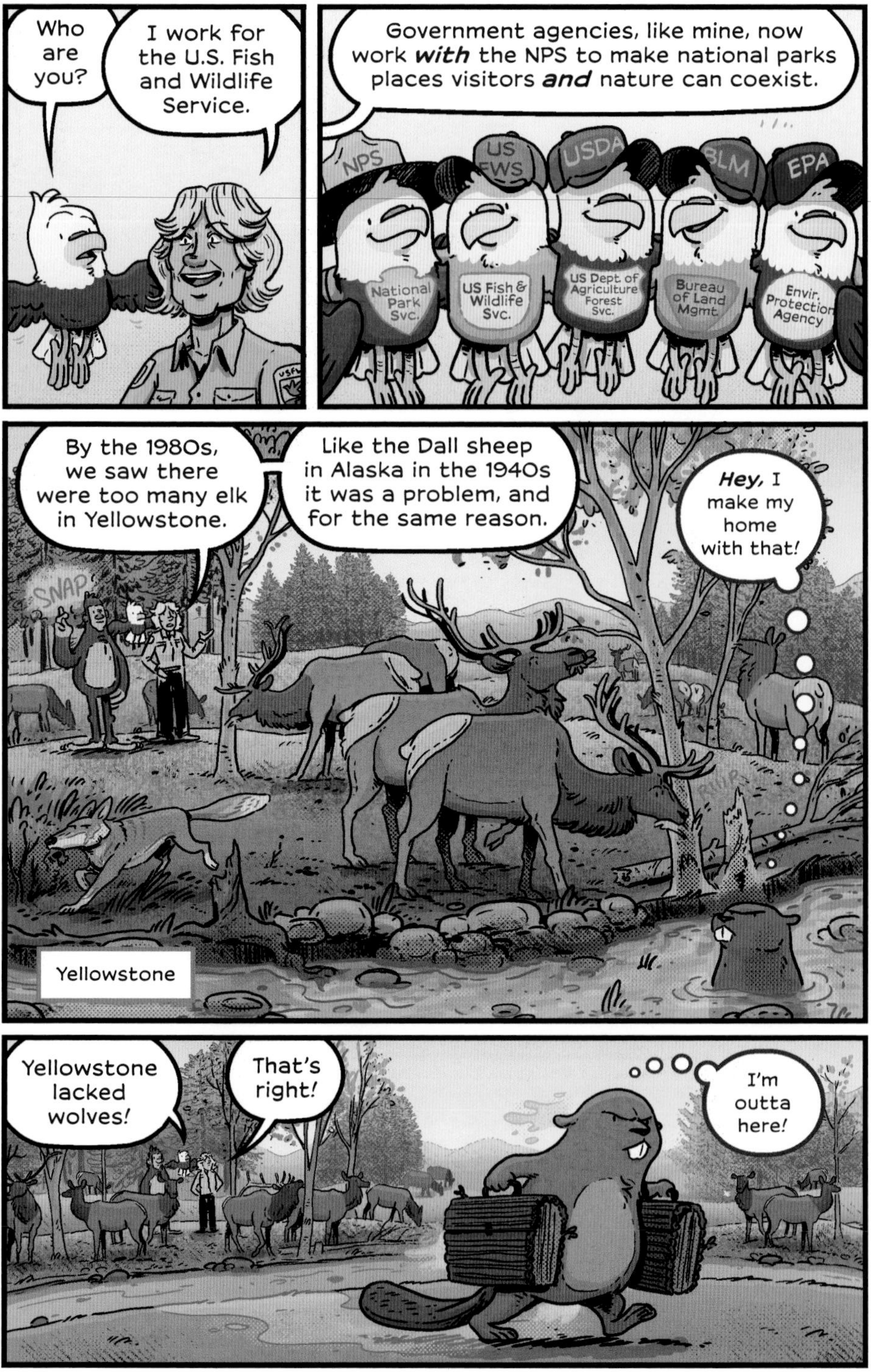
Who are you?
I work for the U.S. Fish and Wildlife Service.
Government agencies, like mine, now work ***with*** the NPS to make national parks places visitors ***and*** nature can coexist.
NPS
US FWS
USDA
BLM
EPA
National Park Svc.
US Fish & Wildlife Svc.
US Dept. of Agriculture Forest Svc.
Bureau of Land Mgmt.
Envir. Protection Agency
By the 1980s, we saw there were too many elk in Yellowstone.
Like the Dall sheep in Alaska in the 1940s it was a problem, and for the same reason.
Hey, I make my home with that!
SNAP
Yellowstone
Yellowstone lacked wolves!
That's right!
I'm outta here!

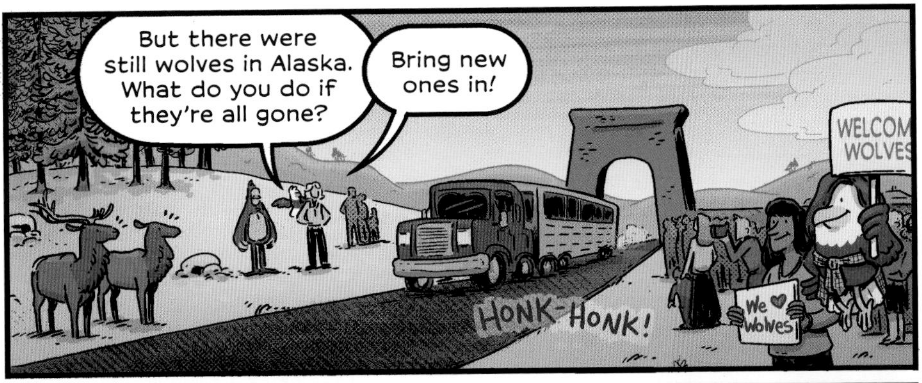
But there were still wolves in Alaska. What do you do if they're all gone?
Bring new ones in!
WELCOM WOLVES
HONK-HONK!
We ♥ Wolves

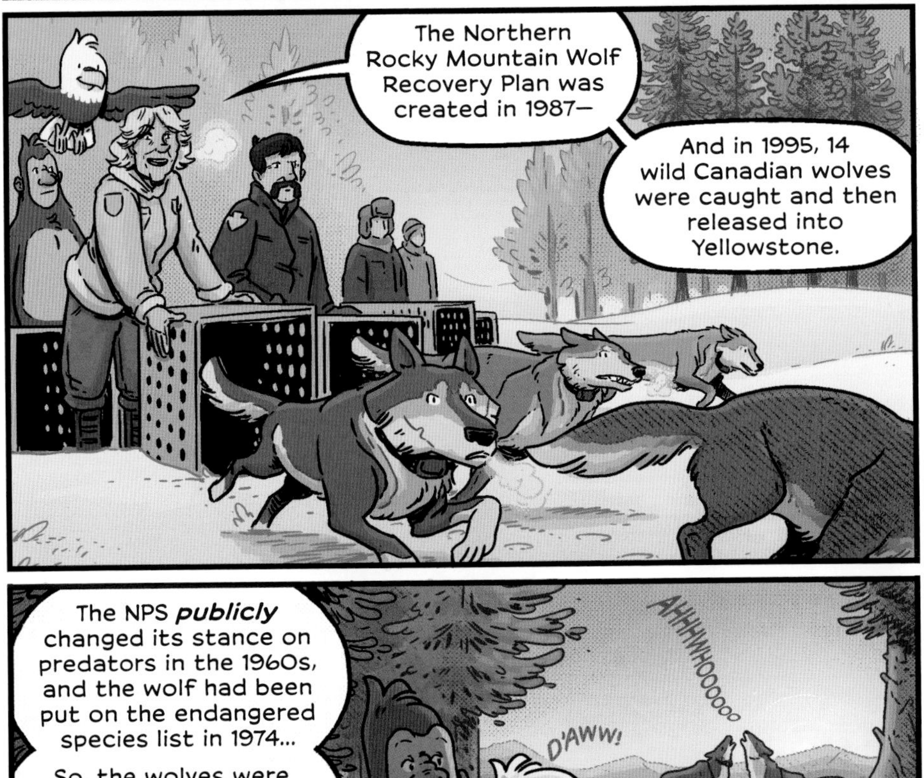
The Northern Rocky Mountain Wolf Recovery Plan was created in 1987—
And in 1995, 14 wild Canadian wolves were caught and then released into Yellowstone.

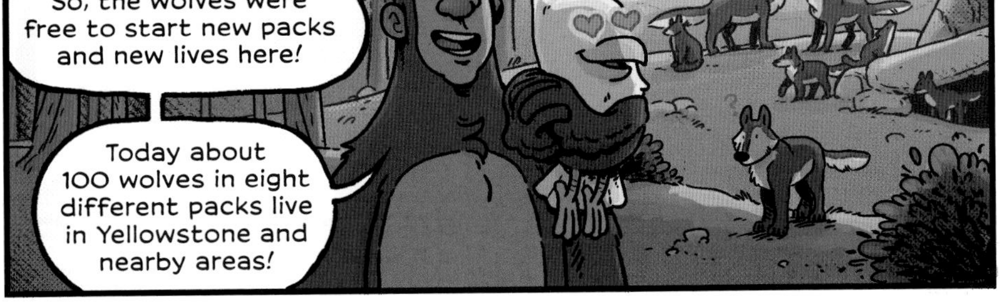
The NPS *publicly* changed its stance on predators in the 1960s, and the wolf had been put on the endangered species list in 1974...
So, the wolves were free to start new packs and new lives here!
Today about 100 wolves in eight different packs live in Yellowstone and nearby areas!
AHHHWHOOOOOO
D'AWW!

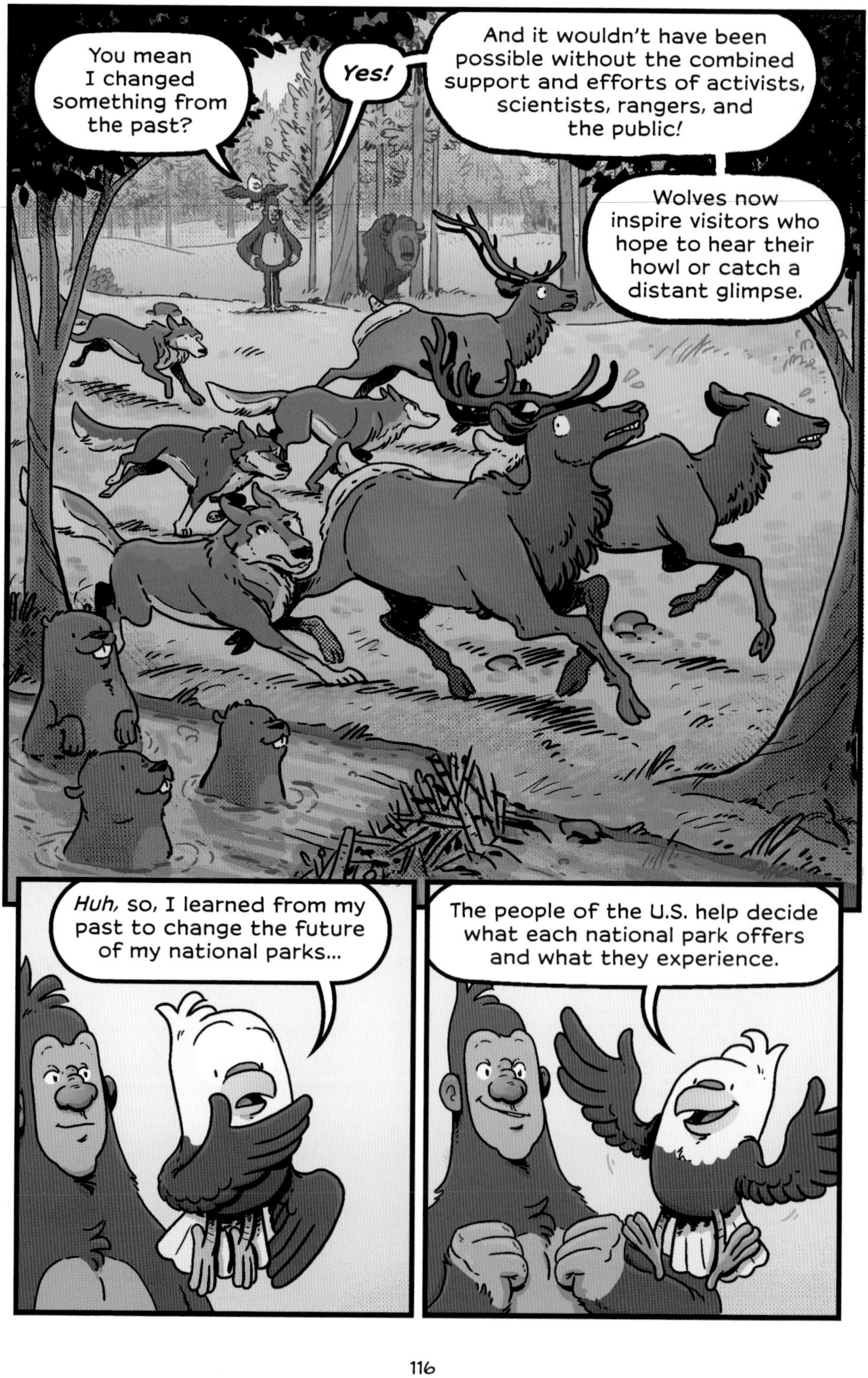
You mean I changed something from the past?
Yes!
And it wouldn't have been possible without the combined support and efforts of activists, scientists, rangers, and the public!
Wolves now inspire visitors who hope to hear their howl or catch a distant glimpse.
Huh, so, I learned from my past to change the future of my national parks...
The people of the U.S. help decide what each national park offers and what they experience.

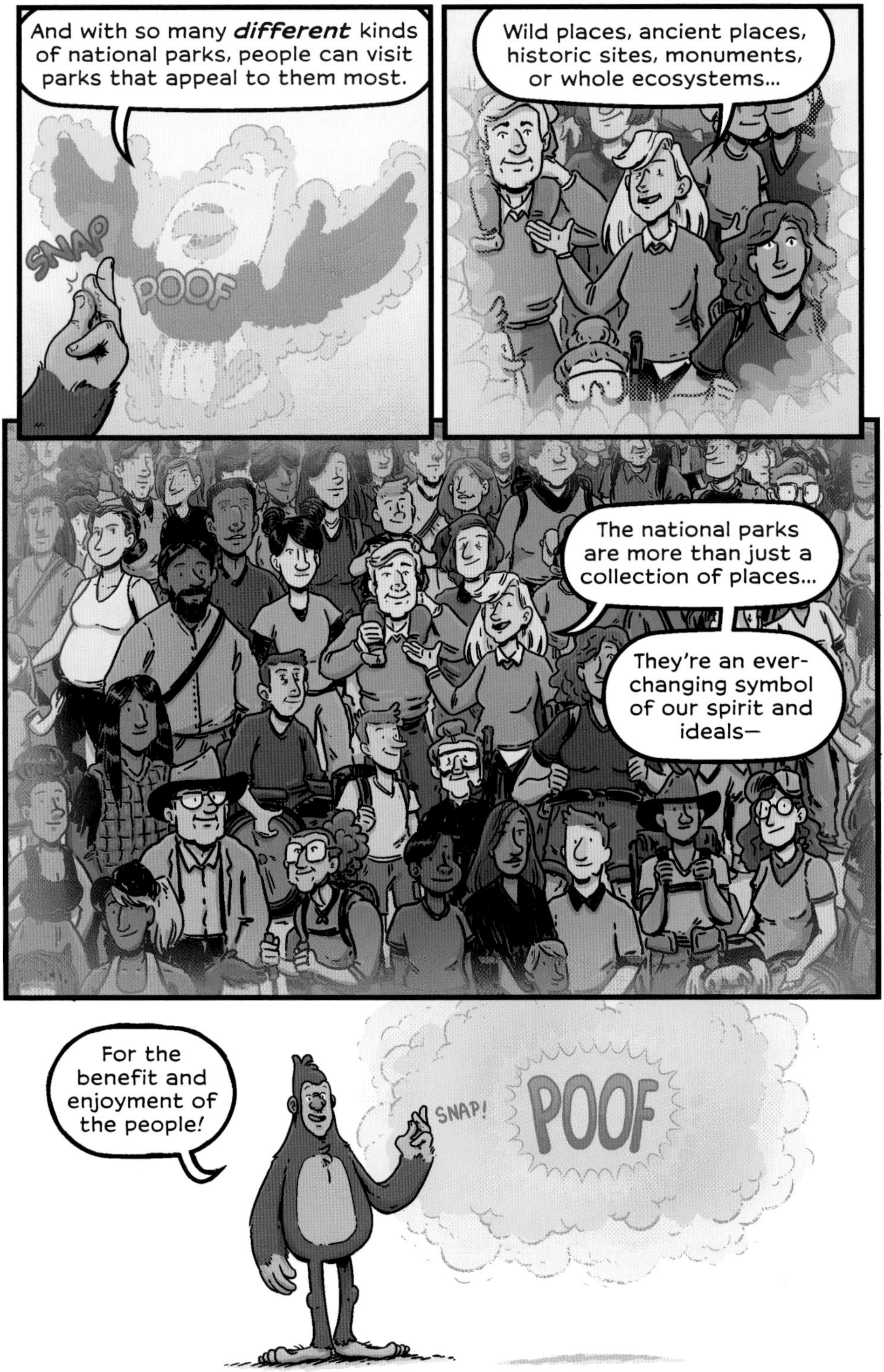
And with so many ***different*** kinds of national parks, people can visit parks that appeal to them most.
SNAP
POOF
Wild places, ancient places, historic sites, monuments, or whole ecosystems...
The national parks are more than just a collection of places...
They're an ever-changing symbol of our spirit and ideals—
For the benefit and enjoyment of the people!
SNAP!
POOF

Afterword

National parks hold a special place in my heart. They aren't just places to visit, they are places to experience! From 2017 to 2018 my husband and I packed ourselves into a van and attempted to see as many national parks as we could. The national parks are a gift for all people who want to see some amazing sights and truly get away from it all. We made it to 48 parks (pretty good if you ask me) and on our adventure, all of these cherished places came to feel like our home. I don't live in a van anymore, but the quest to see all the national parks continues. With new parks added all the time, maybe I never will, and that's part of the fun!

For me personally, the biggest draw to the national parks was nature. The beautiful untamed places are a chance to rediscover oneself and connect with the wonders of the larger world. But I realized from my travels, and from writing this book, that is only one reason why someone might visit a national park. You can also learn more about history, enjoy bicycling and other sporting activities, or just kick back and relax in a jaw-dropping setting.

I think it's important to recognize that history, all history, is filled with imperfect people. Even those with the best of intentions are capable of bad things, and flawed people can create positive changes. John Muir was a pioneer of environmentalism; much of the Sierra Nevada is preserved for us to enjoy today because of him, and others who were influenced by his writing. But Muir was also a racist who believed that white people alone, rather than the Indigenous Native Americans, were the best caretakers of nature. There is no such thing as "being a product of one's time"—people of the past knew what they said and did was wrong, but did not have to face consequences for their words and actions.

As journalist Michael Hobbes said, "History should make you feel weird," and to shy away from the past because it wasn't perfect deprives us of the context we need to appreciate those who eventually broke the mold. Women, minority groups, and the Indigenous may not have been included in much of the early history of the parks but are still passionate about the preservation of our nature and history moving forward. Learning from the past and creating a national park system that's more inclusive should be the duty of all who love the national parks and the national park system.

I hope this book serves as a spark to encourage readers to find the people and places within our park system that inspire them most. With so many parks out there, I'm sure they will.

—Falynn Koch

Further Research

National Parks: The American Experience by Alfred Runte

Dispossessing the Wilderness: Indian Removal and the Making of the National Parks by Mark David Spence

See America First: Tourism and National Identity 1880–1940 by Marguerite Shaffer

National Parks and the Woman's Voice: A History by Polly Welts Kaufman

The National Parks: America's Best Idea by Dayton Duncan

Many people in this book, like Marjory Stoneman Douglas, John Muir, and even Horace Albright, wrote their own books, too!

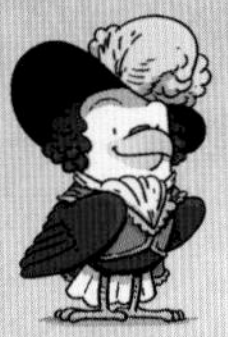

Time Line

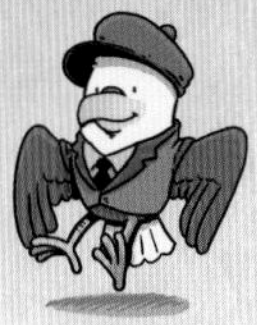

1851	The Mariposa Battalion attacks
1864	Yosemite State Park Est.
1870	Washburn-Langford-Doane Expedition of Yellowstone
1872	Yellowstone NP Est.
1887	The Boone and Crockett Club Est.
1890	Sequoia NP Est.
	Yosemite NP Est.
	General Grant NP Est.
1892	The Sierra Club Est.
1899	Mount Rainier NP Est.
1900	The Lacey Act is passed
	The Colorado Cliff Dwellings Association Est.
1902	Crater Lake NP Est.
	Platt NP Est.
1903	Wind Cave NP Est.
	Theodore Roosevelt's reelection tour
1904	Sullys Hill NP Est.
1906	Mesa Verde NP Est.
	The Antiquities Act is passed
	Devils Tower NM Est.
1908	Grand Canyon NM Est.
1910	Glacier NP Est.
1913	Hetch Hetchy dam approved
1914	John Muir dies
1915	Rocky Mountain NP Est.
1916	The National Park Service is Est.
	Hawai'i NP Est.
	Lassen Volcanic NP Est.
1917	Mount McKinley NP Est.
1919	Zion NP Est.
	Lafayette NP Est.
	Grand Canyon NP Est.
1921	Hot Springs NP Est.
1926	Great Smoky Mountains and Shenandoah NPs approved
	Wolves in Yellowstone eliminated
1928	Bryce Canyon NP Est.
	The Tropical Everglades National Park Association Est.
1929	Grand Teton NP Est.
	Lafayette NP renamed Acadia NP
1930	Carlsbad Caverns NP Est.
	Stephen Mather dies
1931	Sullys Hill NP changed to wildlife refuge
1933	Federal National Park System Est.
	Wildlife Division NPS rangers Est.
1934	Great Smoky Mountains NP Est.
	Everglades NP approved
	Shenandoah NP Est.
1935	The Wilderness Society Est.
1936	Geogre Meléndez Wright dies
1938	Hetch Hetchy dam complete
	Olympic NP Est.
1940	Kings Canyon NP Est. (General Grant NP absorbed into it)
	Isle Royale NP Est.

1941	Mammoth Cave NP Est.
1944	Big Bend NP Est.
1947	Everglades NP officially Est.
1956	Mission 66 approved
	Virgin Islands NP Est.
1961	Haleakalā NP Est.
	Hawai'i NP becomes Hawai'i Volcanoes NP
1962	Petrified Forest NP Est.
1963	Mission 66 stopped in McKinley
1964	Canyonlands NP Est.
1966	Guadalupe Mountains NP Est.
1968	The Firefall ends
	North Cascades NP Est.
	Redwood NP Est.
1971	Arches NP Est.
	Capitol Reef NP Est.
1972	Ute Mountain Tribal Park Est.
1974	Gray wolf added to NP endangered species list
1975	Voyageurs NP Est.
1976	Platt NP changed to Chickasaw National Recreation Area
1978	Badlands NP Est.
	Theodore Roosevelt NP Est.
1980	Biscayne NP Est.
	Channel Islands NP Est.
	ANILCA passed
	McKinley NP renamed Denali NP
	Gates of the Arctic NP Est.
	Glacier Bay NP Est.
	Katmai NP Est.
	Kenai Fjords NP Est.
	Kobuk Valley NP Est.
	Lake Clark NP Est.
	Wrangell-St. Elias NP Est.
1986	Great Basin NP Est.
1987	Northern Rocky Mountain Wolf Recovery Plan approved
1988	NP of American Samoa Est.
1992	Dry Tortugas NP Est.
1994	Death Valley NP Est.
	Joshua Tree NP Est.
	Saguaro NP Est.
1995	Wolves reintroduced to Yellowstone NP
1999	Black Canyon of the Gunnison NP Est.
2000	Cuyahoga Valley NP Est.
2003	Congaree NP Est.
2004	Great Sand Dunes NP Est.
2013	Pinnacles NP Est.
2018	Gateway Arch NP Est.
2019	Indiana Dunes NP Est.
	White Sands NP Est.

Est.: established
NM: National Monument
NP: National Park
NPS: National Park Service